28 DISASTROUS DATES

28 DISASTROUS DATES

A (Mostly True) Humourous Memoir

POPPY MORTIMER

Poppy Mortimer

Copyright © 2022 by Poppy Mortimer

All rights reserved. No part of this book may be reproduced in any manner whatsoever without written permission except in the case of brief quotations embodied in critical articles and reviews.

First Printing, 2022

This book is dedicated to all the Poppy Mortimers out there who have experienced their own disastrous dates, have questioned their self-worth and wondered where they fit in a patriarchal world that fears female empowerment and independence. You are beautiful, you are powerful, and you deserve a life filled with laughter, love and respect.

ACKNOWLEDGEMENTS

I would like to acknowledge all the wonderful people who have played an integral part in the creation of this book.

Abigail Isaacoff, you were the first person I connected with on the manuscript. Your pointers were pivotal in guiding the direction of the book. Thank you for believing I had my fingers on the pulse of the zeitgeist, and I'm delighted to hear you're having fewer of your own disastrous dates. Abigail can be found making people laugh in comedy clubs across New Orleans.

Arielle Andreano, what a comedic genius! Thank you for seeing my vision and embracing my quirky, non-swearing ways to help create a book that is laugh out loud funny. Thank you for adding your own flavour that punched the comedy out of the park. You are a legend, and I see a bright future for you. Arielle can be found on Twitter @ArielleAndreano.

Jan-Andrew Henderson, thank you for your apology on behalf of men worldwide, but jokes aside, you were the first man to read the book, and I truly appreciate your knowledge, insight and support.

Tracy Tutor, we've never met, but you have been a huge inspiration to me. Thank you for being a powerhouse of a woman, someone who walks the talk, embraces her femininity and has created an amazing life on her own terms. Keep being the authentic, empowered woman that you are. You inspire me.

My lovely mum, whose influence and wisdom have featured heavily throughout this book. You are the strongest woman I know, and I wouldn't be the woman I am today without you. Thank you for your insight, love and belief in me. But most importantly, thank you for being my mum.

My dad, who inspired my entrepreneurial spirit, taught me to love nature and animals, to see the wonder in the stars and passed on his magnetic charm, which has brought me great friendships and wonderful opportunities. I love you.

Sally, thank you for all the support, knowledge and time you've put into so many of my projects. You are a precious gift, and there's never a day that goes by that I'm not grateful for you.

Thank you to Cate Hogan, Joanna Chalmers, Daniela Medellin and Mykola Shelepa for your expertise.

And finally, a big thanks to my wonderful friends who listened to many of these disastrous dates in explicit detail and encouraged me to write this book.

INTRODUCTION

Where do I even begin? Why am I even writing this? The truth is no one would believe some of the following dates could ever happen.

Unfortunately for me, they did!

So, here I am, airing my dirty laundry for your entertainment and edification, sharing my most disastrous dates that have spanned two decades and three continents. I use the term 'date' loosely, as some of these experiences were so shocking, they never progressed beyond texting.

Blame my childhood. As an eleven-year-old and a child of divorce, I turned to films and romance novels about women falling madly in love with the most beautiful men Hollywood and Hollywood's plastic surgeons had to offer. You can already see how I was doomed to fail from the start, right?

So, how weird are we talking?

Recently I got a text from a prospective date.

Let's skip dinner, go back to yours and play Postman, where I'll put my big package in your tiny slot.

Yep. Apparently, that behaviour is 'acceptable' for a forty-year-old man to send to a woman he's never met . . . And now he never will.

But it got me thinking about all the horrendous 'romantic' encounters I've put up with over two decades. And now it's payback time . . .

Before getting into the dating ordeals I want to start with apologies, mainly to my mother.

Mum, I apologise for all references to male genitalia. This is not because I want to talk about male genitalia. In fact, it's probably the lowest ranking topic on my conversational list. It just seems to come up a lot of the time—no pun intended.

Over the years, your ears have bled and eyes burnt by the explicit photos of men's private parts. Thank you for handling them so well. That's another unintended pun.

Thanks for being a great Mum—by the way!

Speaking of parents, I should inform you ahead of time that my dad raised me with the notion that those who curse lack the vocabulary to properly articulate themselves. And since this is my book and my conditioning reigns supreme, I'm going to censor some dialogue, serving up penises with a side of bleeps. Think of this as an opportunity to add your own flair to the book and to mentally add in whatever combination of swear words brings you the most joy.

In addition to the apologies section, I'm including a shame section. While I'm the one making you all envision the horrid scenarios that follow, I am not the one who made them happen. I place that responsibility firmly on the shoulders of all the feral cavemen that have made show-stopping appearances in this book.

And a special shout-out should go to the patriarchy for creating a dynamic where women feel responsible for the atrocious behaviour of the male species.

There may be men reading this who might want to be part of the new world where equality and respect are normal ways of behaving. In that case, I hope this serves as an educational piece on how not to act in romantic situations.

Please, DON'T do any of these things you are about to read. Pretty please. And if you are thinking about it, just stop. Like immediately. And then go to your computer, open your preferred search engine, look up a therapist and start a beautiful journey of self-discovery and growth, with the ultimate goal of not traumatising your fellow humans to the point of them having to write a book about it.

Finally, I'd love any readers (who have probably had disastrous dates of their own) to realise the following:

You are not alone.

Every disastrous date will lead you to know what you don't want, which in turn leads you to know what you do want. That's physics. Or something.

Each date has the potential to reflect your conditioning and that insight can lead you to finding your true self and the right partner—should you want one.

If not, you can still lead a happy, fulfilled life as an amazing single person. Or even as an ordinary one.

So, are you prepared to uncover the looming horrors? You may just throw up in disgust or spit your drink out in shock. Therefore, I recommend no eating or drinking whilst reading.

Proceed with caution . . .

I

MR STRONG MAN

Age: 20
Location: Manchester, England
Where we met: Online dating site
How he asked me out: Via text message

I had recently returned from a six-month backpacking trip around Australia. I'd taken the trip after ending a three-year relationship. What caused the end of a three-year relationship? It turns out three years is precisely the amount of time it took me to realise that I do not, in fact, enjoy being around men with severe anger issues.

Having also finished sixth form around the same time, I thought, what the heck, let's exchange my UK thongs (underwear) for Australian thongs (flip flops) and go on an adventure. Alright, I might have brought some UK thongs with me, too.

The trip was eye-opening, to say the least.

If I could share one highlight, it would be the life-changing coral reef scuba diving trip.

I met twenty lovely strangers and there was a beautiful banquet. I wish I could say that we sat down and devoured that beautiful banquet together, sharing hilarious stories and creating lifelong memories. Unfortunately, that's not what happened. Instead, I got seasick and threw up all over said banquet and had to look those twenty starving strangers in the eye for the two-hour trip back to shore. But every trip has its moments.

On returning to old Blighty as a newly single business student, I became aware that a lot had changed in the dating scene: Cue online dating.

I will mention this though, and my sibling will vouch for me when I say, I'm sure we were the original founders of the online dating idea because when I was thirteen and she was fourteen, we used a CB radio to chat up bored truck drivers. Don't tell Mum.

Unbeknownst to me at the time, this first online dating experience would foreshadow a twenty-year span of some of the most bizarre experiences of my life.

My typical type was the tall, lumberjack kinda guy. You know, the ones you'd see cutting wood, showcasing chiselled abs and topless in the middle of a snow blizzard? Yep. That was my physical type to a tee. At twenty, my selection criteria were, how do I put it politely? Basically . . . well, basic. Just basic.

So, when I came across Mr Strongman on an online dating site, he clearly ticked my lumberjack box. The thing about lumberjacks is they share a lot of similarities to Neanderthals. It's kind of like being able to tell a crocodile from an alligator. Only nerds and those who've experienced the relevant trauma can tell right away.

His profile read that he was almost seven feet tall—an extra-large human. It also mentioned that he competed in strong men competitions around the world; you know the ones where contestants carry massive boulders and pull ten-tonne trucks with mammoth-sized ropes? Impressive. Apparently, he'd reached his sports goal and was now seeking a relationship with the right woman. So far, so good.

The Date

We begin with the usual exchange of numbers, which leads to some flirty text banter, learning about each other, you know, the usual fun and games. Textbook modern courtship right here. After several hours of back and forth, he says the one sentence I love more than 'You've won the lottery and your mum will live forever': *Let's go on a date.*

Please note, for all the men reading this, I find nothing more unattractive than a man who texts and texts and texts and never asks for a date. I want a passionate evening I can reminisce about on my death bed, not a pen pal. Second to that is the guy who asks for a date and doesn't organise anything. If I was a professional party planner, we'd be a match made in heaven, but since I'm not, move along. So, when he uttered those golden words, it was an instant yes!

Let me explain what happened next.

His text read, *Let's go on a date*, but it didn't finish there. That wasn't the end of the sentence. It continued:

Let's go on a date, but first I need to ask you something important.

Oh, here we go. That's one hundred per cent a set-up for something I'm not going to like. Is he married? Does he have herpes? Is he only in the area for a month so even if we fall madly in love, it can only be a short-term love affair ending in inevitable heartache that I'll sigh about in quiet moments for years to come? I'm worried, but, okay, I'll take the bait. What's this very important question?

His response, *It's easier just to show you*. Not the short-term love affair, then.

The first image that comes through—the first of twenty—is a close-up of his man bits in tighty-whities; his schlong is wrapped into a kind of mister whippy ice cream formation. Looks like an anaconda taking a nap. Think elephant, then double the girth. This is something nightmares are made of, let me tell you.

You know when you can't believe what you're seeing? When your brain ceases to function, whilst it's trying to comprehend what's happening? That's my current experience. My jaw falls open. Has he photoshopped it or something?

As promised, there were nineteen other photos and sadly, no, they did not all come together to form one giant life-size image of his member. The nineteen other photos that follow reveal more of the monster in the flesh. One of which shows him holding it like a proud fisherman, celebrating the catch of the world's largest sea slug.

I text the following: *What the heck, is it real? It's massive. I've never seen anything like it.*

His response? *Yeah. It's real.*

I get the sense he's proud of it. The delusions of a male mind.

Is it natural? I feel like David Attenborough discovering a new sea creature that has lurked at the far depths of the ocean—never before seen by human eyes.

Well, not exactly. I've always been extra-large. After achieving my sports ambitions, I needed something new to focus on, so, my new goal is to have the largest penis in the world and see my name printed in the Guinness book of records.

Owwwkay. Firstly, when did the *Guinness World Records* begin recording the largest penis? And who are you not yet beating out with this submission? Secondly, I am curious to know how he got it to be such a mammoth beast.

So, if it wasn't always this big, how have you grown it? I text back.

Instead of a text, he sends through another photo.

Erm, say what? This photo shows him standing in front of a walled mirror where a large rope, like the ones used to moor boats to the port, is tied around the girth of his you-know-what and at the other end dangles a kettlebell. The dang monstrosity is literally hanging below his knee, and remember, this guy is seven feet tall.

A text follows: *I swing the kettlebell back and forth to train the muscle. As you can see, I've had outstanding results.*

It's like he's trying to sell me a penis extension programme and if I buy today, I'll get half off.

No, sir, you have not achieved outstanding results. You have literally created what resembles a monstrous sea slug.

Was I in a nightmare? Who would do such a thing? And who the heck took the photo in the gym? Is this a new trend? Are there groups of men over the world training their junk in gyms and rotating who takes the pictures?

Out of curiosity, what happens when you get an erection? So many questions, so little time.

To be honest, it's impossible now, as I pass out.

Wow. I've suffered the angst of my man passing out after a bonking session, whereas this guy passes out before it's even begun. At least with premature ejaculators you've got a shot against the clock. You're really not selling yourself, sir.

Surely, there's no way any woman would be able to have sex given the size of it, though?

What I wanted to say was no woman in her right mind would go near that Loch Ness monster, but I'm English so I've been conditioned to be polite.

That's why I'm talking to you. I am hoping you are willing to give it a try.

Give it a try? That's a question you'd ask if you're offering someone a new flavour of ice cream, not to invade their body with a missile like it's a hostile country. Besides, do I look like a woman harbouring a Eurotunnel vagina?

In my silence he continues, *Women have babies all the time and they're fine.*

Yes, that's how large it is, he is comparing sex with him to giving birth to a human being. Every woman's favourite sexual experience.

Seriously, we both know those words could only emerge from the mouth of the male of the species. Does this man know most women swear off ever having another child after giving birth because of the immense amount of pain they go through? Not to mention the trail of destruction on their body resulting from literally passing another human being? This guy has lost his marbles. What is romance to this guy? *Fancy a quickie, love? I've already bought you adult diapers and sorted a month of leave from work for your recovery period.*

In between texts, I forward the photos to Mum. She responds with one word, 'Run.'

Forward to sis. Her response, 'Photoshopped.'

I send this text, *I'll be honest, I'm not sure you're going to find a woman on a dating site who can physically engage in intercourse, let alone wants to give it a try. Sorry, but I'm out. Good luck.*

As you can imagine, a man whose main goal in life is to have the world's largest penis also has an ego that somehow rivals the size of the medical marvel between his legs. He did not like my response and instantly blocked me. Dang, I was going to suggest a business idea. I'm certain there's a market to help men who are on the smaller side to grow it to a size they are more comfortable with. Don't you think? My entrepreneurial instinct going underappreciated once again.

Needless to say, I didn't hear from the monster sea slug again and Mum, apologies for scarring your innocent eyes. For life. Forgive me. You will never be able to unsee those images and neither will I. Sorry.

Lessons I learned from this date: Firstly, size does matter, but not in the traditional sense women talk about and men feel insecure about. As we've seen from this story, bigger isn't always better. Perhaps we should change the narrative and say there's a perfect size for everyone. Think of Cinderella and the slipper.

2

MR TUNNEL OF TERROR

Age: 20
Location: Manchester, England
Where we met: In the restaurant where I worked as a waitress
How he asked me out: His friend asked me for my number on his behalf—not a red flag, but perhaps a light pink one.

After the trauma and bizarreness of the text conversation with Mr Strongman, I believed the online dating world was full of penis training weirdos. So, I deleted my profile. But the universe had other plans for me in the form of an archaic style of courtship few people alive have experienced—meeting in person!

I met date number two when I was mustering up extra

cash working as a waitress at a local eatery. He was a fireman and came in for a Sunday roast after a shift with his fiery friends. Don't you just love a man in uniform? Not unless he's got good character to back it up!

He didn't say it directly, but I could tell he was blown away by my banana split making skills. I did give him extra cream. Plus, when I placed it before him, his eyes widened like full moons. I took that to mean joy, but it could also have been horror or some other fearful emotion.

I was still on the hunt for an Adonis, and date 2 didn't disappoint. He was a strapping-looking lad of six foot four (hopefully his . . . other features were not so towering). Model appearance and a physique out of a bodybuilder magazine. He was the type of guy women all over the world swoon over.

During one of our phone conversations, I suggested our first date be at the amusement park, Blackpool Pleasure Beach. Fun for the whole family, apart from one attraction: The Tunnel of Terror, an interactive walkthrough experience where all of the most ghoulish horror films come to life. But, no one could ever know how terrifying it is until you are in there and unable to escape.

I'd heard the experience had a high fear rating, so figured it would be a fun date. I based this conclusion on an article I read that suggested—and I don't know how true this is—if you go to a horror film or share a scary experience with someone, you will appear more attractive after the event because the sweaty palms and heart palpitations a person feels after psychological arousal is misattributed to a feeling of sexual attraction to the other person. Fascinating, right? Maybe that was date one's tactic all along: traumatise, then woo.

My date's response through laughter was, 'Oh, those things aren't scary, but if you want to spend the day at the amusement park, I'm happy to go.'

Yipppee! A guy who loves a bit of adrenaline, like me. Love it. Tick.

The Date

I hear the peep of a horn and jump down two stairs at a time, hollering goodbye to Mum on the way out. Yes, I still live at home.

After a two-hour drive, we reach the car park at Blackpool Pleasure Beach. He parks the car and grabs our bags from the back seat where he hands me my trusty rucksack. He must have noticed my struggle to get one of the straps over my arm because he immediately comes to my assistance. What a gentleman. He pulls it over my shoulder and taps me on the back twice.

'Ready?' He tucks a stray hair behind my ear.

'Ready.' I tug the straps down to tighten it more snuggly against my body and we stroll hand in hand towards the park entrance grabbing our tickets at the kiosk. I wave some money at him, but he bats my hand away. I'm already mentally planning our destination wedding to Hawaii.

Through the turnstile we go and the first attraction on the left in big letters is The Tunnel of Terror. This is going to be fun.

A ghostly figure sits above the entryway, fake blood dripping from its mouth. I guess this is a taste of what's to come.

I grab my date's forearm, 'Are you scared yet?' Giving him a cheeky poke in the ribs.

'I'm not scared, don't worry, I'll protect you.' He grins and strokes my hand that's now wrapped around his massive forearm. I think he enjoys my touch. I like that he wants to protect me. Definitely a quality I desire in a man.

An attendant wearing a scream mask guards the rope that blocks our path. 'Just a few minutes until you'll be running for your life.' With menacing eyes staring into my soul, she taps the rope with a large—hopefully fake—machete. I laugh, knowing nothing in there could be so scary as to send me running.

A loud screech bellows from the walkie talkie she's holding. 'Send in the next victims.' Maniacal laughter follows the announcement.

'Here we go.' I clutch my date's arm a little tighter, but the corridor is single file, so I push him ahead. My palms begin to perspire.

It's pitch black and deathly quiet. Why did I suggest this? I'm already regretting it as I feel my stomach churning. I could have chosen to take him to a mild horror film like a normal person but instead I've forced us into hardcore psychological thriller cosplay.

My date continues taking steps forward at a good pace. That is until bloodied arms dart out of the corridor wall trying to grab him. I hear a blood-curdling scream and assume it's coming from one of the actors until I see the gaping mouth of the fireman. Wow. He's taking the horror film cosplay to the next level.

You know how I said I'm polite because I'm English? Well, it turns out that only applies in situations where I'm able to control my reactions because as he's screaming like he's just seen his mum murdered in front of him, I am laughing hysterically in his face.

The laughter momentarily eases the tension in my body. So much for not being scared. Have you noticed it's always the huge men that are like teddy bears inside? Big softies. I find it quite endearing.

We continue through the first corridor until an opening and light appear at the end. Looks like we'll be entering the first room. Oh crap, fear starts to bubble up in my chest.

In the centre of the room, a dark-haired, female figure sways back and forth in an old wooden rocking chair. Long murky hair falls over her face and terrifying gurgling emerges from her mouth. If hell exists, it's *The Exorcist* and I'm living inside it right now. My only hope is we get out of this room before she starts to projectile vomit. The fireman and I huddle in the corner. We have to walk past her on three sides before we can reach the door to the next room. Current fear factor—ten. I'm shaking as we edge around the rocking exorcist, our backs pressed firmly against the wall, our eyes pinned on her, our hands ready to block any stray vomit, faux or otherwise.

Halfway down the first wall, sounds resembling demonic chants echo around the room.

'Help me.' The gurgles increase in volume.

'Help me.' The gurgles morph into shrieks and the rocking increases in momentum.

'Help me.' She violently hurls herself out of the rocking chair towards us, accompanied by ear-piercing screams.

Her razor-cut arms claw in our direction. I grasp at my date's shirt, but he's too quick. I forgot to mention he plays rugby at the weekends, so he's agile and has disappeared into the next room leaving me to fend for myself. Hopefully, this is an isolated incident.

Feeling pure terror, I close my eyes and sprint in the direction of the next room where I crash into the back of my date. He lets out another almighty scream, continuing a targeted, personal attack on my ears.

The fireman is frozen on the spot.

A crack of metal-on-metal reverberates off the walls. My eyes are drawn ahead, where a bloody ghoul scrapes a steel rod across the prison bars, accompanied by deranged cackling. He's locked in the cell, but the gap between the cell and wall is a distance of only a few feet, so he can easily reach through the bars and grab us. Terrifying does not cut my fear level right now.

Escaping to the next room is our only option.

Before I can communicate this to my date, the prisoner and I lock eyes.

'I'm going to kill you both.'

I'm gonna take a hard pass on that one. My heart is pumping out of my chest. I reckon it'd be easy to have a heart attack in this place. I feel all the blood drain from my face as the prisoner opens the gate that's keeping us apart. My date still appears to be glued to the floor. Well, this isn't part of the fear contract we all mentally signed before I agreed to enter!

The chill of fear engulfs my body as I try to push past my date. He blocks my path with his humongous arm, forcing me backwards and leaving me as prisoner bait, whilst he sprints towards the next room. I'm curious to know which part of firefighter rescue training includes this tactic.

I manage to dodge the prisoner as he yanks off the cell door and chases me with his crowbar down the corridor. At least someone's paying attention to me on this date.

I hear screaming, but this time it's my own and once again I slam into the back of my date in the next room.

'Thanks for leaving me.' My hands are trembling. 'What happened to protecting me?'

No response.

My thoughts are obliterated to silence on observing the terrifying scene before me. Still no response from my date. I put my hand on his back, it's wet from sweat. In a shaky voice that increases in volume with each word my date utters, 'I can't do this. I just can't. I can't do this. I need to get out of here.'

Really? You were handling it so well.

I grab his shaking hand. His eyes are wide and terrified, darting around, probably looking for an exit? He starts screaming, 'Let me out' and banging on the walls, then, with violent intensity, punches a hole through the wall and darts back into the previous room.

I'm left in a freezing cellar with hanging carcasses all around me. I take a moment to admire the design aesthetic of this circle of hell.

I hear a voice over the speaker. 'Can the large man please turn around and go back to the last room. You cannot get out by going back, there are more groups behind you. Can the large man running back through the rooms please turn around and continue forward to the exit, immediately.' I'm pretty certain they are referring to my date.

I hear the fireman's screams increasing in volume and heading in my direction. He rugby tackles me out of the way, and I'm flung into the wall, which I slide down, landing on my bum.

The sounds of a chainsaw starting to rev engulf my ears and to my horror, I see the blades cutting through one of the carcasses where a whole human arm extends out. Holy freaking crap. I claw at the wall desperately trying to scramble to my feet. My mind is blank, then I'm sprinting. The chainsaw psycho is fully emerged from the carcass and is on my tail. I feel the air from the chainsaw kiss my neck as I dart around a carcass and throw myself through the next door. The door swings open. My date is curled in the foetal position on the floor a few feet away. I don't have time to avoid him. I trip and fly through the air crashing to the ground on my side.

Sounds of hysterical laughter echo around the room.

I raise my gaze to see we're in the middle of a jam-packed café, where onlookers are enjoying lunch, and we're the live entertainment.

I didn't realise at the time, but the patrons had viewed our entire journey through The Tunnel of Terror. One young patron is struggling to breathe through laughter, tears streaming down his face. I guess he, like me, takes joy in people's misfortune. Maybe this is my karma for laughing in my date's face moments before he thought he would die.

I glance at my date. He's still in the foetal position. As the pace of my heart begins to regulate, I fake smile for the patrons and scoot across the wooden floor on my bum until I reach him. I put my hand on his back. He jumps to his feet, holding out his fists ready for combat. I forgot to mention he's also a part-time boxer. It turns out all his pastimes have combined to make him the least perfect haunted house patron of all time, aside from, perhaps, a rabid bear on crystal meth.

'It's okay.' I stroke his arm like a nurse calming a patient having a psychotic episode. 'It's over.' I speak in a soothing tone. His eyes—deer in headlights. I continue with long strokes along his arm as I guide him like an old-age pensioner towards the exit.

There's a bench close by, so I gently nudge him to sit. I grab water out of my bag, tip his head back and pour it into his mouth like supporters do for participants on the running part of an Iron Man competition. He seems incapable of doing anything for himself right now. I hope he hasn't sustained any long-term trauma and he's at least able to visit the toilet without assistance.

'How are you feeling?'

He looks up and his eyes have softened.

'I guess I am scared of things like that after all.'

No sh*t, Sherlock!

For the rest of the date, we enjoyed much less scary rollercoasters, much to the relief of my date.

Well, my findings suggest the psychology behind experiencing something scary on a date has some truth to it because the fireman and I ended up dating for six months. Who knew? It didn't last, though, because when a man doesn't have a natural protective instinct and I have to step into those shoes, I end up feeling more like his mother than a partner.

Because of this, my desire to bonk him diminished to zero, and we all know what happens after that, don't we? Cue *The Sound of Music* 'So Long, Farewell' track.

What I learned from this date: Firstly, there is something extremely endearing when a man is vulnerable and shows his emotions. It's one thing I thank my dad for. I remember being in Dad's arms dancing around the living room to 'Fairytale of New York', seeing tears in his eyes. Dad had no issue crying or expressing himself, and so for me, it's normal male behaviour and helps build connection. On the other hand, a man who acts like he's dead inside is not normal.

Secondly, men without natural protective instincts, who happily throw their partner under the bus to save themselves, are not the men for me. Due to this role reversal, I felt forced to take on the masculine role. Result—zero sexual desire.

Thirdly, the experts were right! Experiencing something terrifying with a date definitely creates a bond and an attraction right off the bat. I am living proof. But think twice before bringing a giant boxing, rugby player to a haunted house, for everyone's safety.

3

MR INCREDIBLE HULK

This date has a warning on it. Critical language and aggressive behaviour ensue. As you are well aware, I don't swear, so I can't bring myself to type such profanities.

Age: 21
Location: Manchester, England
Where we met: He was a bouncer at a bar, and I was a patron
How he asked me out: Face to face

Six months later, I was taking great delight in my degree as it was reigniting my passion for entrepreneurship and business.

I'd inherited these passions from Mum and Dad who were a dynamic duo. Mum came up with the ideas. Dad executed them. I became a blend of the two mindsets. I even bickered with myself. So, it was natural to start my first business at ten years old with my eleven-year-old sister.

We'd been posing as models for the cover of an indoor hopscotch game—one of Mum and Dad's genius ideas—but during production, they'd made too many discs. Think drink coaster size, which was the indoor equivalent of the stone you throw in outdoor hopscotch.

Inheriting our parents' entrepreneurial thinking, my middle sis and I decided to make up a game called Skimmers.

Skimmers had the same rules as marbles, where you skim them across the floor and if you hit your opponent's disc, it's yours. It became a huge hit at the local primary school, and we became even more successful than the schools' resident drug dealers selling discs to hungry ten-year-old cronies.

The business was going great guns until Mum decided to do a clean-out of the garage and flood the market by emptying all the boxes into a skip. We felt like little English Escobars watching our empire fall. Picture throwing money into the air in a crowded room and everyone's goal is to grab as much cash as possible. That was the scene of the neighbourhood children in the skip, scrambling to steal as many discs as they could get their grubby hands on. Needless to say, my first business was officially dead. Thanks to Mum being a total narc.

Another thing that was officially dead was my relationship with the fireman. It was the best decision to end it because, strangely, I had zero desire to bonk a man I always had to protect. I'm looking for an equal partner, not a child. So, in typical uni student fashion, I decided to take time out for myself and have some fun with the girls; a night on the town, which involved the primary goal of getting hammered and being dragged into a taxi at the end of the night by fabulous friends. At the ripe old age of twenty-one, I still hadn't evolved beyond my typical gym junkie type, so when I met date number three on the door of a nightclub, my racing twenty-one-year-old hormones went wild.

It was a freezing cold night in England and the black daisy dress I was wearing was hardly a barrier to the cold. I remember feeling gorgeous that night, albeit on the verge of hypothermia. But every English lass would agree, they'd rather freeze than wear a coat.

It wasn't uncommon to see old, bald bouncers on the doors of clubs and bars, but that night, at the Sunshine bar, there was a different kind. Six foot four, rugby player body, chiselled jawline, beautiful eyes, curly dark hair, cut short. The only way to describe this man is Greek God, even though I was certain he was not Greek, or a God—pasty white skin is a sure giveaway and I'm pretty certain God wouldn't be wasting time working a door.

We locked eyes and butterflies swarmed my belly. I love that feeling. It feels like my body is shouting, 'Procreate with this man, woman!' He unclasped the rope so we could enter, and I gave him a cheeky wink as I passed.

'Hey.'

I heard the shout from behind and turned around. 'Can I help you?' I laughed at my candour.

Yes, I am that person who laughs at her own jokes. I'm having a riot alone in a room right now, editing my own book.

'Well, you're a cheeky one, aren't you? I wanted to see if you'd like to go on a date.'

'Where are you taking me?'
'Well, where's your favourite place?'
'Alton Towers.'

I was half-joking given I'd only just met the guy. But the reality is, Alton Towers is my favourite place on earth. It's the most marvellous theme park in England. If you love thrills, please put it on your bucket list of places to visit. But I do suddenly feel the need to advise you to choose your companion wisely. No reason, just a feeling . . .

So, that was that. He arranged for us to visit Alton Towers and the date was happening the following weekend.

The Date

The following weekend rolls around and it's not like I've been counting down the days or anything. I feel the energy of excitement bubbling up in my belly. I'm eager to get to know my date and excited for the rides. I am an adrenaline junkie after all.

A loud knock reverberates through the front door, followed by Mum's voice. 'He's here.'

I make my way down the stairs. Mum has let him in. He's standing inside, leaning against the wall and I feel like a prom queen making her grand entrance. Mum gives me the look of, holy moly, he's a cracker. What can I say, Mum and I have similar taste in men. I raise my eyebrows and nod in her direction. Perfect communication, no words necessary.

We head outside to his car. He's twenty-four-years-old and his car is a bomb, but no twenty-one-year-old cares about their date's car. Well, I didn't anyway. I get in and he kicks over the engine. It splutters and spits, but after a few minutes, it settles and off we go.

On our drive I quickly establish my date has missed his vocation in life—as a stand-up comedian, albeit with no concept of political correctness. But he is English and most English people pride themselves on being as politically incorrect as possible. His delivery reminds me of that comedian in Australia, Carl Barron, who's mastered the art of observational humour. Although my date's forte seems to be in Dad jokes.

'My last date was cross-eyed. It didn't work out because we could never see eye to eye.' He follows the punchline with loud, bellowing laughter. Nice. Something we have in common—we both find ourselves hilarious.

After an hour, my cheeks are aching, and I have to retrieve my emergency tissues to wipe away the mascara that's streaked beneath my eyes. What a fantastic start to the date.

Twenty minutes later, the car starts to spit and splutter, and the worst thing is we're on a steep hill. This is a funny start to an adventurous date, and I look forward to what jokes my date makes to ease the tense moment.

'Don't do this to me, Gladys.'

Who the heck is Gladys? I check the back seat, just in case.

'Gladys, not now, not today!'

I realise Gladys must be the car because my date begins to bang the steering wheel accompanied by a string of cuss words whilst intermittently shouting the name Gladys. And when I say bang, it's more like trying to smash his fists through the wheel. Road rage on steroids, except he's not screaming profanities at a fellow driver who will soon be out of sight. He's in a fight with his own car. I also realise this means there won't be any fun jokes about this moment. At least, not for about twenty years, and I'm not sure I can live with that.

The engine does one last splutter and drops to silence.

'No, you bleeping piece of junk.' His voice is loud and the veins on the side of his head are protruding. Yikes!

He pulls over, yanks up the hand brake, jumps out of the car, kicks it three times and screams, 'F-you, Gladys, F-you, F-you!' I assume to the car because my name is not Gladys and there's no one in the back seat. Either that or he has a multiple personality disorder.

The door swings open and he throws himself back into the driver's seat, forcing the key into the ignition in another attempt at turning over the engine. Nothing. Dead as a dodo. He grabs the gear stick with such force the head of the stick comes off in his hands. The only way to describe his response —pure rage.

A dark shade of purple swells his face as the blood surges into his neck and head. He hurls the knob. Smack. It hits the glass and like an Olympic athlete the crack races across the windshield.

Cue approximately one thousand bleeps.

I remove myself from the vehicle to escape the energy of this lunatic. Watching on from the side of the road, I plug my ears with my fingers, so I don't have to endure the never-ending string of bleeps as he accosts Gladys. There is zero chance I'm going to be able to get through to him in this state, so instead, I call a tow truck.

An hour later, Gladys is towed away, and I assume the

date is done, but, unfortunately for me, my unhinged date is surprisingly organised and resourceful and has booked us a bus that goes to Alton Towers. Oh, happy days! As a little girl, I always dreamed of being swept away by a rageaholic who had no control over his emotions. Eye roll.

We make our way to the bus stop and step aboard when the bus arrives. I scan the bus. The only seats available are right at the back, behind two sumo wrestling-looking guys. We shuffle down the corridor in single file, trying not to bash people's heads in with our bags until we reach our seats. I squeeze into the window seat. My date slides in next to me. He's a mammoth beast of a man, and so, in my attempt to prevent any further outbursts, I squash in as close to the window as possible, providing as much space as I can. Have you heard of the saying, once bitten, twice shy? Yep, that's me, subconsciously adjusting my own behaviour to curb my date's reactions. It's almost as healthy as my date's reaction to minor inconveniences.

The bus engine revs and jerks into motion. It seems my date's emotions have neutralised because he pipes up with a joke, 'A woman in labour suddenly shouts shouldn't! Wouldn't! Couldn't! Don't worry, the doctor said, they are just contractions.'

It's funny and I can't help but chuckle. He seems to appreciate my response as he continues with a second joke.

'What's the best thing about Switzerland?' He motions his hand for me to respond.

'Tell me.' I'm enjoying this side of him.

'Don't know, but their flag is a big plus.'

'That's hilarious.' I laugh and playfully nudge him. 'That's a good one. Love it.' Note to self, tell joke to Mum later. She'll like that one.

I hope this light-hearted version is a sign of what's to come on the rest of the date, and he doesn't revert to *The Incredible Hulk*. Positive thinking, activate!

The universe must have confused my positive thinking for jinxing because the guy in front decides to put his seat back. I feel relief exiting my body quicker than a sneeze as I turn to view my date. That shade of purple has returned with a vengeance, veins bulging.

You can guess what happens next. All hell breaks loose as my date kicks the back of the seat with such force that the poor guy is thrown forward into the seat in front of him. Here we go again. And this time, there's no Gladys to pin it on.

'Bleeping put your seat forward, you bleeping bleep.'

Everyone on the bus turns and stares. One mother covers her daughter's ears who looks close to tears. I grab my date's arm.

'Hey, what are you doing? You are scaring people.' I use a firm and assertive tone. For extra impact, I stare with the intention of the world's most powerful laser penetrating the side of his head.

He looks at me. His breathing is short and sharp through his nose. Picture a bull about to charge. The guy in front turns around. Oh crap, World War III is here. I always figured England would be involved, but I never pictured it would start quite like this. I inhale deeply and brace for impact.

'Sorry, mate.' The sumo wrestler jerks his seat back to an upright position.

Oh, thank goodness he's not a nutter like my date. Most

guys in this part of town would have pummelled his head in by now. My heart is beating so fast. I hate confrontation.

'Let it go. Just relax. It's not a long ride to Alton Towers.' I rub his back to try and calm him down. I feel like the mother of a rebellious infant who is in the phase of the terrible twos. Tantrums abound. My date slumps into his seat, his arms crossed. He looks like a sulking kid who's been given marching orders.

Attraction level—zero.

He removes his baseball cap and throws it to the ground. I notice he's balding, and his eyes are sunken with a yellowish tinge. Is he not feeling well? He's young to be going bald, but it does happen.

Overhead I see the Alton Towers' sign. I literally can't wait to get off this bus. Cue hurdling the seats.

The air pressure releases the doors that fling open. My fellow passengers begin to stand so I can't impress them with my world-class hurdling technique, so I settle for following the line of fellow prisoners exiting the bus. Passengers. I mean fellow passengers.

My date has already bought our tickets, so we get our bags checked and push through the turnstiles into the park. I need to go on a rollercoaster to release the stress of the morning. The Oblivion will do the trick. I check the map that came with our tickets and head in that direction. I feel a hand grabbing onto mine, big and meaty. He does have nice hands. His energy seems to have relaxed again. Please let it stay that way as I can't handle another outburst. I find actual rollercoasters are preferable to emotional ones.

Two cable cars and approximately a mile of walking later,

we reach the Oblivion. The queue is short, which means it won't be long until it's our turn.

'Can we go on the front row?' I jump and tug on his sleeve like a little kid. I'm hoping my light-hearted energy will rub off on him.

He seems to enjoy my enthusiasm. 'Okay.' He says it in a tone a dad would use to an excitable child. Not the sexiest exchange, but any emotion other than rage is fine with me right now.

Another three rides come and go before we're at the front of the line. My date goes ahead and sits in the far-left seat. I slide into the middle one next to him.

I'm not sure if you're familiar with rollercoasters, but the ones that go upside down require much harsher safety requirements, presumably so people don't get catapulted to their death mid-ride. Because of this, I am not surprised when the attendant comes around and pulls the over-the-shoulder bar down and pushes it tight into my body, with an additional push and click for good measure. Crikey! It's hard to breathe, but at least I know I'll survive the upside-down loops.

I feel the excitement rise in my stomach. This is going to be so much fun!

The attendant pushes my date's bar firmly into his chest, which is followed by, 'Bleeping hell, mate, that's bleeping tight. What are you bleeping playing at, you bleep? I can't bleeping breathe, mother bleeper!'

You have got to be kidding me! Round three, ride rage.

Fortunately for the attendant, but not for me, the ride moves on its tracks, so guess who's stuck listening to his endless cursing and yelling? Moi. Now, I really am a prisoner.

I feel like cursing myself. So much for the ride releasing my stress.

We reach the top, where the car hangs precariously over the edge. I peer down at the black cavity far below; smoke rises from the darkness. My date seems oblivious as he continues to belt the chest bar like King Kong. Fruitloop comes to mind.

Whoosh! The car tips over the edge, and it feels like we're free falling. The sensation is exhilarating as a rush of adrenaline courses through me. I appreciate the momentary silence. That is until we emerge from the tunnel, and my date catches his breath and returns to his favourite word in the whole wide world—bleep.

The ride pulls back into its station, and thank goodness there's a different attendant, although that seems to make no difference to my date. 'You'd better tell that mother-bleeper he's a bleeping idiot. He almost killed me. Bleeping bleep.'

Oh, my goodness gracious, this guy is from another planet . . . *Planet of the Apes* perhaps? I'm starting to wish the attendant hadn't strapped him in at all because all participants in this conversation would be in a much happier place right now. I'm dreading going on another ride because he's probably going to have another meltdown. What can we do that's low risk?

'Let's go to the arcade.' I yank the arm of my date, pulling him away from the attendant who is politely nodding. No one deserves this kind of abuse, let alone a poor teenager who makes minimum wage dealing with kids puking and adults screaming.

I slide my hands into my jeans' pockets to avoid holding

his hand. My happiest place on earth, which is Alton Towers, has turned into a nightmare. Surely, he wouldn't have a problem in the arcade? Would he?

On approaching the arcade, I notice a stall where patrons throw bags at tin cans to win prizes. Maybe this could help him let off some steam? I notice my thoughts now revolve around keeping this beast in his cage, exactly how you want to feel on a date. There will be no second date, that's for sure. Trouble is, I'm currently still trapped on the first one.

'Why don't you have a go?' I smile, pointing at the stall.

My date's face still looks like purple hell. He seems to have zero awareness of how his behaviour impacts those around him.

We walk over and the guy on the stand hands us three bags. They look and feel like they are filled with rice. I am thankful that there are no sharp objects around in case my date finds a problem with the contents.

In between outbursts he'd informed me that he plays baseball on the weekends, so he should have a strong and accurate throw. Please, for the love of God, let him be good. There's no combination worse than a delicate ego and no skills.

He aims and throws.

Miss.

Oh no, please let him hit one. My chest tightens.

His face turns a slight shade of pink.

I've learned this is the first sign of a meltdown and my heart beats a little faster.

Second throw. The bag makes contact, and the top can topples to the ground, leaving the remaining cans intact.

Face shade—red.

I attempt to ease the tension by shouting, 'Nice shot' and clapping my hands with such vigour that passers-by might think I'm doing an impression of Jolly Chimp—the cymbal-banging monkey toy.

My date remains transfixed on the cans like a lion ready to pounce on its prey.

Please let this next one hit.

Third shot. Miss.

Face shade—purple, veins popping. Unleashing of *The Incredible Hulk*—imminent.

My date propels himself over the stand like he's Jason Bourne and with one crazy punch sends the remaining cans flying in every direction. This is accompanied by about fifty bleeps, and, apparently, does not qualify him for a prize.

I hear the attendant on his walkie talkie, 'Security urgently required at stall 666.'

My date tears down teddies hanging around the stand and kicks them about on the ground. It's a scene from a teddy massacre.

Three beefed-up security guards charge past me, hurdle the stand and wrestle my date to the ground, placing handcuffs on his wrists. Is this really happening at my favourite place on earth? Or is this another horror house? Designed specifically for me?

I follow about ten steps behind as my date is escorted out of the park and thrown onto the grassy verge. He breaks down in tears.

Remember my first observation of him having road rage on steroids? Seems I was on the money. He confesses he's been on steroids for the last five years. This makes so. Much.

Sense. When I google steroids, I find balding, sunken eyes and hormonal imbalance are side effects. And guess what, there's a thing called roid rage! That's what I'd been subjected to all day long—normal guy, Incredible Hulk. Normal guy, Incredible Hulk.

First step—stop taking steroids!

I declined further requests for a date but was always pleasant when I saw him on any doors of nightclubs. I don't want to be on the receiving end of anymore roid rage.

Lessons I learned from this date: Firstly, this experience has drilled it firmly into my head that first dates should only be for an hour. Maybe going to a local café for a cup of tea, not a whole day with someone I don't know from Adam.

Secondly, I'm not interested in guys who take drugs. It's something I refuse to tolerate.

Thirdly, any behaviour a man displays in front of me means one day that behaviour will be directed at me. Thank you, Mum's counselling training. Fingers crossed he gets help and no, I didn't recommend him to Mum for counselling. I love her too much to send him her way.

4

MR FODDER

Age: 22
Location: Manchester, England
Where we met: In a local nightclub
How he asked me out: He didn't. I asked him.

After the disastrous date with Mr Incredible Hulk, I figured why not try a different type of guy. The last three had all been confident. Some verged on arrogant. So maybe it was time to change it up and try a shy guy.

To provide context for this date, I need to broach the subject of food. Who doesn't love a good feed? I know I do. My fellow Taureans would agree that eating is one of our most pleasurable activities, followed a close second by sleeping. I love a good snooze. But, for me, food reigns supreme, which is why I have to keep my relationship with food somewhat in check. If I allow my appetite for deliciousness to rule, I'd end up the size of a double-decker bus.

I do have a second theory around my love of food, and by food I, of course, mean chocolate and cake. It's a vice I share with my two older sisters. Mum would send us off to school with ... wait for it. One. Single. Digestive biscuit.

Erm. Yep. Mum, bless her heart was thinking about our health. But what happened to all three sisters was when we got to an age where we could buy our own food, well, the best way to describe it is by picturing the cake-eating scene from *Matilda*, where Miss Trunchbull forces Bruce Bogtrotter to eat a whole eighteen-inch chocolate cake. Instead of being forced by a terrifying and formidable woman, we were forced by a decade's worth of chocolate deprivation.

'You're going to be clinically obese by the time you're thirty.' Mum would say this, accompanied by a shake of the head every time she observed my careful placement of an entire Sara Lee double chocolate gateau into the microwave. On the ping, I'd take a serving spoon and mix it until it resembled a massive pile of goo, then, open sesame and down the hatch. You'll find this is the official recipe and serving instructions for chocolate gateau at La Maison Dessert Paris.

Moral of the story ... maybe Mum should have upgraded our snacks to CHOCOLATE. Covered. Digestives.

At this time in my life, when I was not inhaling Sara Lee gateaux, I was necking back cask wine and partying at local bars and clubs, which is, of course, a requirement for any undergraduate in the UK.

One evening I was on the dance floor, busting out some

crazy moves with some random guys when I caught his eye. He was leaning against the bar, standing alone, holding a beer.

Later, I'd discover it was his friends I was busting out funky moves with.

He was the type who didn't know how attractive he was. You know, the guy who's hot but doesn't know it? That was him. I wouldn't normally go for a shy guy, but after the trauma of my last few dates, I was considering an entire lifestyle change. I figured before taking on a new identity and moving to Vatican City, I could consider starting with small changes, like asking a guy out for once. I wrote my number on a napkin and put it into his hand before leaving.

The Date

I will note this is our third official date. We'd had two dates prior to this one, but I didn't realise their significance until we'd had this third and final date.

I rap the knocker on his parent's front door and tug at my jeans that are digging into my waist. Crikey, they feel so tight. I've noticed the same thing with a few other items of clothing lately. My thoughts are interrupted by the door swinging open.

'Hello, beautiful.'

He pulls me in for a hug and I throw my arms around his muscular shoulders feeling butterflies in my stomach. That's always a good sign. His parents are away for the weekend, so we have the house to ourselves. Party time!

'Come in, let me get you a drink.'

A promising start to a raucous evening. I prepare to

answer 'tea, please' to the typical offerings of cocktails, coffee, or tea when I see a saucepan of steaming hot chocolate sitting on the gas top. The sweet scent floats into my nostrils. I'm momentarily surprised, but I take a seat at the island bench and admire his magnificent physique.

'How often do you go to the gym?'

'Every day, for like an hour. Never miss a session.' He flexes his bicep.

Wow. That's commitment. Personally, I don't like the gym, so I don't go. I'd much rather do things I love, like galloping through the forest on horseback, dancing the salsa or hiking through the wilderness.

He grabs two big bags of marshmallows and a pack of chocolate flakes. The entire contents of each bag end up in the mountain of cream that streams down the sides of the mammoth mug. I feel my mouth gape open when the hot chocolate de extravagance comes into view. Mental note: ask Mum why she never made cocoa this epic for me as a child. Mum served us honey and lemon. No comparison really.

'Take a sip.'

He watches intently as I enjoy the smooth taste of velvety chocolate liquid sliding down my throat. Yum. Decadent. I've noticed he loves to watch me enjoying a meal or drink. Most people like to see people enjoying food they've prepared, don't you reckon? So, I don't think much of it. He takes a sip of water.

'You didn't fancy one?'

He shakes his head. 'I've got to keep myself trim, otherwise, you'll be off with another lad.'

I laugh out loud as it's so far from my character. The

Taurean bull is loyal to a tee, and when we love, we love extremely hard.

'I've made us some delicious dishes for tonight. Why don't you go and relax and enjoy your hot chocolate while I prepare the food?'

Could this guy be my dream man, taking care of me, making me scrumptious food? Can a girl get too much of a good thing?

I scoop up my hot chocolate and walk into the living room. This is the first time I've been at his parents' home. They clearly love the dark wood look—reminds me of an old English pub. I scan the family photos. Pretty much all of them are of the two parents and a chubby kid.

'Is this you?' I grab one with a silver frame and head back into the kitchen, flashing it in front of him.

'Oh God, don't look at those. I look hideous.' He rushes into the living room and proceeds to turn all the photos face down. That's odd, right?

'Hideous is pretty strong. I think you were cute.'

He ignores my compliment and busies himself in the kitchen. Okay then. Obviously, a touchy subject. I'll leave that one alone. I flick on the TV and enjoy some *You've been Framed* comedy, whilst devouring the remains of my hot chocolate extravaganza.

'Food's ready.'

I'm seriously stuffed from the hot chocolate. But I can't be rude, that's not the English way. So, I force the food down while he watches on joyfully.

Two hours later, I'm sprawled on the couch in a food coma. This evening has turned from home alone party time to early lights out at Nanna's house. I feel like Violet Beauregarde in blueberry form, only bigger. The only way I'm going anywhere is if my date literally rolls me off this couch. My eyelids feel so heavy, I can barely keep them open.

In the next moment, I wake to a tap on my shoulder, followed by a whisper, 'Wake up, beautiful.' I raise my hand to shield my eyes from the light flooding the room from the side table lamp. The red digits on the alarm clock read 3.32 am. What the heck? Why am I awake at this ungodly hour?

'What's going on? How did I get into bed?'

'I carried you upstairs. I've brought you a midnight snack.'

Now don't get me wrong, you know I adore food, but who eats at 3.32 am in the morning, unless you're staggering home from a pub and wandering past a kebab place? I'm certain I've already consumed my week's calorie quota from the hot chocolate alone.

'Thanks, sweetie, but I'm not hungry. I just wanna sleep.' I shut my eyes and roll onto my side.

'Babe, look what I brought you.'

I feel a weight land beside me on top of the covers. I blink open one eye. There's a tray of what appears to be ten boxes of chocolate chip cookies, piled in a massive heap. Holy moly.

'Come on. It's fun to have a midnight snack. Let's celebrate our first overnighter together.'

He clearly has never watched the movie, *Seven*, with Brad Pitt. I'll remind you, the gluttonous guy carks it.

He hauls me up to a sitting position and does the 'here comes an aeroplane' like parents do to kids to make them open their mouths. I'm so tired, I can't be bothered protesting so I open wide and eat the cookie. He places a mug of steaming hot milk into my other hand. I peer down at my newly formed muffin top hanging over my pyjama pants. My waistline is starting to resemble Santa Claus's. Two hours later the cookie pile is half its original size and I'm the only one chomping down on them. My date looks delighted. Is he training me up to win one of those pie-eating contests? Or perhaps he's going to roast me alive and enjoy me with fava beans? Middle of the night theories are never solid, but this one is feeling too real for comfort.

The following morning, I wake feeling groggy as heck. I'm not used to broken sleep and following Santa's midnight eating routine.

Remember the Oompa-Loompas rolling Violet's ballooned body out of the chocolate factory? That's me this morning, landing with a thud onto the carpet and crawling like a sloth into the bathroom. I love sloths. After dressing and poking around at the dark bags under my eyes, I notice scales beneath the sink and step on them. I gaze down in my sleepy haze until the numbers finally stop. WHAT THE ACTUAL HECK? . . . sixty-eight kilos? In the two and a half weeks I've been dating this guy I've put on eight kilos. Surely that cannot be right, can it?

Feeling alarmed by the sudden and massive weight gain, I jump down the stairs two at a time into the kitchen, where on entering I observe my date breaking a large number of eggs into a bowl. One, two, three . . . I count twenty eggs. What's he making? Breakfast for a rugby team? I watch him as he adds dollop after dollop of butter until he forgets about the dollops and puts the whole pack in, then whisks. A huge pile of grated cheese sitting on the cutting board gets dumped into the bowl as well. Is he catering for a party? Is he expecting guests?

Don't get me wrong, before I culled animal products, I loved butter and cheese. But even then, I was appalled by the idea of twenty servings worth mixed into one heaped mountain of eggs.

He tosses the entire contents of the bowl into the pan, and a few minutes later, yells, 'Babe, breakfast's ready.' He then slides the massive omelette onto a humongous dinner plate.

OH. MY. GOODNESS. GRACIOUS. GREAT BALLS OF FIRE. That twenty eggs, one kilo of cheese, whole block of butter heart attack of a breakfast is. JUST. FOR. ME. That's like 7,000 calories and goodness knows how much saturated fat. Is he secretly trying to knock me off? Maybe my midnight premonition was accurate.

I can see the headline now, Death by Omelette: Twenty-something female dies on date from massive heart attack after consuming world's largest omelette.

My mind floats back to all the other times we'd spent together.

After the first meeting at the nightclub: I saw him again at the kebab shop where he'd kindly ordered extra-large hot chips for me. At the time I thought he was just a generous guy, but clearly, this was all part of his ingenious plan.

He handed me the bag of chips. 'How much do you weigh? You're so little.'

'No idea, I don't own scales.' I stuffed a chip into my mouth and contemplated the oddness of the question.

'I reckon you're around fifty-eight kilos,' he nods, sizing up my waist.

It's not a topic that interests me unless I can no longer fit into my clothes. Mum taught me as long as I'm happy in my own skin it doesn't matter what I weigh.

A quick note, out of curiosity, I did weigh myself at a friend's house and lo and behold, he was close, only two kilos out; I was sixty kilos.

First Official Date: He took me to an all-you-can-eat restaurant where he ordered four starters, four mains and four desserts. He piled food into my mouth, and when I protested that I couldn't fit in another morsel, he pleaded not to waste the food when so many people were starving across the planet. It's now all making sense.

Second Date: Just desserts. Ten desserts later, I could hardly move due to the food baby I was nursing, until the waitress politely asked us to get the heck out so she could go home.

Between Dates: He dropped off chocolates and sweets and insisted on watching me eat them. Mum and I believed they were kind gestures, but on seeing this omelette, I'm one hundred per cent sure this was not coming from a heart-centred place, after all.

Do you see a pattern forming? I know I do.

He turns around and sees me standing by the entryway and my expression must have said it all because he drops the spatula.

'Have you intentionally been feeding me up?'

He rushes over, falls to his knees and tightly cradles my hands. 'I'm sorry babe, I was just scared of losing you.'

'I'm confused. What has feeding me so much food got to do with losing me?'

'If I'm being honest, I never thought a woman like you would ever want a man like me. I figured if you put on a lot of weight, you'd be less attractive to other men and you'd be happy staying with me.'

'Wait. What? Let me get this straight. You're fattening me up like those poor Christmas turkeys so I would look and feel unattractive?'

Needless to say, that was our last date. My weight returned to normal a few weeks later after consuming more appropriate levels of sustenance.

What I learned from this date: Firstly, sometimes deceit is presented as kindness. By bringing awareness to the intention of this person's actions, it led to the truth.

Secondly, I'm extremely confident in my own skin. I'm not perfect by any stretch of the imagination, but I value a man who owns and likes who he is. After having three disastrous dates, I'd discovered I was more compatible with confident guys. Give me an average-looking Joe who oozes confidence, over a hot model who is insecure. And even though these dates had been disastrous, I was learning what characteristics I liked and what I didn't like. Let's call it refinement.

5

MR JET SKI

Age: 24
Location: Perth, Australia
Where we met: At a petrol station
How he asked me out: He didn't ask me out. He kind of stated he would pick me up and assumed I'd be there. He assumed correctly.

Welcome to Perth, Western Australia!
I'd completed my degree with honours. Go me! And since my last disastrous date, I'd entered into a relationship for two and a half years and subsequently dumped him. We'd moved in together and it became apparent his domestic skills were equivalent to those of a toddler. Actually, that's unfair to toddlers; they're capable of at least pretending to cook. It was so bad I'd open the spare bedroom cupboard and there'd be empty hangers and a humongous pile of every

item of clothing he owned in one stinking—literally stinking—pile!

Something about me—I cannot stand domestic duties, so, I was never going to be that girlfriend who took on the responsibilities of my partner's chores and it seems neither was he. If he could have had it his way, our home would have permanently looked like a frat house on a Sunday morning.

Shortly after culling the relationship, I'd met a Turkish man who informed me he never wanted to set foot in the kitchen and desired a woman to bear his children. My response: Sir, you're looking for a maid and a surrogate, which you can find online for a variety of reasonable rates. See ya!

Saying adios to my ex's smelly socks for the last time and vowing never to become a maid-surrogate seemed perfect timing, as Mum was over living in the cold and rainy land of Manchester. After half a decade of feeling chilled to the bone —Mum's words—she'd had enough and carted me and my middle sister off to Oz with her new husband, boring Barry. Mum wanted to relocate to somewhere in the world that had the most days of sun—cue emigration to Perth and a whole new pool of men. Prospects were looking up.

I'd only been living in Perth for a few days, so, being new to the area I was still finding my way around. This was before the likes of phone GPS or navigation systems in vehicles. I'd purchased a road map from a spotty-faced teen at the local petrol station. Unbeknownst to me, after hearing my foreign accent, he'd charged me one hundred dollars instead of twenty-five and had pocketed the change. Thieving little bogan!

I was leafing through it out the front, trying to figure

out how the heck to get home, when I felt the presence of another person.

'Need some help?'

I glanced up to see a cute face with shoulder-length dirty blonde hair. Aussie Aussie Aussie, Oi, Oi, Oi! He had the typical Aussie appearance you see on the likes of *Home and Away* and *Neighbours*. So, you can imagine my surprise when he spoke in an English accent. Apparently, I wasn't done attracting British men. Though I must say, I do love the cheekiness of the Brits, so it wasn't that surprising.

'I'm trying to find my way home.' I pointed to the location of where I lived on the map.

'Aren't we all,' he snorted, giving me a cheeky wink.

'You're trouble.' I shook my head, enjoying the flirt.

'Me, trouble? Those two words don't belong in the same sentence.' His laugh was loud and deep. 'Let me help you.'

Before I could respond, he'd pulled the map out of my hands and pointed to this road and that road until he saw my vacant expression.

'Follow me. I'll get you home.'

What a gent!

I got in my car and followed his ute out of the petrol station. Ten minutes later we arrived at the house I'd been living in with Mum and sis for the last week since we emigrated. Ironically, it's on Notting Hill Street. How very English. All the Brits seem to congregate in the northern suburbs of Perth, so it seems.

I pulled into the driveway, got out and thanked him for going above and beyond.

'It's my pleasure. I'll be your Perth tour guide. I've got a jet ski that we can take out tomorrow. I'll pick you up at 8 am.'

For the second time, he didn't give me a chance to respond and jumped into his truck. He did this kind of salute goodbye, which for some bizarre reason made me do the same gesture back. What, am I on a royal visit to the commonwealth, seeing the sites and saluting the Queen's Guard at Buckingham Palace?

The Date

The next day at 7.55 am he honks his horn. Isn't it against the law to honk before 9 am? Maybe it's different in Australia. I come to realise Aussies get up early, like 5 am early because by seven in the morning, the incinerating heat of the Perth sun means you can't go out for the rest of the day without burning to a crisp. Hence why they are making all sorts of noise before 9 am. Ugh, I detest getting woken up. I will also add that I don't enjoy getting burnt to a crisp. Why am I living in Perth again?

I grab my belongings. Yell goodbye to Mum and head outside.

He's leaning against his ute with shades on, looking very suave. He knows he's hot stuff. He greets me with a hug, lifts me over his shoulder and spins me around. That's an interesting greeting! He puts me back down and the blood drains back out of my face.

He opens the passenger door, where there's an actual step to get into the truck, it's that big. Come to think of it, it resembles those monster trucks that you see driving over piles of cars on television. I'm surprised there wasn't a full staircase waiting beside it.

It's a beautiful day, not a cloud in the sky. I hope this will be fun. We make small talk as we head down the Mitchell Freeway and in no time at all, he's reversing the monster truck down the boat ramp.

I remove my skirt, leaving on my bikini bottoms and long-sleeved sun protection shirt. Being an English lass, the sun tends to turn my milk bottle skin into a lobster within minutes. With the double whammy of the sun reflecting off the water, it will not end well if I risk wearing only bathers.

Ten minutes later, he's manoeuvred the jet ski into the water. He's helped me into the seat behind him and my hands are around his waist.

'I hope you like speed.'

Yes. Yes, I do.

'I hope you like speed too.' I shout back over the sound of the engine as we hurtle across the whitecaps of the Swan River.

Oh, it's a heavenly feeling crashing through the waves with the ocean spray on my face. I am convinced it's going to be a brilliant date. Maybe that thought cursed it because, after ten or so minutes, I hear my date holler over the wind, 'Fancy a go?'

'Heck yeah.'

He skids the jet ski onto the beach and with all the grace of an elite gymnast, dismounts into the water. In my mind, I hold up a score of ten for his perfect performance. I shimmy forward into the driver's seat, and he jumps on the back, placing his hands on my hips. Cheeky.

Unbeknownst to my date, it wasn't my first rodeo on a jet ski, nor going fast, so I figure I'll show him what speed really is.

I jerk the throttle backwards and the jet ski takes off at lightning speed. I feel his hands grip tightly around my waist. He's clearly surprised.

I swerve left, then right, followed by three tight consecutive doughnuts at full throttle. His tight grip is now accompanied by sudden bursts of screaming, which make me holler. I try not to laugh, but it just comes out. I am having so much fun.

After ten minutes, his screams are hurting my ears, so I head back to the beach and jump into the water. His face is red; probably needs more sunscreen, or less screaming, perhaps?

'My turn.' His tone is low, and he has a crazed look in his eyes.

The last ten minutes of pure joy mean I don't fully register his emotion, so in my ignorance, I jump on the back and hold on tight.

He yanks down on the throttle and within seconds we're at breakneck speed, going in one direction, straight ahead. Speed increasing and increasing. I feel my grip tightening, the elation feels electric, but his energy feels different, more chaotic this time. Faster and faster we go in a straight line. What's he playing at? Where's he going? We hit top speed and then he yanks the handlebars down hard and to the right. The jet ski skids into a hairpin turn. The next thing I remember is flying through the air, followed by a headfirst crash landing, smacking my neck hard against the surface of the river. Now I'm submerged. I pull my way through the water, back to the surface, gasping frantically for air and feeling intense shooting pain through my neck.

'My neck.' I put my hand to it and it's excruciating to touch.

My date laughs hysterically. 'Was that enough speed for you?' He smirks.

'I think my neck is injured,' I yell over the wind.

'What?'

'My neck. It's hurt. We need to go back.'

His expression turns from laughter to concern as he pulls the jet ski alongside me and hauls me onto the back.

Guess where we spent the rest of the date? Yep, you guessed it, the emergency room. Where love comes alive and beautiful memories are made. He must have apologised a hundred times and I kind of felt bad for the guy, but after multiple chiropractic appointments and twenty years on, there's still a weakness. Damn you Mr Jet Ski and damn the male ego.

What I learned from this date: Firstly, insight from my two-year relationship—he does NOT expect me to be his dang maid and is adequately domesticated.

Secondly, the male ego is one hundred per cent a real thing. It seems this guy didn't like getting as good as he can give and had to restore his ego by proving he was stronger and faster in an extremely dangerous way. From this date, I realised I need a man who can keep his ego in check and appreciate my independence and passion.

6

MR CAPTAIN

Age: 24
Location: Perth, Australia
Where we met: On a yacht Meetup
How he asked me out: Yelling from afar, whilst I was making my getaway in the opposite direction.

Have you ever had a guy protesting that age doesn't matter? A guy contacted me online who was forty years my senior. I politely responded saying I was looking for a man closer to my own age, to which he announced, 'Age doesn't matter.' I replied with, 'If age doesn't matter, why aren't you going for eighty-year-olds?' He blocked me.

I was still new to Perth and wanted to increase my circle of friends and what better way to meet people than through the online platform—Meetup. No, I am not getting endorsed by Meetup, but if you are the owner, I'm happy for you to take me out for a thank you drink, just sayin'. Unless of course, you resemble any of the men featured in this book.

How this situation came about was through my insatiable desire to learn new things. As you are now well aware from the jet ski date, I love getting the adrenaline moving through my body, so on one sunny afternoon, I decided I would join a Meetup where I could learn to sail yachts, you know, as you do. Marvellous idea, right? WRONG. So wrong!

This wasn't a date, and I wasn't looking for one. This was an experience where I wanted to run for the hills, but due to the fact there typically aren't hills to which one can run in the middle of the ocean, I was stuck. Unfortunately for me, it was with an exceptionally forward older captain with whom I got an instant feeling of ick.

The Non-Date . . . just to be clear

I rock up at the local jetty along with eight eager, wannabee sailors. Everyone is making small talk and eying the surroundings for the owner of the yacht.

Around the corner saunters a tall, athletically built-looking chap who must be in his late seventies, early eighties. I call him chap because when he starts talking, he speaks in the Queen's English. He is also adorned in a dapper sailor's hat, coat and neckerchief. Serious old-school sailor attire.

'All aboard,' he shouts through a make-shift hand megaphone.

We make eye contact, and he does a double-take. Seems he doesn't catch many attractive women out at sea. I wonder why they're avoiding him and wish I'd received the memo.

We form a line, each person taking a step on board, one at a time, with the help of the captain's hand.

I'm the last to board, and he holds my hand much longer than necessary. I politely yank my hand away and smile in an attempt to cover my increasing feelings of discomfort.

'I'll be chatting to you later, missy.' He winks and blows me a kiss.

My immediate reaction is to take a running jump off this boat, but as you will quickly learn, as an English lass I have been conditioned to believe I should not make a scene, no matter how uncomfortable I feel. If I were ever recruited for a flash mob, my instincts would kick in and I'd pretend to be one of the surprised and slightly affronted spectators.

The captain begins his announcements, but instead of distributing his gaze evenly across the group, he stares directly at me, eyeballing me up and down, up and down. It's a look every woman on the planet knows when a man is ogling her. Yuck!

Looks like this half-day is going to be more uncomfortable than a smack in the face. Time, please go fast, I pray.

I check my nails to avoid his stare. I want to give a clear and definite signal there is zero interest on my part. More accurately, it's less than zero. It feels more like repulsion. The trouble is, he doesn't take the hint and as a result, I'm assaulted by the burning gaze of his lustful stare scanning my body. Gross! And now we're too far away from the port for me to abandon ship without drowning, although I'm not completely ruling that out as a viable option.

Being stuck in my head, I don't notice the announcements have ceased. In the next moment, I feel a strong presence in front of me, accompanied by the smell of Old Thyme aftershave that arouses my nostrils. My eyes dart upwards. It's him. Within inches of me.

'You will sail the yacht.' He grabs my hand and guides me to the wheel.

Now I'm going to be stuck on this boat for four hours with this creepy old guy jammed up behind me, stinking my airways out with Old Thyme and doing that thing guys do at golf. You know, when the man stands behind you and scoots in extremely close. The woman puts her hands on the golf club and the man places his hands on top of the woman's hands to direct the swing of the club. You see the golf move in many a romantic movie. I'm certain it's somewhere in a man's dating guide of moves to hit on women. But I'm not in a dating movie, and this move is far from welcome. Don't get me wrong, if this is happening with a guy I'm into, bring it on, I love it, but, if it's by some guy I don't like, ewww! Violation station.

Unfortunately for me, it is the latter, and it looks like I am going to be creeped out by this guy doing the sailing version of the golf move on me for the foreseeable future. How did I end up here?

I consider putting us on course back to shore when he takes the wheel. I intentionally step about a metre away, but, unfortunately, I'm still accosted by the mixed scent of his sweat and aftershave. He begins telling me about his yacht and how he feels like it is an extension of his penis. Okay, that isn't exactly what he said, but reading between the lines, you know I'm right.

After more mansplaining about the workings of the yacht,

the dreaded moment comes for me to take the wheel. Every part of my body is screaming no, but my conditioning of not wanting to say no trumps my impulse to throw myself overboard. So, here I am, on a romantic date with a feral old man and nine spectators. His hands are on mine, moving to the right, moving to the left. I can feel the heat from his body. He is that close. Ick central.

After what seems like forever, he moves away and sits on the ledge behind me. Probably to take in the view. Eye roll.

'So, what do you do?'

Sigh. Doesn't anyone on this boat want to come talk his ear off about sailing? Any takers? No?

My short reply, 'I'm currently looking for work.'

'What are your interests?'

'Looking for work.'

'Where's your husband?'

Oh, that line. So smooth. Urg, I don't want to tell him.

'I'm not married. But if you know anyone *close to my age*,' with extra emphasis on the 'my age' part, 'send him my way.'

It's passive-aggressive, but seriously sir, you're like sixty years my senior. It's never going to happen. Read the freaking room. Even if I did like you, you'd likely be dead in less than ten years from either old age or being thrown overboard by another younger woman and where does that leave me? No, thank you.

'I'll let someone else have a go at steering now.'

I don't give him a chance to object and hastily retreat to the furthest point away from him on the yacht.

A delightful twentysomething Singaporean girl jumps in my spot.

I feel a huge sense of relief being out of his personal space as I take a seat and I'm finally able to take in the setting sun. Now, these are moments where I feel at peace, at one with nature and the planet. I close my eyes and take in a deep, pranic breath of the salty air. Heaven?

Nope, not today.

It's not salty air I smell, it's the heinous concoction of his body odour and Old Thyme. Is that why they named it Old Thyme? Because it's the preferred scent for creepy, old-timers?

I keep my eyes closed and hold my breath, praying it was the upwind bringing his scent into my nose, and I'm safely away from him at the other end of the boat.

'Hey!'

Dang. Please, no. I snap open my eyes to something nightmares are made of. About a foot away and in my direct eye line is a bulge, wrapped in a striped rainbow budgie smuggler.

His bare foot is positioned on the side of the yacht, creating a right angle with his grey hairy leg. He stands with one hand on his hip, trapping me in the corner, striped rainbow bulge in face. The captain has stripped off to get some vitamin D, apparently.

The dilemma is if I try to stand, to get away, I will touch the bulge and there is no way in hell I am going to get any closer to it than I have to. On the other hand, the bulge is a foot from my face, and it seems like it's not going anywhere fast. Note to self: do not go on another yacht meetup. Speaking of which, I have no idea what one is like because I've been playing whack-a-mole with an octogenarian this entire time. How is everyone else doing? Enjoying yourselves? I'm glad someone is.

Bulge in face or touch bulge to escape? They are my only two options. My brain can't think of a third option at this point (see third option in the lessons learned at the end of the chapter).

After some deliberation, I resign myself to the fact that I am officially trapped, and I have no choice but to select option one—bulge in face. I slump back into my seat feeling defeated and repulsed simultaneously. It's a new feeling, and I'm not a fan.

'Do you like animals? I'm vegetarian for ethical reasons.' He taps his foot which results in a slight jiggle of the rainbow bulge.

At last, could this be a potential way out?

'Yes. I love animals. I don't eat meat either.'

At least there is one saving grace to this experience, as I do enjoy hearing when a man has chosen a kind lifestyle. Perhaps this coffin dodger is simply oblivious to how his behaviour is making another person feel? I notice myself making excuses for his inappropriate conduct based solely on the fact that he doesn't eat meat. I recall Hitler was also vegetarian and look at what he got up to.

'Oh, really.' His eyes light up. 'I'm a gynaecologist and women who don't eat animal products always smell the best downstairs, if you know what I mean.'

Oh. My. Goodness. Did he just say that? How vulgar. Could I have misheard? Please let me have misheard. He did not say that to me with his striped bulge jiggling in my face? Is he a medical doctor? If he is, that's the most terrifying part of this whole experience.

For the next three hours, I am trapped in the same corner

talking to his bulge, holding my breath every few seconds to avoid his sweaty ball odour assaulting my airways. Everyone else on board is, I don't know, sailing? Why is no one coming to rescue me? Surely, they can see what's happening? Or maybe they're simply enjoying the view. Sigh. I would take any view other than the sweaty rainbow bulge of this alleged doctor right now. Seems the young Singaporean girl is a natural. Damn it. Where the heck did she learn to sail? This meetup is for beginners.

'Time to get back.' I tap my watch.

'I've been enjoying talking with you so much, I lost track of time. We should do this again.'

I ignore his absurd comment.

'You had better help her. You don't want her to crash your yacht.'

The girl is waving frantically at us for assistance. Finally, freedom from his sweaty crotch. I feel like doing a Mel Gibson from *Braveheart*: 'You may take my fresh air, but you'll never. Take. My freedom!' I imagine all the other women who have been subject to the captain's sweaty balls, breathing fresh air in unison.

Thankfully, the captain is distracted with mooring the yacht and I take the opportunity to seize my belongings and be the first to the area where we boarded. As soon as it's safe, I leap off the vessel. Oh, the relief I feel as my feet hit the earth. Freedom doesn't quite cut it.

I hear the captain hollering my name as I pretend to have sudden and temporary hearing loss. Never in this lifetime will I go on another yacht meetup.

What I learned from this date: Firstly, I am now one hundred per cent convinced I have been conditioned by society not to cause a scene and make someone else feel uncomfortable; even when the other person is doing something that is so unacceptable to me that I want to throw myself overboard. Accepting behaviour from others that I find deplorable and not using my voice to speak up is something I need to work on. I also realised I need to let go of the belief that as a woman I should sacrifice my own feelings in order to protect someone else's. I knew this was going to be a hard one to crack after twenty-four years of silencing myself, but I was up for the challenge. After all, Anne Sullivan was able to communicate with a blind, deaf, nonverbal woman. Miracles do happen.

If I could re-live this date I would have said, 'Sir, I find having your privates in my face and sweaty ball odour in my nostrils incredibly inappropriate. Please remove your bulge from my eye line as I'm not interested in spending my whole day talking to you or your man parts. Find someone your own age to pursue.' Mic drop.

7

MR YOGI

Age: 25
Location: Perth, Australia
Where we met: Online dating app
How he asked me out: Via phone call

Since my traumatic experience with Mr Captain and my close encounter with his rainbow budgie smuggler, you'll be pleased to know I'd started volunteering at the local animal shelter and I'd scored a cool job in sales for a national drinks company. Apparently, according to my boss, I could sell ice to Eskimos. Challenge accepted.

'It's your natural charm and British wit.'

She'd then hug me tightly, probably because I was making her a small fortune in commissions. I wondered if the less accomplished salespeople also got hugs, or perhaps just a sad pat on the shoulder.

Both Mum and Dad had sales skills, so thank you for passing them down. I will add that I was top of the charts smashing the highest targets across all states. So high, in fact, that I'd continually get flown over to the east coast to coach the entire team on how to increase their sales. Pretty good for a twenty-five-year-old with questionable cooking skills. I try not to boast, but I don't have a humble bone in my body. I needed a good dose of self-praise after staring at the not humble bone on someone else's body. It lifts the spirits and I highly recommend it. Dating-wise, I'd purposefully not put myself in any situations where I couldn't easily escape. Attending a yoga studio in the middle of the day is a safe bet. Right?

This was the first time since Mr Strongman that I had ventured back onto the online dating platform. This was long before the likes of dating apps. The good thing was, there was a lot more effort and information put into profiles, so you'd know a lot more about the person prior to the actual date like, say, what their hopes and dreams were or their last name.

When you think of a yogi, what comes to mind? Peace? Serenity? At one with everyone and everything? Yes. Me too. But apparently, I'd found the only yogi on the planet who did not fit this bill.

In my ignorance, the above mentioned were attributes I was expecting when I matched with Mr Yogi. He was a tall, dark-skinned, half-English, half-Madagascan yoga studio owner. Being an avid yoga-goer, I thought this common interest would be a bonus should we end up together. Couples who asana together, create nirvana together—I just made that up.

We'd arranged a phone conversation, which flowed nicely.

But I did notice he talked fast and kept saying, 'How much energy do you have? I have an insane amount of energy.'

He repeated this statement about twenty times during this initial phone conversation. My innocent mind interpreted it in a way most people would—this guy simply has a lot of energy. Maybe that's why he started his yoga practice. To centre himself amidst all the excess energy. Plain and simple, right?

The Date

We agree to meet at his yoga studio the following morning and it's a beautiful day in Perth. The sun's shining, the birds are singing. What more could a girl ask for?

Midday arrives.

I knock and peek through the glass door. The business name is embossed in bold gold letters above a golden lotus flower.

He walks towards the door and brilliant, he is way more attractive in person. I love it when that happens as it's so rare. Most online daters know people often look worse and sometimes way worse in real life. So, tick, what a fantastic start.

For the record, I am told I look better in real life, which is either a wonderful compliment about my appearance or means I need to improve my lighting setup for photoshoots.

The encouraging start doesn't last more than thirty seconds because that's when I begin to understand in more detail what he meant on the phone by having an insane amount of energy.

I greet him with a warm hug, and he embraces me. How to describe this hug? It feels like a headlock, but for the entire body. That would be an accurate description. I can also feel something poking me in my nether regions. Please let that be a penis-shaped key or a veggie sausage he's saving as a snack for later. As I pull back, he must have noticed my eyes fixed on his crotch, because in the next minute he pulls a TV remote out of his pocket. I breathe a sigh of relief and we recline onto some comfy beach-style lounge chairs in the sitting area at the front of the studio. Definitely from IKEA. I admire his casual, chic and plant design choices. I especially love hanging plants. I should get some for my apartment.

I start the conversation by explaining how earlier that morning I'd seen a cute, elderly couple holding hands and cuddling during my morning stroll and expressed how wonderful it would be to have that at their age.

I avert my attention to his face. He's blushing. My initial relief at the TV remote is short-lived as I observe some rather unusual behaviour. He's pulling his T-shirt down over his crotch area. Weird. Why is he trying to cover his crotch? And what is it with me and men's crotches lately?

He cuts me off mid-sentence, 'Can we not talk about cuddling?'

The rouge on his cheeks has expanded across his entire face, which is accompanied by another firm tug of his shirt over his privates. Has he wet himself or something? How has this got so weird, so quickly?

Now, come on, if someone doesn't want to talk about a topic, and an innocent one at that, wouldn't you be curious?

'Cuddling, why not?' Must. Find. Answers.

His eyes widen and the volume of his voice increases.

'Please, don't say that word.'

'Cuddling?' I am so confused right now. Are you confused?

'Yes, or anything related to it, like hugging or holding hands.'

How does a person respond to that? Why would he have a problem with those particular words? His face is getting more and more flushed.

'Okay.' I try to rack my brains for the possible reason for his reaction. Maybe he was one of those poor, neglected babies abandoned to an orphanage manned by people opposed to physical affection, and thinking about what he never had is simply too much for him. Though that still doesn't explain the T-shirt tug of war . . .

Before I can string another sentence together, he diverts my attention, 'Let's do some aerial yoga.' He points to the cocoon-like hammocks suspended by chains hanging from the ceiling.

'I'll be back in a second, I need to wash my hands.'

When he re-enters the studio, it seems like he has pre-planned the actions that follow. He gives me a look that says, check this out, as he pulls the white T-shirt up over his head to reveal a body chiselled by the Gods. Body fat—0.01%. Perfect, dark luxurious skin. Wow! Impressive.

Get in, he motions, wagging his finger at the silky cocoon, peeling it open so I can climb in.

'On your front.'

He helps me to twist onto my front so I'm lying face down with my arms by my side.

'It feels like you're flying when you're face down. Ready?'

He doesn't wait for my reply and instead grabs one end of the cocoon and pulls it as high as he can towards the ceiling, then let's go. Whoosh, I'm off. He's spot on; the sensation feels wonderful. It resembles how I imagine it feels to fly. The pull of gravity when I hit the lowest part of the swing feels the best, as it reminds me of the sensation of experiencing a big dip on a rollercoaster.

I will say this, the good feeling is short-lived because he does this next—he crawls beneath my swinging cocoon and forms a backbend directly under the central part. This means as I reach the lowest point in the swing, my front body brushes against his front body.

How in the world do I get myself into these situations?

How can one agree to some plain and simple aerial yoga and end up playing the starring role in some fruitcake's sex fantasy? The worst part is I can't move. I feel like a caterpillar in its transition to becoming a butterfly. No person on the planet could have predicted this. Yoga was supposed to be the easy escape option! I didn't count on being attached to the ceiling in what feels like a straitjacket.

The force of gravity means I can't wriggle onto my back. I'm literally stuck here until the momentum stops. Great! Yet again I'm in another hostage situation.

Through the silky cocoon material, on every whoosh our eyes meet, and I see his face staring up at me with the most joyful smile I've ever seen. I close my eyes and picture myself ALONE on a desert island, counting down the whooshes, each one slowing in speed.

Fifteen whooshes later (yes, I counted each one), the cocoon comes to a stop, and I wriggle like a lunatic onto my back in an attempt to escape.

'Help me out.' I want out of here. Like yesterday.

He rolls out from underneath the cocoon and holds out a hand. I notice how rough and callused they are. They are blistered on the palms near the fingers, commonly found on men who spend their days lifting heavy weights in the gym or labouring hard. Given his chiselled abs, I assume it's from long sessions in the gym. Never assume anything Mum says and as you'll discover, Mum is right again.

His other hand holds the chain steady. He pulls me to my feet. Freedom.

'You must spend a lot of time lifting weights.' I stare at his hands.

'These blisters aren't from the gym.' He nods his head a few times with raised eyebrows.

'What do you mean?'

'Well.' He rubs his palms together. 'You know I said I have a lot of energy, well, I mean, a lot of energy down there.' He points to his nether regions.

My expression must have clearly communicated, *Are you freaking kidding me?* because he hastily adds, 'I've always had a lot of energy and so earlier, when you were saying words like cuddling or holding hands, or even if I see an elderly couple walking down the street being affectionate, I get, you know, an erection. That's where these blisters have come from.'

He pauses, staring hard into my eyes. 'At least ten times a day.' He utters the word ten quieter than the other words before displaying both hands before me so I can see the evidence.

It dawns on me he did not, in fact, go to the bathroom earlier to wash his hands, although I seriously hope the trip ended with a wash.

'Oh. My. Goodness. Wow!'

It's exceptionally difficult to disguise an expression of horror with neutrality, even though I've had a lot of practice. Inside, all I'm thinking is holy heck I need to get out of here. How can I be with this man? I already know a considerable percentage of my vocabulary would need to be culled. We'd be banned from visiting my grandparents in the old folk's home. How would I explain to everyone, 'No, don't worry, he's not some pervert, he just gets aroused when he sees old people being affectionate.' And ten times a day? How does he get anything done? No way. Not for me.

I intentionally stare at my watch. 'I'd better get going.' I drum my forefinger on the glass face, avoid a goodbye hug, thrust open the entry door and speed walk the heck out of there.

'Do you want to go on another date?' he yells from the yoga studio door.

'I'll let you know.'

Do not look back. Eyes forward. Mission—get back to car, pronto.

What I learned from this date: Firstly, don't agree to activities where I can't easily escape, but seriously, who could have seen this coming?

Secondly, I come back to the trusty one-hour coffee date in order to suss out some of this freaky stuff. But let's get real, I'm still not learning this lesson, and to be honest, it's because I'm a vibrant woman and a one-hour coffee date is so boring.

The third lesson is compatible sex drives. So, now, whenever a guy mentions he has a high sex drive, in my experience it means two things—they don't have a passion they can funnel energy into—read the chapter on sex energy in *Think and Grow Rich* by Napoleon Hill if you want to fully understand what I mean by this. And, as Mum always advised, avoid men with high sex drives, as apparently my days will be spent trying to evade capture from my caveman partner who is constantly in the pursuit of using my body to get himself off, and that's the worst kind of sex. Either that or he'll always be a distant memory because he'll be 'washing his hands' in the bathroom ten times a day. As always, thanks, Mum.

8

MR VEGAN

Age: 28
Location: Perth, Australia
Where we met: Vegetarian dating site—a site for people who share a similar eating lifestyle.
How he asked me out: Via phone call

By the time this date happened, I was six months out of a two-year relationship with an Australian guy. We'd had a lot in common in terms of our love of animals, like when I'd ask where we should go out to eat, he'd reply with one of five of my favourite plant-based eateries. Oh, the ease.

Trouble was, that's where our similarities ended.

My ambition level—Napoleon Bonaparte.

His ambition level—less than a housecat that at least keeps a strict schedule of eating, napping, stretching and cleaning.

My accomplishments in the last two years—I'd finished

up with the drinks company, actioned the goal of owning my own dog walking business, which had become a raging success, and I'd also written a book on dog psychology.

His accomplishments in the last two years—wake up. Roll out of bed. Go to a job he hates. Complain about that job. Spend his wages on crap. Rinse and repeat.

There was one significant realisation that came from my relationship and that was the ease of being with someone who had similar values around animals and shared the same diet. I was keen to experience this in my next relationship, so, that's why I went on this specialised dating site, specifically for vegetarians and vegans. Bring on Mr Vegan.

I am genuinely interested in how a man treats two things —his mother and animals. For me, these are key indicators that show his values around respecting women and revering innocent life forms. If he passes these two, chances are he's got a good heart and I will be treated with the same regard.

I had several phone conversations with this date prior to meeting and we got along like a house on fire. He told me he was vegan because he loved animals. Tick! And he had a loving relationship with his mum. Double tick. He also owned his own successful tech company. Had I hit the trifecta? It was almost four weeks after our initial conversation that we ended up meeting, as our schedules were out of sync. Because I felt like we knew each other pretty well I was delighted when he sent this text:

Margaret River is whispering your name. This Saturday. Pick you up at 10 am?

I had vowed to only go on trusty one-hour dates; however, I'd also established I wasn't the trusty one-hour date kinda girl. Strangely, my current strategy was effective in some bizarre way, because each date showed their true nature very quickly. These revelations meant no time was wasted having a second date. And one thing about me, I detest wasting time.

I hadn't been to Margaret River since I'd visited for a hot air balloon ride to celebrate a friend's birthday and thought it would be lovely to take the opportunity to revisit, explore the vineyards and muse at the rolling hills. How bad could a day trip be after a month of phone conversations? Plus, he hadn't used the phrase 'lots of energy' in the entire month we'd been talking. In my hopeful innocence, my text response was as follows:

That sounds like a fantastic idea. Count me in! Looking forward to it.

The Date

Saturday arrives and, glancing at my watch, I see I have thirty minutes before his arrival. Light denim jeans on, hair styled with a slight curl so it lands squarely on my shoulders, cosy, pink, polar neck jumper, so soft and comfy. My brown bag will go nicely with my cowboy boots.

I'm downstairs. Black Audi. No rush. See you soon.

I like that he said no rush. He must understand that most ladies need an extra few minutes to finalise things. I contemplate how much of a woman's life is spent getting ready. If she spends forty-five minutes a day every day for seventy years of her life, that's equivalent to 19,162 hours, 798 days and 2.18 years. Holy moly! At least I have established a solid, long-term relationship with my own face.

I had better get a wriggle on. I grab my bag and jacket and am out the door. I press the button marked 'G' in the elevator and a few seconds later the doors open, and I say a little prayer—please let this date go well. Pretty please.

Parked on the street next to my apartment is a shiny black Audi. My date sees me and casually steps out of his vehicle. Attractive. Nice. He's smartly dressed in a crisp white shirt and dark jeans. What woman doesn't love a sharp dresser? And no signs of him pulling his shirt over his crotch. Bonus.

I stand on the concrete steps and hold out my arms. 'If I jump, will you catch me?' Gotta open with a good flirt. He grins and his laughter suggests he's happy with my cheekiness. He holds out his arms and I jump into them as he swings me around. I feel like a little kid.

He opens the passenger door. Yay, a gentleman. A woman doesn't get treated that way often, nowadays, but I truly appreciate it.

He shuts the passenger door behind me, hops into the driver's seat and we begin our journey. He glances over and smiles, and I return the favour.

Margaret River is approximately a three-hour drive from my apartment, so I get comfy in my seat. My date turns on some chilled tunes and when a song comes on I like, I do a little dance, which my date seems to find highly amusing.

'So, if you were on your death bed and could have one final meal, what would it be?' I don't know why, but a person's answer always intrigues me.

He grins, 'Burgers and fries.'

'You mean like a veggie burger?'

I notice his cheeks flush a little, which is an interesting reaction. 'Erm, yeah. That's exactly what I mean.'

He keeps his eyes firmly on the road ahead and doesn't ask me what my last meal would be. Okay, I guess that conversation is deader than whatever went into his final burger.

The concrete landscape transforms into lush greenery. We must have been driving for a few hours by now. Only one more hour to go until we reach the winery. A delectable lunch and a wander around the art gallery awaits us. What a delight.

I press the window button to let in some air. There's nothing better than fresh, country air, don't you agree? By mistake, I hold down the button for too long and the window retracts all the way back into the door. As I attempt to fix my mistake, I notice a tiny four-legged figure standing alone on the roadside. It's the smallest lamb I've ever seen, still with the umbilical cord attached.

You know that IKEA advert where the woman rushes out of the store with loads of bags and screams, 'Start the car!' I'm pretty certain that's what I sounded like when I frightened the living daylights out of my date by screaming, 'STOP. THE. CAR.'

My date hits the brake performing a perfect emergency stop and the Audi screeches to a halt. I must say, I'm impressed with the efficiency of the braking system. My date is seemingly less impressed with me as his expression resembles one of 'What the bleep, woman?'

'There's a lamb on the side of the road.'

I'm assuming he's as alarmed as me as I run to the little

darling and immediately pick him up and hold him close to my chest.

'Where is your mummy?' I stroke his head. He bleats. He's cold to the touch. He needs warmth. The umbilical cord dangles. He must be only hours old, and the little munchkin is standing alone on the side of the road. Oh, the injustice of this world.

I hear the door slam and my date appears alongside me and Alfie—this is the name I've given him.

'It stinks.' My date's face is wrinkled with disgust.

What the? That's an odd response for a person who claims they love animals. And poor Alfie's out here freezing to death and you're criticizing his stink when the poor thing hasn't even been alive long enough for a proper bath. I'm sure he's not thrilled about the situation either. So rude.

'Shall we see if there are any paddocks with sheep along this road?'

'No, it's going to stink out my car.' He shakes his head with intensity. 'No way.'

I'm taken aback. How could anyone, let alone a self-professed animal lover, leave a newborn lamb shaking and alone on the side of a massive highway? I have a feeling Alfie has fallen off the back of a truck, you know the ones that transport them to their death. That thought makes me feel even worse knowing where his mother is heading.

'I thought you loved animals?' I'm genuinely perplexed at his reaction.

My date hesitates and looks at the ground like he's weighing something in his mind. 'Okay, get in. There'd better be a paddock of sheep close by.'

I feel extremely awkward as he opens the car door because he looks seriously ticked off. I don't know if you've attempted getting into a car with a live animal before, but it's tricky with no arms for balance or support. I manage and within a few minutes, we are driving down the country road looking for sheep.

Unfortunately, ten minutes go by and there's still no sheep in sight, only empty paddocks.

'We should take him to the vet. He's shivering and probably dehydrated.'

My date huffs. 'There won't be a vet for miles.'

I'm getting a strong sense my date doesn't give a crap about Alfie and so, holding Alfie in one arm, I grab my phone out of my bag and google the closest vet which is a twenty-five-minute drive in the direction we are heading. I show my date who seems relieved for the first time since finding Alfie, as he punches the address into the GPS.

We both put our windows down a few inches as Alfie is a tad pongy, but I'm sure it will air out once he's safe with the vet.

'We're doing a good turn. This experience will bond us.' I'm pulling out all the stops to lighten the mood, but my date's expression remains neutral and silent. I hope this doesn't put Alfie off father figures.

Thirty minutes later, we arrive at the veterinary clinic. It took five minutes longer than what the GPS said, likely from the windows being down and the resulting wind drag. Relief. My date doesn't get out of the car but instead turns the air conditioning on full blast and rolls down all four windows. I cover Alfie's eyes so as not to add insult to injury. This poor little angel is going to need some serious therapy when he grows up to be a sheep.

I enter the reception, where I'm greeted with a warm smile. That is until her eyes land on Alfie. 'How can I help you?'

'I found this newborn lamb on the side of the road. He's only a few hours old. Can you help him?'

The receptionist glances at Alfie and then back at me. 'I'll go and get the vet.'

A moment later a short, stocky guy with grey hair enters the room. 'I can take him, but we'll have to put him down as we don't have the resources or time to re-home him.'

I'm sorry, what did you say? 'Two seconds ago, I rescued him, I'm not going to let you kill him after I've just saved him.' I instinctively hold Alfie closer and take a step backwards away from the vet. I envisage the vet taking him home and yelling to his wife, 'Honey, I've brought dinner.' I bolt out of there like I'm running on hot coals as the vet yells in the background, 'Every vet will tell you the same thing, sorry, there's nothing else I can do.'

So, that was that. He wasn't going to help my little Alfie and there is no way in this lifetime I would hand him over to be killed. No chance.

I walk back to the car park. My date is shaking his head and appears to be gripping the steering wheel tightly.

'You are kidding me?' He grits his teeth as I struggle to open the door and climb in with Alfie under my arm.

'He's going to kill Alfie. We haven't saved him so he can be killed. Let me call a few more vets.'

My date gets out of the car, slams the door behind him and storms off. I'm starting to feel I'm on a date with a complete d*ck. I call other local vets. Vet after vet says the exact same thing; Alfie will meet certain death if I drop him at their clinic.

What is this, Old MacDonald's death cult? I thought vets loved animals. Surely, they have contacts and networks to rescue shelters. That's it, a rescue shelter. I dial the number for the RSPCA, and I blurt out Alfie's story and pretty much beg the woman for help.

'Of course, we'll take him.'

'He won't be put to sleep, will he?' Which is the PG version of asking if they are going to murder him.

'Definitely not. We have lots of farm animals. He'll have lots of friends here.'

Oh, my aching heart. Thank goodness!

I pick Alfie up so his beautiful eyes are looking into mine, 'Did you hear that, angel, we've found you your new home. You're saved.'

I holler through the open window at my date who seems to be pacing and talking to himself.

'Hey, I've found help.'

My date walks back to the car and peers through the driver's window. His face is beet red.

'Good news. I've found a home for Alfie.'

'Where?' He looks seriously annoyed.

'RSPCA.'

I put the address in Google. Oh dang, it's a two and a half-hour drive back towards the city.

'Isn't that almost back in the city?'

Seems my date is also a mind reader, or perhaps just good at geography.

'Erm. Yep. I tried all the local vets and they all said they would put Alfie down.'

'You've already named him?' He stares at me like I'm from another planet. 'So much for a nice day in Margaret River. My car already reeks.'

Well, maybe you should drive straight into the river. I'm sure Margaret Whicher would love to meet your acquaintance.

'What else can we do?' I start to feel panicked.

'Leave him with the vet.' He rolls his eyes.

I activate my best puppy dog eyes, silently pleading inside.

He does the loudest huff of the date, then jumps in the driver's seat, turns on the ignition and spins the car out of the parking lot at a speed that makes pebbles and dust fly up behind us. From the thrust of momentum forward, something flies out from under his seat. I glance down into the footwell and you will not believe what I see.

A freaking lamb burger wrapper from a well-known takeaway joint!

I had brought Alfie into a death chamber where his kind had been chomped down on possibly earlier that same day! Maybe he's feeling guilty because he's got Alfie's cousin, Jimmy in his belly right now! Okay, stay calm. Don't jump to conclusions. Could the wrapping be from his friend?

'How come you have a lamb burger wrapper under your seat?'

My date blushes red.

'Cos I'm a bleeping carnivore, okay!'

That explains the final meal he mentioned earlier. He'd lied directly to my face.

'If you're a carnivore, why were you on a veggie dating site? And why did you tell me you were vegan?' I feel the knot in my stomach turning into rage.

'Because I wanted to date you, okay, it's not a big deal. And I do love animals. I love eating them.'

What the heck? That's like saying 'I love children, that's why I dress up as a clown to murder them on weekends.' What an insensitive jerk. Not a big deal? Lying is a massive deal.

Before I can respond, poor Alfie starts trying to wriggle free, probably from feeling the crazy amount of rage coming from inside me. I feel something warm and wet on my jeans. Pee? Oh crap. I peer down, not pee, I see diarrhoea all over my jeans and on the car seat and I fear a couple of cracked windows might not save us.

'What the bleeping hell. Now we have to sit in bleep, for the next two hours. For bleep sake. Why the bleep did you have to bring him in the car? Look at the bleeping mess he's made on my seat. What the bleep. Bleep. Bleep. Bleeeeeep!'

Needless to say, all four windows needed to be lowered in order for us not to throw up every few seconds, and I'll be frank, it was still difficult to hold down the vomit.

Silence and high blood pressure make up the remainder of the journey, and when I get out of his car at the RSPCA, he throws my bag at my feet and yells, 'I'm never dating another vegan again.' He speeds away like he's participating in a Formula One race.

Crikey.

That was the last time I heard from him. I call Mum, who picks me up and brings along some baby wipes and clean clothes and affirms it was good I found out what type of man he was before things got serious. You know, more serious than saving a baby lamb together. Wise words. Thanks, Mum.

Less than a month later, Mum texts me: *Look what I saw in the local paper today.*

Accompanying the text is a photo. I spread my fingers across the screen to increase its size. There, in the photo, is my little Alfie. He is surrounded by children who are four or five years old. It says Alfie is making the rounds at local primary schools as part of an initiative to teach young kids how to take care of farm animals. Oh, my heart feels like it's about to explode with joy. Alfie has found his purpose and look at how much joy he's bringing to these children. I feel the heat of warm tears welling up in my eyes and let them fall down my cheeks. It feels like an affirmation from the universe that my efforts were for a bigger purpose and a reminder that every life is equal and important.

What I learned from this date: Firstly, stress shows the true nature of a person. Lying is not okay and is something I refuse to tolerate. This date also made me realise how important it is for me to be with a man who is respectful and is the type who would rescue newborn lambs from the side of the road. I need to put in more filters to ascertain if someone is telling the truth. Food for thought—yes, I'm sure you're starting to gather that I love puns.

9

MR SALSA

Age: 28
Location: Perth, Australia
Where we met: At a bizarre dance class
How he asked me out: Face to face as we were dancing what I would later refer to as the 'boob dance'.

After the date with liar, liar, pants on fire, or should I say, Mr Carnivore, I'd once again scrapped my online profile and was focusing on doing things I loved. You should now be familiar with the fact that I'm partial to busting out a few crazy dance moves from reading my previous dates and the truth is I enjoy experimenting with different styles. My least enjoyable, being grinded down to the floor doing the bachata by a stinky old man. Eww. My absolute favourite dance style of all has to be the waltz; Disney princess vibes all the way. But the most fun dancing experience I've ever had was being part of a line-dancing troupe with gay cowboys back in the UK. Two things were guaranteed to happen during each rehearsal: (1) hysterical laughter, and (2) the tallest and most jacked up cowboy would complain that HE wanted to be the princess that gets lifted up at the end of the routine—I was the current princess. At the end of rehearsals, we'd all grab a drink and share our disastrous date stories. They had their own fair share. It affirmed that sexual orientation had no bearing on how disastrous a date could be. I miss those guys! It's too bad I'm not a gay man.

The dance class where I met date number nine was none of the dances described above. In fact, I had no clue about the dance style until I was in the class. Now, I'm not sure if you've ever experienced the Argentine Tango? Where the male and female hips are pressed heavily against the other? I don't know about you, but this is not my idea of a good time. This is especially the case when my partner is an elderly gentleman, and I can feel his man parts pressing against my you-know-what and I'm not living on the cover of a romance novel.

So, back to the 'boob' dance class. The reason I describe it this way is because the female is moved around the dance floor, not from hip-on-hip action, but chest on chest. Yes, you read that right, chest pressed firmly against chest. And you know what sits on many women's chests? Yes. Boobs. Full marks.

The fact of the matter is, I'm not small chested. So, picture this: my boobs are smashed right up against a complete stranger, who is standing there with the biggest grin on his face and is instructed to manoeuvre me around the dance floor. By. My. Boobs. Do you see the problem here?

To make matters worse, it's not a dance you do with one partner, so I'm palmed off into the arms of the next stranger in the group. In a nutshell, I'm being flung around the room by fifteen participants who are all encouraged to use my boobs as a steering wheel. Do you now understand my living hell?

So, that's where we met. He was stranger number fifteen. An Aussie local. Originally from South America, Chile, to be precise. Rather than grinning like a teenage boy like the other buffoons, he said it how it was, 'Don't you feel uncomfortable having all these random guys pushing you around the dance floor with your boobs?'

Yes. Yes, I do. One hundred per cent. Nail on the head, sir. Glad you understand my pain.

After laughing about my predicament, he asked if I'd like to do some salsa with him at a local nightclub later on that evening. You don't know this about me, but I'm an excellent salsa dancer and as far as I know, private parts are not involved. So, my answer was, of course, a hell yeah!

The Date

I enter the nightclub. Multi-coloured streamers hang from the ceilings. Loud, fast beats bounce off the walls and the place is packed with vibrantly dressed patrons. The energy of this place feels more like a festival. I love it. At 9 pm, we meet at the bar, which is dotted with Pisco Sours. My date approaches. He looks sexy in his bold, flowery shirt with the top buttons undone, showing a good amount of dark, curly chest hair. I must say, I am partial to chest hair, but not shoulder or back hair. Not sure what the logic is there, but hey, that's my personal preference.

My date grabs my hand and kisses it twice. 'Let's dance, my beautiful.'

His sexy Chilean accent definitely adds to his appeal.

In the next moment, I'm getting dragged through the crowd, and this place is packed like sardines. It seems they have little issue with zero personal space. Being English, I prefer a reasonable twenty-metre radius to feel at ease.

We arrive at the centre of the dance floor, and he pulls me straight into a *Dile Que No*, followed by an *Enchufla*. Oh, he's a dream to dance with. An excellent leader. He manoeuvres me smoothly between moves making it feel effortless. This guy knows how to dance, and you know what they say about men who can dance?

The other fabulous thing about my date is he smells intoxicating. You know when you catch a whiff of a person's scent, and it makes you go weak at the knees? His pheromones are off the charts. I feel my whole body instantly get hot solely by being close to him. I guess this, right here, is mother nature's way of saying, yes, you two would make exceptionally healthy offspring, so get humping!

Plus, I'm not even ovulating right now, which is usually the time when my body is turned on to any man with a pulse. Even if he was ten feet tall and wore dirty underwear for a hat, my body would still scream for him to impregnate me and pronto.

Our chemistry is electrifying and so when the tempo changes to the Bachata, which can be slow and intimate, I can't think of anywhere else I'd rather be. Bring on those delicious pheromones.

My date is sensual in his movements and even though we aren't physically bonking, onlookers would term it—dry humping—which is humping fully-clothed.

Unfortunately, moments later I am rudely forced out of this state of bliss by loud shouting in Spanish. A short brunette wearing massive killer heels yanks at my date's arm, pointing aggressively in his face. I can see the whites of her eyes glaring at him.

Side note, how the heck can she walk in those shoes, they must be at least six inches high?

I take a step backwards in my much more conservative heels. My date retaliates loudly in Spanish and bats her pointed finger away, signalling towards the exit.

What the heck is going on? Who is this woman?

After one last extremely high-pitched scream in Spanish, the killer-heel-wearing brunette pushes my date forcefully and storms off the dance floor.

Okay. That was awkward.

'What is that all about?'

My date doesn't seem phased and instead pulls me in close and says, 'Forget about it, it's nothing,' as he grabs my hips and sways me down towards the ground. Must have just been some crazy lady who had one too many drinks. When we return to an upright position, I see the brunette stomping out of the exit. Well, at least she's gone. I glance around the dance floor and see three ladies staring in our direction: A redhead, a lady with luxurious long black locks, and a platinum blonde.

If this is the start to a great bar joke, I must be the punchline because they're all scowling at either me or my date.

As I am *Enchufla'd* from side to side, I see the redhead pushing her way past dancers on the main floor, knocking a Pisco Sour out of one man's hand and not even glancing back. She swoops in between us and hits my date over the head with her handbag and starts yelling. It was extremely loud in the nightclub, but I could make out the following words as they were in English, 'You bastard! Why won't you pay your child support? You're a complete waste of space!' The yelling was accompanied by intermittent bats to my date's head.

By this point, the platinum blonde and black-haired woman had also made their way to the centre of the dance floor. Fingers pointing in his face ensue, along with blows to the head with handbags. A large space has formed around the commotion, and I'm forced to step backwards to avoid any errant bag swings. My date is now hollering at all three of them, flailing his hands around his head with passion and flair. By the fourth woman, I'm starting to think maybe woman number one wasn't a crazy drunk after all. But what is the deal? Obviously, he has a child with one of them, because of the accusations of not paying child support, but what about the rest?

Bouncers intervene, hastily escorting them out of the building. Patrons dance into the empty space and I'm left standing in the middle wondering what the heck just happened.

A man with a hefty moustache taps me on the shoulder. 'Be careful with him, or you'll be number six.' He walks away before I can ask questions and disappears into the crowd.

I head for the exit and as the cool night air hits my face,

I hear screaming in both English and Spanish. I see the back of my date legging it down the street and the four women—the first one had obviously joined the group of three—were wielding their bags around their heads and chasing him in their stilettos.

Gees. I'd hoped for a drama-free night of dancing and ended up in a telenovela. I walk back to my car, drive home and by the time I enter my front door, I've got a missed call from him. Obviously, the angry mob hadn't done him in.

I don't know if I should call him back, but I'm kind of curious. Why were those women so mad? Plus, what did that guy mean, saying I'd be number six? I dial his number.

'Hey, what happened?'

'I'm sorry about that. They were my exes.'

'What? All four of them?'

'Yep.'

Crikey, you don't see that every day, unless you're on the *Jerry Springer Show*.

'Why were they all there and screaming at you to pay child support?'

'Erm. I was hoping I didn't have to tell you this until we knew each other better, but . . .' he pauses and takes a deep breath, 'I have kids.'

'Having kids is not a problem, but why were all of your exes screaming at you? Why were they all together at the nightclub?'

'Because they know each other.'

He doesn't offer any details.

'Okay, that's weird. How do they know each other?'

'Because I have kids with each one of them.'

'Wait, so, you have four kids with each of those four women?'

'Erm. Well. Not exactly. I have two sets of twins, so seven kids.'

It turns out what they say about men who can dance is true, and he's been doing the horizontal dance with half the town.

'Also, if you want to keep dating me, I have to let you know there is a fifth ex who is pregnant and she says I'm the father, but I'll need to do a paternity test to make sure. It might not be mine.'

If the saying is true and history repeats itself, I would go all in on a high-stake bet that that is your eighth child, sir, since you seem to possess atomic sperm and have no boundaries around who that sperm enters.

So, this guy has five exes with whom he shares at least seven, and potentially eight, children. And I'm the budding sixth woman to bear his fruit? That's what that guy was insinuating at the club. Oh no. That's never going to happen. Not for me. Having five angry exes hanging about is one thing, but not paying child support is a whole other issue. This guy clearly is happy to sow his wild oats, without any thoughts about the consequences.

Is he trying to take over the planet by creating a small army from his own loins?

No. I most definitely will not be baby momma *número seis*. *Adiós, señor.*

What I learned from this date: Firstly, a man who shirks his responsibility as a father says a lot about his character and not in a positive way. And having eight offspring by five women at the ripe old age of twenty-seven, could point to the fact he is not the best at nurturing relationships, don't you think? I love a man who is loyal, devoted, picks his partners wisely and takes pride in honouring his responsibilities, and that was definitely not this guy.

10

MR MUSCLES

Age: 28
Location: Perth, Australia
Where we met: At a local restaurant
How he asked me out: He didn't. I asked him out.

This date occurred not long after I'd ditched Mr Salsa. I was still off online dating sites and was enjoying my own company, as well as spending time with wonderful girlfriends and my furry pals at the animal shelter. You'll be pleased to know my business was still expanding and my dog psychology book was going through the roof selling to clients. Believe it or not, I wrote my first book when I was in primary school. It was about dogs. Go figure! There's something to be said about going back to childhood to find your true passion.

My love of reading and writing started young. Nightly, Mum read us Roald Dahl books and I'd fall asleep feeling the magic of Matilda tingling in my fingers and believing anything was possible. Those wondrous stories expanded my imagination, and Mum always encouraged creativity with painting, nature and dancing.

At school, the other parents wanted to know which dance class Mum was taking me to because of my interesting dance style. What both they and my mum didn't know was I'd got my hot little hands on the early Jane Fonda fitness videos, and we all know what kind of moves were on there.

Speaking of dancing, a girlfriend and I had a regular weekly catch up where we'd attend a local belly dancing class. After that, we'd get dressed to the nines and enjoy a delicious meal along the oceanfront. We were working our way down West Coast Highway, where numerous restaurants with spectacular views lined the street. Some of my best dates ever.

The story of date 10 began one balmy night, after our belly dancing class, in an outdoor restaurant. Picture warm hues of red and orange reflecting off the Indian Ocean, a warm breeze caressing your cheeks and the sounds of laughter from neighbouring patrons. Bliss, right?

I was in my Jessica Rabbit style dress and was enjoying the ambience in the company of a lovely friend. We'd devoured a delicious meal and were now sipping on peppermint tea as we immersed ourselves in deep conversation.

I noticed the table next to us were having some sort of family get together, where several members were using sign language to communicate. Cool! My attention was drawn back towards the roadside with the sound of a loud rev of a sports motorbike.

It sounds cliché, but this is really what happened. The next scene could have easily been taken from *Top Gun*, as the rider pulled off his helmet, shook his locks and displayed a perfect set of Hollywood pearly whites. Jaw drop. This was some guy!

He stomped loudly up the stairs in his biker boots, flipping his keys through his fingers. We locked eyes as he walked past my table and I watched as he removed his bike jacket to reveal a solid, gym body. The edge of a tattoo could be seen before he adjusted the sleeve of his white T-shirt. I must say, I am partial to tattoos. I tried not to stare in awe and drool all down my front as he signed what I figured was hello to his brother. It's clear his younger sibling was deaf, and the rest of the family could hear as their signs were all directed towards the curly-haired teenage boy. This somehow made this Hollywood moment man even hotter.

'He is so my type,' I spoke in a whisper so only my friend could hear.

'He's an attractive guy.' My friend grabbed my hand and giggled.

I kept one eye on him as we continued chit-chatting away and sipping our tea, but to my dismay, thirty minutes after sitting down, the handsome hunk got up and put his jacket back on. He was leaving. He gave me a wink as he swaggered out of the café and the sound of his bike could be heard as he sped away, literally into the sunset. You can't make this stuff up.

'What's wrong?' My friend grabbed my hand.

'I liked his vibe; I wish I'd said something. I'm going to write a note and give it to his mum.'

My friend giggled. She was used to my random behaviour.

This is what I wrote:

Hi there Mr Motorbike, I was the lady in red sitting across from your table. I got good vibes from you, so I was wondering, if you're single, would you like to take me on a date?

I signed my name and printed my number.

'You should give it to his mum as we are leaving so it's not too awkward.'

I nodded in agreement. 'Good idea.'

We split the bill and stood to leave. I walked over and tapped the shoulder of the mother.

'Excuse me, so sorry to interrupt your evening. Please can you give this to the guy who came on the motorbike?'

She smiled sweetly, nodded and put the note into her purse. Her reaction suggested this wasn't her first rodeo in taking notes for her son. I contemplated briefly if he compensated her for this service and whether she was on a monthly retainer.

My friend and I linked arms and made our way down the stone steps. Support is usually required when wearing high heels, something every heel-wearing person on the planet knows.

'Oooh, I wonder if he'll call. You are so bold. You inspire me, lady.'

'I'll let you know what happens, and thanks for a lovely evening. See you at the same time next week.'

We hugged goodbye.

The next day, I awoke to a message from a mystery number. Yep, it was him. How exciting!

Good morning, Lady in Red, thanks for your lovely note. Yes, I am single and yes, I would like to take you on a date, tonight, dinner at my place.

Now, I must say I wouldn't normally go on a dinner date at someone's home on the first date, but I'd already met his family, so it was more like going on a date with an old family friend, right?

I planned my outfit and felt excitement fill my tummy. Little did I know what else I'd be filled with by the end of this date. But, in my ignorance, I felt hopeful this could be my last first date, and sorry to disappoint, but it wasn't the last first date, I've had a thousand or more first dates since, but who's counting? Sigh.

The Date

I walk up to the front door in my sparkly silver heels and say a quick prayer for the date to go well. The door swings open. He looks divine in a white button-down shirt and ripped blue jeans. He runs his hand through his lush black hair. He reminds me of those men in shampoo adverts.

'Come in, my lady in red.'

Cute.

He escorts me into the living room that has a modern, minimalist vibe and places his hand on the small of my back. I love it when men do that. It makes me feel like they are taking care of me. The feeling of ecstasy tingles through my body. That is until a moment later when a foul stench assaults my nostrils.

What the heck is that? Is he cooking eggs? But he knows I don't eat eggs. Maybe he's making something different for himself? I haven't cooked meat in so long, but I can't remember anything smelling that bad.

I try my best to ignore the foul odour, I don't want him to feel uncomfortable, but it seems like his whole house smells of rotten eggs. How am I going to enjoy my food when I'm surrounded by this stench? Impossible.

He gives me a kiss on the cheek and as he bends forward, he lets out the loudest fart I'd. Ever. Heard. In. My. Entire. Life. Are you familiar with that YouTube clip where the hippopotamus is caught on camera farting for an entire minute? That's how loud it was. After I recover from the sheer sonic volume scaring the living daylights out of me, I scope out the room for where the Nat Geo cameras are hidden.

He roars, 'Better out than in,' as he grabs my hand.

Gross. His house is literally the embodiment of his bowels. How did it go from heaven to hell so fast?

He walks off into the kitchen to grab me a glass of water—I'm hoping it will help flush some of his butt toxins out of my throat.

I hear another trombone-sounding fart reverberate through the kitchen walls, followed by a second, third and fourth. One after the other, farts burst from his backside like an orchestra, and his butt is playing all of the instruments. This is not the type of musical I usually enjoy.

I realise I'm going to be subjected to this for the entire night. How am I going to eat my food? A window. Maybe I could open all the windows in the house? Would that be weird? Probably. But not weirder than a house being filled with air that's ninety-nine per cent fart. Following the cry for help from my lungs, I target the nearest window and like a crazy person trying to escape, I yank open the window to breathe some clean air.

'Hey, what are you up to?' He pokes his head around the corner.

'It's too cold outside to open the windows.' He saunters in, presses himself against me as he lets out another large trumpet fart. How has he managed to have a sex life if he can't even walk over to someone without letting one rip? I bet he measures his sexual performance by the number of farts per thrust.

I close my eyes and hold my breath, which for some unknown reason he takes as me enjoying the moment. The next thing I know I'm off my feet and over his shoulder. He's heading to the bedroom, which when I later relay the story to my friends, I refer to as the Dutch oven.

He kicks the door closed, pulls the duvet back and throws me onto the bed, followed by a running jump, letting out the most thunderous-sounding fart I've ever heard. Is there a category in the *Guinness World Records* for loudest fart? I make a mental note to ask Mr Strongman.

I'm in hell. How have I gone from fighting for air by the window to being in a literal Dutch oven inside one minute? I've got to get out of here. I cannot inhale any more of his toxic butt fumes.

I throw off the duvet and like a bull seeing red, charge towards the door, with the main goal of allowing some of the methane to escape.

'What's the matter with you?' He seems surprised.

'I'm so sorry, but I can't handle your constant farting. You are literally gassing me out. I can't breathe.'

He stands up proudly, flexes his pecs and announces, 'This body doesn't happen with no sacrifice. The protein shakes make me gassy. It's not a big deal, I fart about two hundred times a day, at least.'

He counts his farts? I've never heard of that before. He sounds so proud that he's notching up two centuries of farts per twenty-four-hour cycle. He says it like it's normal to be a farting machine, and what's worse, he thinks I should be okay with it. Delusional.

'I'm sorry, but I can't handle the stench. I feel like there's more methane than oxygen in your house. I have to get out of here.'

'Well, if you want to date me, you have to accept me as I am, farts and all.'

I'm doing everything humanly possible to hold down vomit.

'Well, in that case, I don't want to date you and your fart machine arse.'

I dry retch and pounce on the door handle. The door opens and the fresh air enters my lungs. I cannot begin to tell you the feeling of relief. I take in a deep inhale and thank the universe for clean air.

Needless to say, after disclosing this story to my sister, he was forever known as The Farter. She has a way with words. The rest is history, and so was he.

What I learned from this date: The first lesson I learned is I need a man who considers my needs. He thought I should accept being continually gassed by his butt and be okay with it, without him considering my basic need for survival, like, for example, breathing fresh air. Sir, Mars is calling your name. You should go back.

Secondly, it is certainly not worth destroying my health and well-being for a hot guy. Is there a person on this planet who would tolerate being gassed by their mate at a minimum of two hundred times per day, on an ongoing basis? If so, they'd likely die an early death of methane poisoning.

Thirdly, you know I'm working on not sacrificing my own feelings and needs for the sake of another. Once upon a time, I would have sat in that stinking house and inhaled his toxic butt gas without even a murmur. I'd have died silently and would have had to return as a ghost to see what the coroner had officially ruled my death as. Exposure to gaseous butt fumes? Acute colon to lung toxicity? The fact I spoke my truth and got the heck out of there suggests that the old paradigm is in fact shifting. Yay! Kudos to me.

11

MR GIGANTIC COFFEE

Age: 29
Location: Los Angeles, United States
Where we met: On my yoga mat at the Santa Monica foreshore
How he asked me out: Face to face after establishing a similar taste in reading materials.

Yep. I'd moved again. Not house. Country. Why? Truthfully, I was bored out of my mind living in Perth.

In my opinion, Perth is fantastic for retirees or families with small children, but for an attractive, single twenty-nine-year-old, it was not cutting the mustard.

The creativity and vibrancy Mum had cultivated in our childhood, for example, encouraging us to make a crocodile out of grass cuttings, was being underutilised. So, where could I live that had creativity in spades? The only way to find this place was through a creative ritual, so I closed my eyes, plunged my finger down onto a map of the world and there, beneath my finger, lay the city of Los Angeles—my next home.

Let me state a fact: the people of LA are freaking creative. Let me explain. During my first week in La La Land, a 'pregnant' lady positioned herself at a set of traffic lights and moved down the line of cars begging for cash. I handed over some crisp ATM dollars and wished her well.

The following day I was walking down the next street over and guess what? Down a small alleyway, I saw the same lady pull a pillow out from under her T-shirt and throw it into a Porsche.

Yes. A. Porsche.

She got into the driver's seat of that Porsche and zoomed away. I had to give it to her. Definitely creative. And I bet the pillow was a Tempur-Pedic. Creative and well-rested.

So aside from the sheer audacity and blatant fraud I'd witnessed in LA, I can confirm Perth had nothing on the creative minds of the Angelenos.

Want to know another area where the people of Los Angeles beat out the Perthites?

Guys ask you out. Like to your actual face.

In Australia, men stare at you from afar, look away when you make eye contact, then awkwardly leave without saying anything. On the other hand, in LA, getting asked out on dates is an everyday occurrence, even if it's by residents of the Santa Monica homeless community. Either things were looking up or I was about to get a sharp increase in future book material. I chose to be optimistic.

At the time of date 11, I had been living in West Los Angeles for a few weeks and most days, after finishing volunteering at the local bookstore, I would head to the beach to read one of the paperbacks I'd borrowed.

I'd roll out my yoga mat on the grass, park my pillow at the head of the mat, lie down and open the book of the day, raising it just high enough to block the sun so I didn't have to squint.

On this particular occasion, I'd followed my usual mat procedure, and no sooner had I lay down when I heard, 'I love that book,' from a deep baritone American accent; a voice that sounded perfect for radio.

I lowered the book and peeked over the top to see a tall, olive-skinned, masculine hunk of a man standing in front of me dressed in all white. I bet you any money he's Greek. Only a Greek man would have the cojones to wear all white.

'Is the book good?' I secretly admired the boldness of his wardrobe choice.

'Why don't you let me tell you about it over coffee?'

I don't personally drink coffee. If I drink caffeine, I'm awake for five days straight with a train of thoughts on a constant loop careening through my mind. But I had truly had enough of being trapped with crazy, carnivorous, methane-gassing men in inescapable scenarios, so I felt I could find a way to make it work.

'I'll get an almond chai latte.' I held out my hand and he pulled me to my feet. I brushed away the stray blades of grass from my white dress as he took my arm, like how a gentleman would escort a lady in the olden days, although I did have to increase my speed to keep pace with his long strides.

The Date

Some easy chit-chat and a couple of blocks later he stops and fiddles around in his pocket pulling out a few dollars and says, 'Hop on,' motioning me towards a chrome scooter parked on the sidewalk.

'Is this yours?'

'No, we're renting it.'

Well, this is a first. A date on a scooter? I wasn't exactly dressed for the occasion, but, what the heck, you only live once, right? I step onto the back edge with the help of his forearm, which keeps me balanced. Once I'm steady, he jumps on the front.

'Ready?'

I feel gravity jolt me backwards as we propel forwards.

I'll paint you the scene of what happens next. Imagine my white dress flying around like a plastic shopping bag caught in the wind, whilst I'm holding onto his body tightly. I'm pretty sure this is all part of his strategy to move me past the physical touch barrier as soon as possible. Lucky for me, his body is a typical LA body, athletic and strong, so it's not an unpleasant experience. Just saying.

For about twenty minutes the ride is fun. You know the score, wind in hair, cool breeze on cheeks, the constant honking of horns by impatient LA drivers—not fun. The scooter starts to slow, and after a few minutes, we are at a complete standstill. Yep. It's broken and we're almost at Venice Beach, miles away from my car and miles away from the coffee shop. I have somehow managed to turn a coffee date into a hostage situation as well. At least I'm consistent.

I step off the scooter onto the pavement and face my date. His cheeks are rosy, and he looks stressed out, so I grab his arm. 'Don't worry, it's all part of the fun. Let's enjoy this wonderful weather.'

A smile brightens his face, and his clenched jaw softens as he links my arm once again. We walk arm in arm several miles back to the coffee shop; the broken scooter rolling sadly along beside us. We arrive at a cute little corner building with bright red window shutters.

'You have to try the gigantic mugs here.' His tone is excitable as he extends his arms to accentuate the largeness of the mugs.

'I'm up for that. I'll have an almond chai latte, please.'

I shuffle the contents to retrieve my wallet and he pushes it back into my bag, muttering that no woman from LA would ever offer to pay her share.

He motions me with his hand to grab an outside table. There's a quiet corner spot at the back of the courtyard. Pretty white flowers dangle from hanging baskets. I spot a couple getting up to leave, so I head in their direction and slide into one of the seats. The previous bum had warmed it for me. Thank you, sir.

A few minutes later my date is gazing into my eyes, sitting in the opposite chair. He's got a fantastic set of teeth. Everyone does in LA, but have you noticed they have a blueish tinge? Must be from all the bleach.

'Thanks for not making a fuss when the scooter broke

down.' He places his large hand on top of mine and leaves it there.

'It's not a big deal.' The warmth of his hand feels nice against my skin.

A moment later, the gigantic mugs arrive, and he's not wrong about the size. Think soup bowl.

'Is that straight black coffee?' I peer over at the dark, steaming liquid.

He nods. He's going to be as high as a kite after drinking all that caffeine.

The waitress places my chai latte down in front of me with the precision of a surgeon trying not to cut an artery. I assume with the goal of zero spillage. Mission accomplished. They must spend a whole day's training on not spilling out of the massive mugs. I thank her with a smile, as my date takes a sip of his coffee.

It's hard to describe what happens in the next few minutes, as peacefulness is replaced by absolute chaos. I'll describe the event in slow motion as that's how it happened in my head.

My date's lips meet the hot liquid in his coffee cup. His eyes begin to widen until they are bulging out of his head. He starts to rise out of his chair screaming, 'Hot!' in a long, drawn-out bellow.

As he stands, he knocks the table with force. At the same time, chucking his coffee mug into the air that heads in my direction. I feel my arms raise instinctively to protect my face from the fast-approaching mug hurtling my way. At the same time, I let go of my own mug of chai latte. The immense amount of hot liquid from both giant mugs cascade into the air and descend over both of us, splattering each of our white outfits with dark black liquid. On impact, what feels like molten lava sinks through my dress onto my skin, and I instinctively let out an almighty scream.

It's like the splash zone at an amusement park, only it's burning hot and we're the only ones screaming. My date hollers profanities whilst scowling at a pattern of dark splashes on his white attire with a mixed expression of horror and rage.

These moments are pivotal in one's life. Do I react to this situation or respond? I don't have time to make a choice because my date clearly has no concept of responding and instantly reacts by yelling at the top of his lungs, 'For bleep sake! Why did this happen? Why?' I will note the final 'why' was long and drawn out and he's looking up at the sky, his hands clenched in tight fists. Talk about dramatic. Clearly, this Angeleno has taken one too many acting classes that have a whole section on Marlon Brando.

This sudden outburst draws the attention of every patron in the café. You could hear a pin drop. A waitress hurries out with concern written on her face. She hands me a damp towel, which is accompanied by a never-ending string of apologies. She passes a towel to my date, but he swipes it away and starts ranting again, 'Why the bleep would you serve me boiling coffee, you idiot? I'm going to sue the crap out of you.' Again, drawing out the last word for extra emphasis.

Why, when something happens that an American doesn't like, do they instantly think to sue the offending person? Ever thought of trying the proven and efficient strategy of talking it out?

I'm still in a state of shock when he suddenly decides to

leave and walks out of the café, leaving me alone, covered in coffee, with every single patron staring at me in silence.

What the heck just happened? I drink the remaining drops of my chai, apologise profusely to the waitress for his outburst and walk two miles or so back to my car.

Mr Gigantic Coffee had the nerve to text me the following day requesting another date. You can guess my answer.

What I learned from this date: Firstly, we all have moments when we snap, but they should be few and far between. From this date, I learned how important responding to a situation is, instead of reacting to it. Through my meditation practice, I'm becoming more aware that as the emotion arises in my body, there's a split second when I can catch it. From this awareness, I can choose my normal programmed reaction, or I can take a moment and decide how I want to respond. This is a tricky feat, and sometimes I miss the moment, but it is my mission to conquer my programming. I shall succeed!

Secondly, I want a man who has a high level of emotional maturity and can keep his emotions in check under stressful circumstances.

Thirdly, I should meet someone AT a coffee shop for a coffee date in future. I'm leaving no more room for transportation mishaps.

12

MR SHARMEN

Age: 29
Location: Santa Monica, United States
Where we met: Self-Realization Fellowship Lake Shrine
How he asked me out: Face to face after observing him performing some miraculous yoga postures.

Aside from trying to dodge scalding liquids, I did desire to stay in La La Land, but my tourist visa was running out fast. So, how would a normal person try and accomplish that goal? Marry a local? Get sponsored by a company? No. For me, it had to be—get accepted into a prestigious university to complete a master's degree that would allow me to stay for two more years.

Problem solved.

I was a few weeks into my degree and I was loving it. But I need to confess; something strange occurred every time

I'd participate in lectures or discussions. Maybe you could enlighten me.

When I'd speak, the room silenced, and everyone would turn towards me and lean in. I knew it was specific to me because if someone else spoke, others would cut in or talk over them, but for some reason, my voice evoked complete and utter silence.

As you can imagine, I found this extremely odd. Was I overthinking it or did I sound like Donald Duck, and they were in fact trying to decipher my buccal speech?

After putting on my detective hat, I discovered the following possible reasons, other than my Donald Duck theory, which I hadn't ruled out:

1. Americans love an accent, and the English accent has a level of refinement associated with intelligence. So, do they subconsciously believe that when an English person speaks, they know more than they do?
2. Could there be some remnant conditioning that occurred from the British colonisation of the Americas in the 17th century? Do Americans think they aren't as smart as the Brits?

These observations are obviously false since Americans have, shall we say, healthy egos and don't give even a moment of thought to the Brits unless it has to do with Queen Elizabeth conspiracy theories or competitive baking shows. So maybe my first theory was correct—Donald Duck it is. Case closed.

Before I get into the nuts and bolts of date 12, I need to

bring something to your attention, and no, it's not about my newly formed Donald Duck speech impediment. It's about driving.

You may or may not be aware that Los Angeles has different road rules to the UK and Australia, the biggest one being you drive on the right side of the road instead of the left. As a result, the steering wheel and driver's seat are on the left side of the car. If you've always driven on one side of the road or vehicle, driving on the opposite side can be a daunting mental challenge, especially when you're dealing with impatient LA drivers. Do they give their sick friends 'Get well immediately' cards?

After living in LA for three months, I needed some wheels to get around the place as Los Angeles has a poor public transport infrastructure, so I took the plunge and hired a car—a Ford Focus I named Janet. I'd gotten the idea of giving vehicles pet names after the date with Mr Incredible Hulk. Remember Gladys? Janet and I so far had a much healthier relationship. When I first hired Janet, I did a few laps around the car park and figured, surely it can't be that hard driving on the other side of the road? Especially with my new pal Janet by my side at every turn.

Janet and I made it in one piece to my new favourite place in Los Angeles—The Self-Realization Fellowship Lake Shrine. I'd describe this place as a little slice of heaven amidst the chaos of LA, and I'd vowed at least once a week I would perform a walking meditation through their manicured gardens.

From my last few weekly visits, I'd become good friends with the resident swans, Pamela and Simon (the names I gave them), and they proved especially attentive in listening to my dating escapades. The family of turtles didn't care so much about my personal life but reminded me that basking in the sun was a productive endeavour.

During my self-reflection time at the Shrine, it was evident a pattern was forming in my dating life. Whenever I had a hellish date, I immediately vowed never to date again, wondering why I had such a high ratio of crackpots entering my life. That being said, the hopeless romantic in me could never give up on love, so, when I saw date 12 in the meditation garden, I was eager to give love another chance.

I was sitting crossed-legged reading *Emotional Intelligence* by Daniel Goleman. I peered over my book to see a handsome guy doing some impressive yoga poses about ten feet away. I squinted into the sunlight and gave him a smile. He returned the favour. It was less than a minute later when his masculine body blocked the sun and cast a shadow over my face.

'Hey beautiful, would you like to go for a drink?'

Very direct. I like it. I'm not one who enjoys the personality type where a person goes on and on and on for ages, round and round in circles, to make a simple point they could have summed up in one sentence. I'm in a conversation, not the audience of a one-man show. It's evident I'm a strong D on the DISC profile.

I sat up and used my hand as a shield from the sun. The image of being trapped in the cocoon from the Mr Yogi date flashed before my eyes. I discarded the thought. 'Sounds great.'

We exchanged numbers and agreed I'd collect him at 6 pm that evening near Whole Foods, Santa Monica, affectionately known by the locals as *whole paycheck* because you enter with your weekly wage and leave in debt. But I still love that place. My date informed me that he was an eco-warrior and didn't believe in owning a car, which was a polished way of saying I'd be driving. The only thing LA values more than being eco-friendly is having good PR.

The Date

I drive Janet into the Whole Foods car park at around 5.30 pm. I need to stock up on some of their scrumptious white chocolate. Heaven doesn't cut the taste. I grab a few other bits and bobs, head through the check-out and wait outside at our meeting spot.

I'm ten minutes early, which is unlike me, so to stay in my conditioning of being late, when a homeless lady—who I'd come to know as Brenda—with two trolleys, asks me to push one of them to her new home, I oblige.

On the way to the next block, Brenda informs me that she wants a fresh start and needs to escape her current location to get away from her loser ex-boyfriend. I hear you, girlfriend.

She thanks me for my help, and I stroll back to my meeting point, where I see a shamanic-looking man in a blue linen get-up. It's my date. No sweating for you, sir.

I open my arms for a hug. He lifts me up and spins me around, like in an old Hollywood movie when a couple reunites after months of separation. I love it when guys are bold like that. So attractive. He also smells clean. Big tick. You'll be hearing about some less hygienic dates when I return to Australia. More on those later.

I walk around to the right-hand side of Janet and

immediately correct my mistake. 'Brain is still in Australia.' I shake my head and make my way to the other side and jump into the driver's seat. The Sharman slides into the passenger side. I turn on the car and put her into drive. Thank goodness Janet is an automatic and I don't have to worry about gears, as well as everything else.

We take a turn to exit the car park and I'm presented with four lanes: two going in one direction and two going in the other. It's a wide street, but there are no cars on either side of the road when I arrive at the car park exit. I feel tension starting to build in my brain because my normal strategy is to follow the car in front, as that's usually a safe bet.

Unfortunately, on this occasion, there are no cars in front. My brain freezes. Crap, which side should I be on? In the rear-view mirror, I see a car pull up behind me. Great. I know what's coming next . . . horn honking!

If there's one thing that's exceptionally annoying about driving in LA, it's if you stay stationary in a car for more than a millisecond when you're at an intersection or red light, every driver behind you starts honking their horns in loud, offensive streams. It shocks the heck out of your nervous system. It also means every time you're in a similar situation, your body automatically goes into freeze mode, which impedes your brain's decision-making faculties. It seems driving classes in Los Angeles teach you the primary objective is to get all cars in front of you out of the way, even if that means sending them into oncoming traffic.

Unlucky for me and Janet, the driver behind is a typical LA honking lunatic, and when the loud, extended honk begins, I feel instant pressure to move. Crap. Left or right. Left or right. Honk. Honk. Extended honk.

I put my foot on the gas, cross my fingers and go left. No sooner have I made the choice when I hear loud pitch screaming coming from my date's mouth. His eyes are terrified and wild, and his scream is loud and primal. He's pointing forward and when I avert my eyes to the windscreen, I see rows of cars in both lanes heading Directly. For. Us.

Again, I'm not fully versed in American driving rules yet, but I'm pretty sure that's not supposed to happen.

Now, something interesting occurs in this precise moment. Obviously, my brain is trying to make sense of the situation, so guess what my brain concludes? Why are these drunk people driving on the wrong side of the road? Thanks, brain. At least you've got my back.

My date's screams morph into screaming words, 'You're on the wrong side of the road.'

It's only when I hear his words, do I realise it's I. Me. *Moi*. I'm the one who's driving on the wrong side of the road and I'm not even drunk.

The oncoming cars swerve left and right. The honks are all in unison, a never-ending stream, loud and piercing. My date is screaming. I'm screaming. I'm sure every person in the oncoming cars is screaming. All I can do is keep going straight ahead and pray they get out of my way.

About twenty honking cars later, there's an opening across all four lanes. Hallelujah! I go for it, pulling the steering wheel down hard and left. Janet skids into a hairpin turn. My date holds onto his door handle for dear life as smoke burns off Janet's tyres. I straighten up and pull a hard right onto a side street, where Janet grinds to a halt.

Holy freaking moly! I'm shaking from the adrenaline surging through my body. My hands are clammy, and the windscreen is fogged, possibly from the heat of terror coming off my date. My date is bent over with his head in his hands, but at least he's stopped screaming.

'Oh, my goodness! I'm so sorry, are you okay?'

My date lifts his head. Even with his dark complexion, he's pale. The blood drained from his face.

'My life flashed before my eyes.'

The part of me that's still in date mode thinks, *Oh, tell me more about this life!* Right, back to the pressing matter at hand.

'I'm. So. Sorry. I'm so freaked out right now.' I take in some deep breaths in an attempt to calm my nervous system. Thanks, yoga training. 'I don't think I can drive. Can we go somewhere closer? I need a stiff drink.'

My date nods and slowly manoeuvres himself out of the car. I get out and shake the nervous energy out of my hands. My date is silent, undoubtedly still in shock, but he starts to walk, albeit a tad shaky. I follow until we reach the first bar we come across. I guess this is the one we'll be attending.

We sit on a couple of bar stools and my date orders a whiskey, straight, even though he's been a teetotaller for years. I can't blame him; he did see his life flash before his eyes. I order some chilli fries with dairy-free aioli. Maybe food will help calm our nervous systems or, at the very least, drown the remaining screams left in my body with aioli sauce.

Our drinks arrive and my date takes an extra-long sip. It must have been potent because his shoulders instantly drop down from up around his ears and relax down his back. Thank goodness. I hope he's not scarred for life.

'Feeling better?' I rub his arm.

He nods. 'What a first date!'

It's a good sign he's loosening up. I follow suit until we are both holding our bellies from laughter. The release feels good.

The conversation flows and he's an exceptionally interesting guy who travels all over the world, exploring his spirituality and his connection to the divine. What a grand life purpose, finding one's true meaning in life. It's the purpose for all humans, in my opinion, to live fully as divine creative beings. Good on him for following his path. I feel extra glad that I didn't get him killed, as I have a feeling car crash by English lass was not supposed to be on said path.

The chilli fries arrive, and we tuck in. The aioli is especially creamy today and, in a few minutes, the bowl is empty. I feel more relaxed, but still nervous about driving Janet again.

My date must have sensed my hesitation because he says, 'Don't worry, I'll drive,' then holds my hand like a kind, enlightened sage and I feel instant relief. Hopefully, the relief lasts longer than it has done on other dates.

'Oh, thanks so much. I really appreciate that.'

'It's my pleasure to take your stress away, and you never know, it might become a hell of a story we tell our grandkids.'

He leaves cash, grabs my hand and we walk back to the car.

Janet sits in the side street, calm as a cucumber like nothing has happened. Can you believe the cheek?

We get into our respective seats. My date turns on the ignition and reverses—slowly—out of the laneway and back onto what I believe should be renamed The Terrifying

Boulevard. This time he goes into the right lane, both literally and figuratively.

After about five minutes or so, we merge onto Pacific Coast Highway and the crescent moon shines brightly against the darkness of the sky. There's something so mysterious about the moon. I notice I'm more emotional when there's a full moon; that must be where the term lunatic comes from. I'll google that when I get home.

My date winds the window down an inch and warm evening air floods the car. Heaven! I close my eyes for a minute and enjoy the serenity. I'm alerted to the hum of the car moving over the rumble strips and casually blink open one eye. Sure enough, we're drifting towards the steel rails, the barrier between road and beach.

I glance across at my date. What the absolute heck? His face has blown up like a balloon. His lip is drooping downwards, with saliva dribbling down his chin. His right arm dangles lifelessly by his side, with the other one white knuckling the steering wheel. This is not the relaxing ride back I had hoped for.

'What's happening to you?' My voice is loud and trembling.

My date responds with a weird, incomprehensible grunt as we veer further over into the left lane towards the steel barriers. Oh, my life, not again.

I grab the wheel and try and pull it to the right, to straighten the dang thing up. What's with this car? It's a death trap. Suddenly Janet starts increasing in speed. My date's right foot is flat to the floor on the accelerator and Janet seems to have no intention of helping me out.

You have to forgive me, but a string of bleeps leaves my

mouth—sorry Dad—as I yank off my seat belt, jump over to his side and grab his right leg, hauling it off the accelerator, which causes the car to slow. My heart is pumping so fast right now, I need to stop Janet, whom I'm considering renaming Jolene because she's clearly trying to take my man.

The lights of a gas station in the distance catch my eye. Maybe they can help. Janet is almost at a crawl now and I'm praying there will be enough speed to get us into the gas station. The familiar sound of LA honking ensues from the rear. Long strings of F-words leave my mouth. Finally, we make it and roll to a stop as I yank up the hand brake, hard.

Now for my date. I jump out of the passenger seat and bolt around to the driver's side. My date slides, like a sack of potatoes, out of the car and onto the ground.

Bleep. Bleep. Bleep.

I rush into the gas station. 'I need help. Please. Now!'

The attendant races outside behind me, where a group of people have gathered around my date. He's not responding. 'What do I do? What's happening to you?' I can hear myself yelling.

Under his breath, he murmurs, 'Dairy.' And an onlooker speaks out, 'Is he allergic to dairy? Could be a severe allergic reaction?'

'We haven't eaten any dairy though. But the aioli did taste extra creamy. Maybe they gave us the wrong one?'

'He needs an antihistamine, like now.' The gas station attendant sprints back inside and comes out with a pack of pills and pops two onto my date's tongue. Another lady pours water into his mouth, as my date splutters and spits, water spraying everywhere, but eventually, he swallows.

I prop his head up with my jacket and trace my fingers across his forehead. 'Don't worry, everything will be okay.'

Please let everything be okay. I'm not cut out to be a suspect in a manslaughter case, especially when the US government already classifies me as an alien.

A few minutes later, I hear the sirens of an ambulance getting closer. Thank goodness someone remembered to call them. My date gets strapped onto a stretcher and lifted into the back of the ambulance. I am so scared to drive death trap Janet, but I need to make sure he's okay, so I thank the group and still fearing for my life, drive Janet behind him, freaking out the entire way and telling Janet I'll be booking a couple's counselling session because this is giving me Gladys flashbacks.

You'll be pleased to know my date did survive and it was confirmed he had a serious allergic reaction to dairy. Poor guy.

We didn't have a second date as he decided to travel to Peru to heal from the PTSD he incurred from our date. Last time I heard he was doing a five-day Ayahuasca retreat. I hope it helps.

I returned Janet to the rental shop. I figured Janet and I just weren't a good match—like every date thus far.

I continued to drive in LA and sure, I still screamed when I came to a four-way intersection—I mean, how do you know who's meant to go first if you all arrive at the same time? But luckily my travels were all pleasant from then on, minus the constant honking from the locals. People of Los Angeles, take note: go easy on the honking, you're scaring the tourists.

What I learned from this date: Firstly, even though it had diabolical consequences, what I appreciated was this date took the lead and put me first when he knew I was feeling scared to drive. I did have to save his life, and take over the driving shortly after, but it's the thought that counts, right?

Secondly, I need to buy my own set of wheels.

Thirdly, I need to take a course in US road rules.

13

MR OH MY GOD

Age: 30
Location: Santa Monica, Los Angeles
Where we met: Online dating site
How he asked me out: Via dating site messaging

I'd been living in Los Angeles for about three months, and you'll be delighted to hear that to celebrate taking the leap into my flirty thirties, I bought a convertible Beetle in eggshell blue I'd named Betty! I just prayed she was not related to Janet.

Betty and I had taken a sunset drive to Malibu beach to celebrate this momentous occasion. The transition into my thirties was going well as I wrote prose for my new book on how to start a successful dog walking and pet sitting business whilst at the same time savouring each bite of my favourite white chocolate. All set against the backdrop of the day's sun disappearing over the horizon. Betty certainly knows how to treat a lady.

I had hoped for a peaceful transition from my twenties to my thirties with some self-reflection over the last year, but it wasn't meant to be.

'Hey!' A raspy male voice hollered from a large beach house on stilts.

Two guys motioned me over.

I stood up and then pushed my feet through the sand to where they were sitting, their bare feet dangling over an expensive-looking glass balcony. This is beach living at its best.

The first question out of their mouths, 'What do you do?'

It was the first question anyone in LA asked me unless I'd spoken first, in which case the question was, 'Are you from London?'

When I divulged that I owned a dog walking business and had written a book on dog psychology, they spent the next two hours trying to convince me they could get me my own show. Think, *The Dog Whisperer*. I wasn't surprised, as it's exactly how Hollywood portrays the place to be. I'd be a hoot on TV. But my biggest barrier to world fame was I had zero desire for everyone on the planet to know my name. I mean, I'd only just properly introduced myself to Betty and we knew each other intimately. So, in my predictable ladylike manner, I politely entertained their absurd ideas with intermittent nods. When they'd finished their pitch, it was dark, so I made my excuses to leave and vowed never to walk that part of the beach again.

My frequent visits to Santa Monica foreshore meant there was no shortage of dates, but no keepers. The more dates I had, the more it felt like so many people in LA were having a crisis of identity that had them more lost than I was trying to navigate the LA freeway system. So, one sunny morning I thought, let's see what the American online pool has to offer.

Let me tell you, this pool was online dating on steroids. Every man clearly had a professional photographer at his disposal. The pearly whites glared out of the screen like sunbeams and, interestingly, it seems every man in LA was either an actor or entrepreneur—go figure!

Ironically, date number thirteen started off comparable to a Hollywood movie. You know the narrative, where a guy goes above and beyond to meet the girl of his dreams, travels across the country for days and sends the most adorable messages until the final hour of meeting. Sounds so thoughtful and romantic, right? Have we learned nothing on this journey together? Wrong!

Let me start at the very beginning (that's a very good place to start). His photos were cute. He had the entrepreneurial mindset you've come to know I love. He had big dreams and it made for a fun phone conversation. He was out in the midwest, and I was in LA, so, when he offered to travel to meet me, understandably I was flattered. Could this finally be the Disney princess moment I've been waiting for?

A few red flags popped up when his journey began, and every hour he would stop and take a photo and send it to me with an accompanying text:

This beautiful tree reminds me of your strength and vitality, only 28 hours until we meet.

It would have felt romantic if I'd met the guy, had feelings for him, and he knew anything about my strength and vitality.

But he could have been talking about a resilient houseplant. When I receive these kinds of messages from a guy I've never met and only spoken to via phone, it feels—let's be honest—too much.

Twenty-seven hours and twenty-seven messages later, I felt overwhelmed with a heavy feeling of dread that felt like a lead weight sitting in my stomach. I couldn't cancel because I felt a sense of obligation since he had travelled so far to see me. Damn my English conditioning and the lack of ease in American transit systems. I felt like I was stuck between a rock and a hard place; if the rock was also spiked and the hard place was the door to Hell. I needed to suck it up and meet the dang guy. It's only an hour of my life, right?

The Date

The dreaded time arrives, and I walk down Santa Monica Boulevard to the start of the pier where we'd agreed to meet. I see a guy looking around. He's extremely short, has dirty blonde hair that looks freshly cut, and he's standing with a straight, upright posture. Have you watched that show, *Meerkat Manor*? Where the meerkats pop out of their burrows and stand perfectly straight with their heads darting around, taking in their surroundings? That's him, right now. But seriously, that can't possibly be him. His profile stated he was six feet tall.

Dating tip: I've learned from years of online dating guys tell fibs about their height. Knowing this, I allow for a two-inch height lie, but this guy was way shorter than me and I'm five foot six. He's definitely less than five feet. I know to be classified as a dwarf a person has to measure less than four foot ten in height. That surely can't be him.

I, on the other hand, clearly look exactly like my photos because he starts waving like a maniac in my direction, and I begin to regret representing myself so accurately. You know those fast waves kids do? That's his wave. I'm not going to lie; I'm already turned off.

I put on my best fake smile and walk in his direction. He holds out a miniature hand to greet me. I shake it and feel his tremble. Standing side-by-side, I'm a good head and shoulders taller than him and he doesn't look anything like his photos. He seems nervous because he's shuffling his feet and his eyes are darting all over the place. *Meerkat Manor* is all that passes through my mind.

His nervousness is unsettling, and I want out of this awkwardness as soon as possible, so I attempt a diversion by saying, 'Let's walk to the end of the pier,' and I start walking in that direction.

He nods and we begin our commute. I notice he's keeping a three-foot distance between us, which I'm secretly glad about because his energy is creeping me out.

I need to try and lighten the mood and lucky for me I see the fortune-telling machine coming into view, like the one out of the movie *BIG*, where the robotic genie sits inside a glass case and pops out your fortune on a card. This could be the exact same machine given we are in LA. I did search this later and fun fact, that scene was actually filmed in Rye, New York.

'Let's get our fortunes read.' I skip ahead until I'm in

front of the machine. The fortune teller's black eyes stare into my soul.

'I don't want to do this.' My date speaks in a raised tone with a slight panic in his voice.

'How come?' I watch as my dollar gets pulled into the machine.

'It's bad luck. You're dealing with the devil.' He grabs my arm and yanks it.

I pull my arm back and grab the fortune card that's popped out. 'It's okay. It's just a bit of fun.' But internally I'm wondering if my date has ever had a moment of fun in his life.

'Don't read it out loud. I can't listen to this.' He puts his hands over his ears and starts making noises kids make when they are trying to drown out the sounds of their parents' voices.

Do I have to spend an hour with this guy? My instinct— RUN. I turn away from him and read the card silently . . .

You will find love and fortune with a tall, dark, handsome man.

Well, that's instant relief that this guy is most definitely not the one, but heck, I didn't need a fortune teller to tell me that. I'm starting to think the robot psychic might be a hack.

A spindly hand that can best be described as the hand of 'Other Mother' from *Coraline* reaches around and snatches the card from my fingers, followed by, 'I knew this was a bad idea. This date is doomed. I can't believe my luck. This is the devil's work. I told you we shouldn't mess with dark forces.'

He rips the card up into pieces and chucks them into the air, where they cascade and flutter to the ground. It's like in movies when the snow falls romantically around a cuddling couple, except it is bits of paper and I'm trying to avoid touching a crazy person with 'Other Mother' hands. And seriously, did your parents not teach you about littering?

The fortune teller was one hundred per cent accurate. Plus, he's a litterbug. Mum would not approve.

I get onto my knees to collect the bits of paper and dispose of them in the nearest bin whilst my date continues to rant about the devil and bad fortune. What have I got myself into? This guy's an absolute fruitloop.

I need to break his flow, so I point at the kiddie ride and say, 'Let's go on the rollercoaster.'

His face pales. 'I don't like rides. I can't go on that.' He crosses his arms and shakes his head like a stubborn child.

'Oh, okay. I'll go on my own.' Any excuse to get away from his unstable energy if I'm being one hundred per cent honest.

He follows me to the booth, where I hand over cash for one ticket.

'Sir, we'll need to check your height before you go on the ride.' The attendant comes out of the booth with what appears to be a ruler and positions it above his head. He's just shy of five feet. A twelve-inch lie on his profile. What the heck? Plus, he's got work boots on. He's probably closer to four foot eleven.

'I'm not going on the ride,' he announces to the booth attendant and takes a step back. I make my way up the stairs.

In the next second, I hear heavy breathing in my ear. I turn, it's him, and now he's not only as white as a sheet, but he's also sweating profusely.

'You don't have to come, it's all good.' I want him as far away from me as possible.

'No. I have to do this. I have to face my fear. God wants me to face my fear.' His knuckles are white as he grips the handrail.

God wants him to face his fear? I'd like to call up God and ask why this man absolutely must face his fear today, on my date? Why not tomorrow when I'm safely far away from this individual and enjoying a perfectly nice day by myself? I breathe a heavy sigh. This is going to be a long, tiring date and I'm going to have to do a meditation and energy clearing when I get home to rebalance myself after being assaulted by his chaotic vibes. Lucky for me, Los Angeles is a hub for such rituals, but I secretly hope it's just trending and not because the dating pool has made it a necessity.

We reach the front of the line and his whole body is shaking uncontrollably. The attendant looks concerned. 'Is he okay?'

I shrug my shoulders. 'He doesn't look okay.'

My date's eyes dart in every direction and he's breathing short, shallow breaths. Meerkat.

'Sir, are you okay?' The attendant puts his hand on his shoulder and my date jumps about a foot off the ground. He turns and pushes past the line of ride-goers, almost stacking it down the stairs.

'I can't do this, God. Sorry, not today.'

God might be disappointed, but I'm not.

The coaster pulls up and I get in. Down below, my date is sitting on a park bench, holding a brown paper bag that he's breathing long, deep breaths into. Where did he get that from?

The ride pulls up and I step into the footwell, sit and

secure the seat belt. Three. Two. One. We're off. Gravity thrusts me back into my seat as we speed forward and for the next two minutes, I'm in heaven. There's something wonderful about feeling sensations that one wouldn't normally feel in day-to-day life. Don't you agree?

Dips and turns, left, then right. The view of the Santa Monica pier. I feel alive.

The ride skids to a stop and the passengers disembark. I unlatch the seatbelt, step out and walk down the steps and through the exit. My date is now breathing at a normal pace.

'How are you feeling?' I plonk myself onto the seat next to him.

'I'm okay. Can we go and sit somewhere, please, no more fortune tellers or rides?'

'Sure. Let's get a cup of tea. You should get some water though.' My eyes are drawn to his sweat-stained armpits.

Luckily, a café sits only a few strides away, so we walk over and order at the counter, take our drinks and grab a seat. I take a sip of my soda water. The greater part of me wants to escape back to my apartment, whilst the kind, conditioned, obligated side feels like I should stay and comfort him.

'So, how was the trip?' I figure this topic is God-fearing and dark force free, even though I know full well how the trip went, everything in fact, down to the finest detail.

'It was so cool; I was counting down how long I had until I saw you.'

Oh really? Is that so? I had no idea.

Normally, that would be music to my ears, if I like a guy and there's chemistry, but when you experience feelings of repulsion, the words sound like the cries of Satan.

'How long are you staying?' Please say you're heading home after the date. Please, please, please. I cross my fingers and toes.

'Seven days. I thought we could spend the week together.'

What the heck! No! Panic starts to rise in me. Is panic contagious? Have I caught it off him?

'Oh, right.' Think fast. Think fast. 'I've got plans this week. Sorry.'

Why do I always apologise? Why don't I simply say I'm not feeling it, and let the guy feel what he needs to feel? My fear is he'll have another panic attack and I'll be stuck with him for several more hours, that's why.

My date looks crushed, but a second later his face is within an inch of mine, lips pursed and heading towards my lips.

Sir, read the freaking room! Or at the very least, skim it. Retreat. Retreat. I pull back so far; I almost fall off my chair. I raise a hand to my face as a protective shield to block any chance of lip contact.

My date recoils, rejection written all over his tiny face. His eyes glisten and I'm anticipating waterworks. He rams his face into his palms and starts mumbling, 'God, why doesn't any woman want me? What's wrong with me? Why did you make me so short? God, why do you put these women on my path? I can't take it anymore.'

God's having a rough workday with this guy.

I don't want to touch him, but I once again go against my instincts to flee and instead, pat him on the shoulder. 'It's okay.'

He jerks into an upright position and in a raised tone commences an extensive monologue. 'No, it's not okay. Women are evil. Women only want my money; they don't want me. I married an eighteen-year-old who was pregnant with another man's baby because God told me to. After she gave birth, I adopted the baby and found out she'd been sleeping with the father the entire time and secretly wanted my wealth. We divorced, she took all my money and now I only see my baby that's not even mine, once a month. Why does God tell me to do these things?'

My immediate thought is, *Wow!* My second thought is, *God is not telling you to do these things. Take responsibility for your own decisions and your own dang life, fool.* But as you know, I didn't want to risk another panic attack, so I say nothing and try to figure out a way to get the heck out of there, pronto.

Three hours later, I still haven't said one word and I could write a thesis about his life. I have to do something.

'You should get some rest. You've had a long day.' I stand and pray he follows my lead. He does. Thank you, God.

'Where are you staying?'

He looks puzzled. 'I thought I was staying at yours since I travelled all this way to see you.'

I feel the blood draining from my face. 'Oh, my goodness. I'm so sorry. It's not my house, I'm renting a room and my roommate has a no man policy. Sorry.'

'Where am I going to stay now?' His hands cover his face again and his body folds forward.

Think fast or I'll be stuck for another three hours. I grab his hands. 'It's okay. Let's get you a hotel.'

'No. I never stay in hotels. I hate hotels.'

Maybe that's where the devil likes to stay?

'I'll stay at a hostel where I belong, with the losers.'

Hostels typically house travellers, not losers, but I'm hoping they will make an exception for this one. I quickly google hostels and thank goodness there's one not far from the pier.

'I've found one, let's go.'

I speed walk to the hostel and stop out front. No chance of a hug and dash on this one. It'll be a sprint back to the car. For your information, the hug and dash is when you give your date a hug with enough distance from your vehicle or place of escape, so you can move swiftly out of the hug, then dash away from your date, without any awkwardness. Good strategy, right? You can use it if you like.

'Lovely to meet you. Get some rest.'

It was not lovely to meet you. I don't care about your rest. Please never contact me again. I turn in preparation to sprint away.

'Can we do something tomorrow?'

No. No. No. No screams through my mind.

'Let's see how you feel tomorrow, yeah, you've had a rough day, get some sleep.' I smile whilst adopting a world athlete speed walking technique to the corner and then full-on sprint back to Betty.

Oh, my goodness, that was literally the date from hell. On entering the car, I lock the doors and drive home twenty miles above the speed limit. Once home, I jump in the shower, meditate for five hours and when I'm feeling blissful, check my phone. Twenty-one text messages. I have to cut this off, right now!

It was nice to meet you and thanks so much for travelling all this way for a date. I didn't feel that sparkle I was hoping for, but I wish you safe travels home and I hope you find someone wonderful.

I block his number as I know there will be a bombardment of texts in response, and I can't handle even one more word from him. For the next seven days, I don't leave the house. Just in case.

What I learned from this date: Firstly, my preference is to date locally if I'm meeting with guys from online.

Secondly, I also learned I'm not compatible with anyone with dogmatic religious beliefs who blames God or other people when things go wrong. Very unattractive.

Thirdly, this date also reaffirmed I still have a long way to go in my evolution of putting others' needs before my own. I do want to be kind and compassionate, but where is the line? Should I have left him to wallow in his hateful speech? At what point could I have left that would have still been considering his needs and efforts? Hmmm. I will meditate on this and let you know what I discover.

14

MR PRINCE CHARMING

Age: 30

Location: Topanga Canyon

Where we met: At a Hollywood restaurant, where he worked as head chef

How he asked me out: Face to face. He'd chased me down the street. How romantic. Hollywood all the way.

Are you interested in hearing what I uncovered during my meditation? If I was to honour my own needs but also consider Mr Oh My God's needs, after we sat down for the drink following my ride on the rollercoaster, I should have communicated that I didn't feel that spark and left it in his hands to decide what he wanted to do. Don't you just love hindsight?

Moving on. Did you know LA is one of the leading-edge cities for new trends? Health is at the top, despite the disturbing amount of Botox one observes in faces on a stroll through Beverley Hills. I read that Los Angeles has 7.6 plastic surgeons per hundred thousand residents. There's clearly a demand.

I decided to take a drive through the winding canyons of Malibu. The wind blowing through my hair and the sun rays on my face was my idea of a wonderful time.

At the peak of the canyon, a beautiful, rustic style building stood proudly. Pansies cascaded out of hanging baskets like rainbow waterfalls. A hand-painted sign that read, 'Nature's Sanctuary Health Store' hung over the doorway. How quaint.

I will say I'm an absolute nut for trying new health foods and products, so a smooth turn into the empty car park was my only option. Sounds of whales flooded the space as I stepped into the entryway. I ran my hands through silk scarves hanging off a hand-crafted wooden stand and closed my eyes to absorb the healing energy from rose quartz crystals. Wowsers! This place was the epitome of a sanctuary. Had I found heaven?

'Can I help you?' A shadowy figure emerged through some beaded curtains.

You know that feeling when you're in a Zen state? When your guard is completely down? That was the state I was in, so, when the person stepped into the sunlight beaming through the window, I was so stunned by what I saw that as I took a step backwards in preparation to smash those glass panes and escape, I tripped on the wooden stand and found myself on the floor covered in silk scarves.

Coming into contact with an elderly woman who had so much Botox injected into her face that she resembled ET was beyond shocking. My brain one hundred per cent believed I'd come into contact with an alien life form, and my fight or flight response kicked in and promptly knocked me over.

The next conscious thing I remembered was being back at home, with no memory of how I got there. Had my ET erased my memory?

I will say the extra-terrestrial encounter was a welcome change from the nut jobs, as I was still trying to avoid the trap of going back into the hell that is online dating. So, I was delighted to meet the acquaintance of date number fourteen when I was out having a deluxe meal with a girlfriend. Date 14 was the chef at the restaurant who not only cooked me a meal with every dietary requirement I'd requested but personally served it to me at my table.

Apparently, after clocking me through the kitchen door and seeing I was leaving, he'd decided to make a big first impression by chasing me down the street and placing a folded-up piece of paper in my hand.

It probably wasn't the delivery he'd hoped for because I was in the process of doing my good deed for the day by gifting my leftovers to a homeless man sitting on the sidewalk.

'Here you go. It's a delicious veggie risotto.' I placed it softly into his filthy hands.

At the exact moment that date number fourteen reached me, the homeless guy had taken a peek inside the bag and suddenly shouted this, 'I don't eat no rabbit food.' He then hurled the takeaway container at my feet with such force that the entire contents splattered onto the concrete. It looked like vomit and for all the use either of us got out of it, it might as well have been.

My soon-to-be-date was speechless as he took in the scene of risotto vomit, the homeless man, and me. It clearly wasn't the Hollywood scene he'd pictured moments before, so he shoved the note in my hand and left.

I shook the risotto off my heels, picked up the takeaway container and discarded it in the bin. Mum HAD taught me about not littering. Thanks, Mum. I did feel for the poor person scheduled to clean the sidewalk though.

When I got back to Betty, I read the note:

I love a woman who knows what she wants and isn't afraid to ask for it. Call me.

Of course, I rang him, and after laughing over the risotto vomit fiasco, I'd discovered date 14 was not from LA, he was from New York and the 'executive' chef at the exclusive Hollywood restaurant where I'd dined. I must say, I do love a man who can cook because personally, I'm not a fan. I also loved his note. A man who appreciates that I am opinionated and strong? Finally! What also impressed me was the number of questions he'd asked to find out about the things I liked. It feels so good when a man wants to know more about me. It's a sure sign they're interested and, in turn, makes me feel more attracted to them. This guy had got the questioning down and not in a weird interview kind of way, which is a flaw of my own personality.

So, on to the date. Have you ever been on a date where you were treated like a queen? Where your date picks you up in his car, opens the door for you, takes you somewhere he knows you will enjoy and does lots of small, considerate things that make you feel special? Well, if you haven't, you'll know what that looks like as I describe the first half of this date. Yes, I said first half. The second half was . . . a little different.

He texted me shortly after our second phone chat with the following:

Hey, I would love to take you on the best date of your life. Are you free this Thursday? I can pick you up at 6 pm.

The best date of my life? Wow, confident. He is half-Italian, so I figured his Italian side must have been writing the text. I was curious. I wanted to know where he was taking me.

My response: *The best date of my life? You've got me intrigued. I'd love to. See you at 6 pm.*

The Date

Six pm on Saturday rolls around as I push open the door of my apartment building and make my way down the steps and onto the road. The sounds of an engine revving alert me to a silver Ferrari idling on the left side of the street. Is that him? I walk closer to the vehicle to peer through the window, but before I can bend down, the driver's door swings open and out steps the chef. I take him in. He's a dark-featured guy, about five foot ten, stocky build with a perfectly shaped bald head. It's quite possible the baldness was a result of his high-pressure job. I remember in my teens working as a waitress, where the head chef was an absolute lunatic and an alcoholic. If I asked him to repeat himself, he'd throw a knife at my head, no kidding. I had to perfect my Matrix combat moves to stay alive. I casually check to make sure my date isn't sporting any cutlery.

'Hello.' I open my arms for a hug.

'You look beautiful.' He takes my hand and gives me a spin. My green dress flutters up as I twirl.

'Aww, thank you.' I feel a little heat in my cheeks.

'Let me get that for you.' My date sprints around to my side of the car and opens the passenger side door like a valet. The seat is sunken low, so low, in fact, it feels like I'm about to sit literally on the ground. He gently closes the door as I rearrange my belongings in the footwell. Into the driver's seat he hops and revs the engine that's so loud I might need earplugs for the journey. He glances over at me. I reciprocate with an eyebrow raise and nod, along with a grin that seems to satisfy him as he clicks on the indicator and the Ferrari starts to move.

'So, where are you taking me?' I adjust my dress, so it falls flat over my legs. Don't want him to get too revved up too early—he does seem to have a lot of energy and we know that's a trigger for me now.

'It's a surprise. Do you like surprises?' He holds his gaze on me until I respond. I can tell he's keen to please me and I'm not complaining.

'Yeah. I love surprises. I'm sure I'll love whatever you've planned.' I'm not lying when I say that. I'm easy to please on dates and can have fun no matter where I go or what I'm doing. Well, as long as my date isn't a complete lunatic. That seems to be the tricky part.

Trees are lush on the hilly terrain, which indicates we're leaving the city. The Ferrari moves around the tight bends with ease and grace, even though it's a classic rather than a new model.

'What kind of cupboards do you have at your apartment?'

Random question, don't you think? 'White gloss. Why do you ask?'

'Oh, no reason. I'm interested to know your taste. White gloss sounds very chic, just like you.'

He looks cool in his shades, and I like how much he seems to appreciate that I know my taste.

'So, tell me, boss lady. You obviously love ordering people around, right?' He jokes, but I sense a bit of nervousness in his voice.

'Yeah, I love telling people what to do. I live for it.' Sarcasm is my forte.

Perspiration forms on his forehead and his cheeks flush. He winds down his window and takes in a long, deep breath. Thirty minutes or so pass and we take a sharp left turn. Overhead I see large, black letters that read—Movies under the Stars.

I point at the sign. 'Is that where we're going?'

'Yes, ma'am.' He smiles and nods. His gaze lingers on my mouth.

I clap my hands together. 'Oh, cool. I love watching movies outside. I'm so excited.'

We pull into a parking spot, and he scrambles out of his seat and races around to my side, like he's the butler to a queen. I feel like I should wait in the car so he can open the door for me. He's so eager to please. The door opens and he offers me a hand like a prince asking a princess for a dance, and I'm half expecting him to roll out a red carpet. Since

I'm sitting at ground level, I do need a hand—two hands, in fact. He hauls me out of my seat to a standing position. He's strong.

'I need to get some stuff from the trunk.'

Very American word—trunk.

I sidle around to the back of the vehicle. He's unpacking what looks like stuff for a two-week camping trip. How long is this movie? Is it one of those three-day movie marathons? I haven't brought spare undies.

'Can I carry something?' I have two free hands since my bag is over the shoulder.

'No. You relax. I got it.' He swings one rucksack over one arm, another over the other. He's holding what appears to be a tent in one hand and is carrying two shopping bags in the other. The car keys dangle from his mouth. Somehow, he also manages to grab my handbag off my shoulder and carry that too. I look like a right princess. Hopefully, no one I know is at this event.

'Shall I close the boot?'

He somehow uses his foot to close it. Guess he doesn't need help then.

We walk towards the cinema entrance and on reaching the gate, one by one, he puts everything on the ground, retrieves the tickets and hands them to the guy at the entrance who clicks them and points the way for us to go. I attempt to pick up one of the bags, but my date pushes my hand away, grabs it and organises the stuff back onto his body.

'You don't need to carry a thing, ma'am.'

I'm starting to feel like he's my butler rather than my date. All that's missing is a cap and white gloves.

We enter and pass the huge white blow-up screen and make our way further back. There's a slight grassy incline that would mean perfect viewing of the movie.

'What about over there?' I point at the lush verge.

My date nods and a few moments later, the two weeks' worth of camping stuff is on the ground for the third time. He picks up the item that resembles a tent and begins to unfold it. Next, he blows into the plastic nozzle on the side. What the heck is this thing? A blow-up bed?

My date must have been blowing this thing up for twenty minutes before it starts to resemble anything. Holy guacamole! He's brought a bed. Maybe in Los Angeles outdoor movies are more of a slumber party situation?

Forty-five minutes later the bed is pumped full of my date's breath. All the blood in his body seems to have accumulated in his cheeks, but he appears satisfied, nonetheless.

I take a few steps back, in preparation for a leap onto the bed, but he puts his hand out and blocks me. 'Wait, there's more, ma'am.'

Why does he keep calling me ma'am? Must be an American thing?

He rummages through the rucksack and pulls out two fluffy pillows and two cosy-looking blankets. He lifts one of the blankets that unfolds in the air as he shakes it. He neatens it on top of the bed and places the two pillows at the head.

'Now, it's ready for my queen.' He bows as he presents the bed.

Queen? That was definitely the vibe I was getting.

I crawl onto the right side and lay my head on the pillow. He grabs and shakes the second blanket and carefully places it over me. I feel as snug as a bug in a rug. How lovely. Am I in heaven right now?

'I must say I love the surprise. Thanks for going to so much effort and for bringing me here.' I wriggle onto my left side so I'm facing him.

He grins. 'You look so darn cute, right now. Are you ready for another surprise?'

I nod enthusiastically, like a kid at Christmas.

He reaches into the other rucksack and one by one starts pulling out candles, you know the ones that work on batteries? Apparently, he's not allowed to bring real ones, as they are a fire hazard and forest fires are frowned upon in these parts. He places twenty or so of them around our bed creating soft orange flickers of light against the darkness.

I notice people next to us checking out our setup and hear one woman say to her date, 'You never do anything like that for me.' He's in trouble.

I feel like I'm in a magical fairy tale and I'm blown away by his efforts. Expensive designer ceramic bowls are placed one by one at the end of our blow-up bed. He asks me to sit up so he can start setting up the food. He removes cling film and lids and starts to lay out trays filled with fresh salads, coleslaws, olives, dips, a nut cheese platter with crackers and grapes and if that wasn't enough, he opens another container that is filled with raw desserts—chocolate, mint, salted caramel, tiramisu. Holy freaking moly, this is enough food to feed a small village. My mouth must be hanging wide open because my date puts a finger under my chin, and I feel my mouth close.

'I have no words to express how much I appreciate all this.

Wow! The food looks absolutely delicious.' I reach over and cuddle him with some intensity and his face beams.

'How long did all this take to prepare?' I feel my gaze focusing on the gooey salted caramels.

'I spent a half-day yesterday making the desserts as I needed them to freeze overnight. I made all the cheeses from scratch after our first phone chat, so about two weeks ago, as they needed to ferment to get that bite to them.'

My mouth is hanging open again. This guy has gone to a level of effort I've never experienced before. How special do I feel?

'Dig in. Enjoy.' He hands me a salted caramel dessert. How the heck did he know I wanted that one? Is he psychic too? I take it and sink in my teeth, taking a big bite. The chocolate instantly melts on my tongue and the perfect combination of salt and sweet explode on my taste buds.

'I can tell you're a pro. These are the best salted caramel chocolates I've ever had, and I mean ever. And I've eaten a lot of chocolate in my lifetime.'

My date looks like he's going to take flight from the joy on his face.

'I'm so happy you are enjoying them. If you were my girlfriend, I would make them for you every day.'

Is this guy for real? Have I struck gold? Salted chocolate desserts every day? A girl's dream. Although if I were his girlfriend, I wouldn't let him do it every day, lest we forget my Violet Beauregard moment.

The lights dim and the flickering of our candles create a lovely ambience. I grab a knife and spread the cashew cheese over the crackers and crunch down. Heaven is dancing on my tongue right now. I gorge away at the delights in front of me and notice my date is sitting quietly beside me, staring at me.

'Tuck in, otherwise it'll be all gone.' I nudge him playfully.

'It's okay. I'll eat later.' He turns to face the movie screen.

Strange. There is so much food; delicious food at that. Maybe he isn't hungry? I grab some salad and pop in two olives. This is the best date I've ever been on, although I am getting flashes of Mr Fodder and a part of my brain is on alert.

An hour later, I slowly stuff the last cheesy cracker into my mouth and lean back, nursing my bulging stomach.

I cup his ear and whisper, 'I've eaten so much, I need to lie down.'

He suddenly jumps up and starts to pack everything away. 'You lie down.'

Okay, he's putting the food away. Not another Mr Fodder. I relax again.

'Let me help you.' I move to a seated position. He stops and looks directly into my eyes. 'Please, lie down and relax. Let me take care of you.'

I slowly recline. I feel a bit weird. I haven't helped at all on this date, and he's gone to so much effort. I feel uncomfortable. So much for relaxation.

A few minutes later all the food has been neatly packed away. He climbs back under the covers and reaches down and grabs one of my feet. He pulls it closer to him, which causes my body to twist horizontally across the blow-up bed. He retrieves a bottle from one of the bags and squeezes some of the contents into his hand. He rubs the liquid, warming it between his palms, places his hot hands onto my foot and starts to massage. Feels like heaven. I grab my pillow as I can only see the movie screen out of the corner of my right eye, due to the horizontal positioning. Thirty minutes later, he grabs my other foot and massages until the movie ends.

This date has felt more like I was at a day spa than a date. Can't complain, though. Love spas.

Patrons exit quickly, and we're the last to leave since my date won't let me jump on the bed to help get the air out, so I stand on the sidelines feeling like a spare part. I would quite enjoy the jumping bit. We arrive back at the car, where he dumps all the stuff and rushes to open the passenger side door for me. His expression is one of alarm as I touch the handle.

'Ma'am, allow me.' He grabs the door handle, pulls it open and presents the seat with his hand. This is so bizarre. It feels too much. Too intense.

I wait as he unpacks everything into the boot and gets into the driver's side, starts the engine and thirty minutes later we are back at my apartment.

'Thank you so much for the best date. You were right about that. I'll do something nice for you on the next date if you like.' I lean in to give him a hug goodbye.

My date holds me close. 'Can you do something nice for me now? Can I come upstairs, and you can lock me in one of your white gloss cupboards?'

You know when you hear something and it's so out of context you think you've misheard?

I pull back, 'Sorry, what did you say?'

'I said, I would love it if you locked me in one of your white gloss cupboards.'

I still feel like I'm hearing something different than what

he's trying to say. Maybe there's a British versus American translation fail.

'Cupboards, like kitchen cupboards?'

'Yes. Any kind of cupboard really.' He grabs my hand, and I can feel it shaking. I can sense his excitement.

'I will go in any cupboard you order me into.'

I feel my brain heat up with energy, trying to make sense of what the heck this guy is talking about.

'I could tell from our phone conversations you are a dominant and assertive woman, and I love women telling me what to do. Do you know what I mean?'

Suddenly, I know exactly what he means. Turns out he does not appreciate a woman who knows what she wants. He gets off on it. I feel a sense of dread forming in the pit of my stomach. He wants me to dominate him, order him around and lock him in cupboards. You have got to be joking me. Plus, what woman has room in her cupboards to fit a fully grown man anyway? I could save up for a mansion in the hills? No. Dang, my solution-based mind!

'Oh, right. I think I get what you mean now.' I maintain his gaze and begin patting the door behind me in search of the handle.

He grabs my hands. 'Do you think you could be that woman?'

I retrieve my hand out of his grasp. 'I'm sorry, what you're describing is NOT something I'm into, like at all. Like never in a million years. Like the polar opposite of my taste. Sorry. Thanks for the date, but I have to go.'

I locate the handle and frantically attempt to open the door, but because the car is so low and I'm almost on the ground, it's a real struggle. I end up opening the door and crawling out of the seat and onto the pavement.

He jumps up to come to my rescue, just the way he likes it. He holds out his hand, but I'm not so keen to take it this time. So, in my hesitation, he grabs me underneath my armpits and hauls me up to a stand.

'Okay. Thanks. Bye.' I hurry across the road to my apartment.

That started as the best date and morphed into the weirdest date. Not my thing. At all. Being locked in a cupboard? Do I need to start mentioning these things in my profile? Aren't there sites specifically for this kind of thing? I mean, each to their own, but yikes, being locked in or locking someone in a cupboard does not seem healthy to me. But hey, as they say, variety is the spice of life and if it floats your boat, go for it. Just not in my cupboards.

Lessons I learned from this date: Firstly, when something feels off-balance, it usually is. This date was too good to be true and it was. It has made me realise how important balance is in a relationship. Both parties need to contribute and offer value.

Secondly, I'm not into anything that degrades or demeans another person and locking someone in a cupboard, in my personal opinion, falls into that category. Each to their own, but not for me.

15

MR HOTEL CALIFORNIA

Age: 32
Location: Downtown Los Angeles
Where we met: In a swanky rooftop bar in central Los Angeles
How he asked me out: He slid his business card on the table in front of me.

You'll never guess what happened since my last date . . . I'd actually found a man I wanted a relationship with. I know. Miracles do happen. But, alas, it wasn't meant to be. Sigh. Hence why I am back here documenting more dates. Let me tell you what happened . . .

We'd been living together for eighteen months when one ordinary night, he came home on the verge of a nervous breakdown and spilled his sins to me like he was in a confessional, and I was the priest.

'I can't do this anymore. I can't live this lie. I haven't eaten any animal products these last eighteen months because I know that's important to you, but I ate a cheese pizza the other night and now I can't sleep because of the guilt.'

Now, I am serious about my lifestyle choices, but he said it as if he'd had sex with a cheese pizza, which, if true, would come with a whole other set of problems.

He took a moment to take in some air before continuing, 'I go to dancing classes with you because you love to dance, but I have two left feet and feel like an idiot the whole time. And I only cook and clean and do laundry because I feel this is what you want in a man, but I want a woman to do all the domestic chores.'

He lay back on the couch and breathed a massive sigh, like the weight of the world suddenly lifted off his shoulders and slowly drifted like a cloud across the room that crash-landed firmly onto mine. Dang it!

Wait, that's not what happened. Once upon a time it would have, but it seems reading one hundred books per annum is paying off—I listed my reading material over the course of one year, so the above claim is accurate. Future goal —in-home library. But I digress.

I removed that weight from my shoulders and placed it in the middle of the room so we could both handle it equally.

We decided our values were too far apart. He admitted he was extremely attracted to my powerhouse mind and independent vibe, but his preference was a woman who would stay at home, do the housework and cooking and take care of him when he returned from work. Pretty much my idea of a living hell. I decided I didn't really feel like living in hell since past dates filled my lifetime hellish quota.

When he professed these inner demons had been slowly killing him inside since the day we'd met, understandably, I felt blindsided as it seemed our entire relationship was based on lies.

However, always one to see the silver lining, the breakup meant he was finally free to find himself a domestic goddess, and I was free of living a lie.

The breakup was civilised, but I was still grieving the loss of something that never really existed. My lovely Guatemalan friend had booked a table at a swanky rooftop bar in central LA to cheer me up. I was dressed to impress in my electric blue jumpsuit, but was still feeling out of balance given the recent breakup. In hindsight, my imbalanced energy was a good mirror for the man I would meet that evening and the insane events that followed.

Colourful mocktails appeared on our table. My getting hammered days were a long way in the past, plus, being intoxicated and walking the streets of Skid Row at night was not advised if you wanted to make it to sunrise. I took a long sip of the brightly coloured liquid, yum, a mixture of sweet, sour and tangy on the tongue. Delish!

An attractive guy in his thirties straddled a seat at a nearby table, he was with four blinged-up men who appeared to be in their mid-sixties. We made eye contact. I smiled and returned my attention to my friend. A moment later he was standing beside the table, staring at me with piercing blue eyes, dressed in what looked like a very expensive suit.

He leaned over the table, blocking the view of my friend, 'I'd like to invite you on a date, this evening. We are having a party at my house, not far from here.'

He slid a luxe business card with gold trim in front of me. 'Address is on the back. Bring your friend if you like.' He maintained full eye contact as he walked away.

I peered over at my friend, wide-eyed.

'We should go, there might be other hot guys there for me. Let's check the address.'

We pulled out our smartphones and plugged in the location. The house had the appearance of a medieval castle, like ones you'd find in the UK.

'I reckon we should check it out.'

My friend clearly wanted to go, but, in all honesty, I was not feeling a good vibe about the whole thing. But, as I had done many times in the past, I went against my intuition and agreed to go for an hour.

The group of men got up to leave and my date blew me a kiss as he disappeared out the door.

We followed, headed back to our respective vehicles and braved the LA roads to the American castle, hoping it would be as sophisticated as a European one.

The Date

As I pull up outside the house, I see a group of young women piled in a convertible Aston Martin, holding what look like margaritas and throwing their heads back with laughter. They drive through two massive wood and iron gates and into the property. If this place was in the dictionary, it would be smack bang under the word, fortress. And it seems we aren't the only ones who've been invited.

I park my car on one of the side streets and see my friend standing near the gate entry.

I hobble over small, square brick pavers. Let's just say, they aren't exactly high-heel friendly. My friend struggles in her kitten-heel slip-ons, so we grab onto one another for dear life as we make our way to the grand entrance.

We finally arrive at the front door and are greeted by humongous, double wooden doors. Have they imported them from an old English castle? A drawbridge and moat would make for perfect castle vibes. It takes both of us, plus a random guy who's recently rocked up, to push it open. I've heard LA parties are hard to get into, but I didn't think it would require three people just to open the front door. Once inside, we are met with a double-storey height entryway with polished white marble tiles. Further back, an iron staircase spirals up to a second level, where the landing connects to the upstairs rooms. Undeniably a swanky castle.

My eyes are drawn back to the first level, where there must be at least a hundred people gathered. I glance through the crowd, but my date is nowhere to be seen, so my friend and I decide to have a nosey around. We trot down a ramp from the entryway that leads to another large door. On entering, we are met with a four-lane bowling alley, fully equipped with balls and a seating area. Luxe.

Another ramp leads to a cinema that could easily seat one hundred people. My date must be seriously cashed up to own this property.

We walk back up the two ramps and find ourselves in the

kitchen area. My date appears by my side and pulls me in close. 'I'm so glad you came, you're in for a wild night.'

A wild night? Sounds ominous, but maybe that's how Americans describe a good time.

My date interlocks our fingers and walks me into the neighbouring room, which is kitted out as a full bar. My friend turns to chat to a group standing in the kitchen.

'What's your poison, Miss?'

'Do you have any tea? I'm driving.'

'You're not drinking? Come on, have one.'

He ignores my request for tea, and instead, orders a glass of sparkling French champagne. The guy behind the bar places it on a gold-encrusted napkin and slides it in front of me. I pick it up and pretend to take a sip to appease my date.

He places his arm around my waist, and we walk to the back of the room. Before we can strike up a conversation, one of the blinged-up sixty-something-year-old guys from the city bar sidles up next to me but ignores me and speaks directly to my date.

'You managed to persuade blondie to come, nice work.'

Is that an odd thing for a person to say? It seems odd to me. I also see him slip some dollar bills into my date's hand, which feels even odder. But who knows? Maybe they're sorting out their party fund.

Before I can compute what just happened, the wealthy old guy addresses me directly, 'An English lass who is "tea" total?' He smirks. 'I thought it was a myth!'

You know when you meet someone, and you instantly feel uncomfortable? That's how I currently feel. He aggressively puts his arm around my shoulders and pulls me in. Yuck!

'How about me and you go and have a dip in the grotto. You can bring your cup of tea, petal.'

He says all of this in a crappy attempt at a London accent that might rival Dick Van Dyke's performance in *Mary Poppins*. I love dick . . . Dick Van Dyke that is, as he reminds me of my dad. Side note, you need to get your mind out of the gutter. Moving swiftly on, my accent is northern, but for some reason, every American thinks if you're English, you're from London. There are many more cities in England than London, my American friend. A total of fifty-one to be precise. Check out a map.

I observe my date who has a neutral expression on his face. Doesn't he care that this guy is clearly hitting on me, right in front of him? I suppose Americans are a little looser with romance. Free love and all, right?

I take a quick peek out of the window and see there are many grottos dotted in all corners of the grounds.

'Sorry, I don't have my swimming costume.' I inch away from him hoping to gain some personal space.

He pulls me back in, 'Babe, why do you need a swimming costume?' He laughs a loud obnoxious laugh. I notice a number of Armani-clad men enter the room flashing diamond-encrusted Rolex watches. Who were these guys?

The wealthy, older guy is persisting in trying to convince me to take a dip in the grotto with him even though I've said 'no' in every way humanly possible. The more I try to escape, the more interest he shows. He's like a needy, untrained puppy except with stranger-danger vibes instead of a tail. And my date is standing there smirking. Read the room, sir. Not interested. He doesn't get the hint. How can I get away from him? Why is my date not saying anything? The bathroom. Good escape plan.

'Where's the restroom?'

I'd learned that Americans call the bathroom a restroom. It makes sense why the English call it a bathroom because it houses, drum roll, a bath. Not sure why Americans choose that room to rest in. Anyway, I digress.

I smile sweetly, trying to hide my true feelings of repulsion. This whole place is feeling seriously off and it's becoming evident that it might not be the Disney princess castle experience I had envisioned.

'Up the stairs, on the right.'

I see my friend is still talking to the same group in the kitchen. I hastily walk over, grab her arm, drag her out of the room and up the stairs.

'There's something weird about these people. This place is creeping me out. I feel like I'm in The Hotel California.'

My friend giggles. 'A drunk lady told me that that old guy who was hitting on you owns the house, and they have orgies here every weekend.'

If I remember correctly, tonight is Saturday. Surely not. She's drunk. She's out of it.

We take a peep in each of the rooms to eat up some time, in the hopes that the wealthy old guy has moved on to his next target. Ten minutes later, we head back down the staircase. I grip the iron banister for support. I have to question why I continue to wear shoes I can't even walk in.

We arrive at the bottom of the staircase and speed walk outside onto the patio overlooking the perfectly manicured lawn. I glance back, no one is in sight. Perfect, we've gone unnoticed. The grounds are beautiful, with lush greenery creating privacy for the grottos. We tiptoe across the grass to prevent our heels from getting stuck in the ground and lean over and gaze into the water. The lights at the bottom of the pool give it a warm, magical glow.

Do you hear that? Sounds of what seem to be sex noises come from behind the bushes. 'I think someone's bonking,' I whisper to my friend. A moment later, my date hops out, zipping up his pants, with the guy from behind the bar following shortly after. My date doesn't even acknowledge me. Erm. I guess that's him and me done!

I hear the annoying fake London accent of the wealthy old guy approaching from behind. 'Blondie. You said you didn't want to take a dip.'

I feel the weight of his muscular arm land around my shoulders. I roll my eyes at my friend.

'Just admiring.' I step forward, so his arm falls away.

'I need some water.' I hold up my empty glass.

'I'll get it for you,' he speaks in a firm tone. He repositions his arms around both mine and my friend's shoulders as we reluctantly tiptoe across the lawn and back into the castle.

On entering, we observe an extremely drunk woman lying on the kitchen bench snogging the face off one of the billionaire guys. The reason I know he's a billionaire is because he suddenly announces it between snogs. Next, another girl starts taking the guy's shirt off, and another starts to undo his belt. Maybe my friend was right after all . . .

My friend, the wealthy rich guy and I stare at them. This is more awkward than a room full of one man and all his baby mamas, and I would know. Out of nowhere, the drunk woman dramatically thrusts the billionaire guy off, propels herself off the countertop, grabs my arm and drags me into the next room and starts hysterically pleading for me to stay the night. This is a joke, right? I guess that explains why my 'date' didn't care that I was getting cracked onto by another guy, and now the three women jumping on the billionaire guy in the kitchen. Could it be that instead of a sophisticated, swanky castle this was, in fact, an expensive den for orgies?

'Please will you stay,' she begs, slurring the 's'.

What do I say? There's no way I'm staying here with these fruitcakes. Think fast.

'Please stay. I really need you to stay.' Her sobs get louder, escalating into a kind of howl.

'Please. I'm begging you.'

I pull her hand off my arm that's gripped so tightly that when I remove it there's a handprint outline, which refills with blood. I shake out my arm. 'I'm so sorry, I can't. I have to go home tonight.' I eyeball my watch. 'I have to go now.'

'Please. I'll do anything.' She grabs my arm again, even tighter than before. She's strong for someone so small in stature.

'I'm sorry, I have to take care of my cat and need to leave immediately.'

The Hotel California, where you can enter but never leave, had failed to mention the reason you can't leave is because female participants will grab you with the vice-like grip of a world wrestling champion, and beg you to stay for group bonking. I'm starting to think hostels are the way to go moving forward.

I hurry back into the kitchen and grab my friend. 'We

need to go, like right now, we are at their weekly orgy and we're the fresh meat.'

Now, one thing I haven't expressed about my friend is this—she is incredibly naïve. I'm trusting, but hers is another level. Plus, her awareness of her environment is non-existent. We could be in a car surrounded by men wielding knives and she'd insist on rolling down a window for some fresh air.

'Oh, it's fine. Let's stay.'

A feeling of desperation takes over me. 'If you want to be the central attraction for this week's orgy, go for your life. I'm getting out of here, right now.'

Feeling frustrated, I push my way past her and head straight for the castle door we entered through. I reach the exit, but dang, the monstrous doors are locked. And even if they weren't locked, I know I'd need at least two other people to get them open. How the heck do I get out of this fortress? There must be an exit button here, like the ones you see in libraries or hospitals.

I scan the walls on either side of the door, but my attention is brought back towards the kitchen when I hear a high-pitched scream. I turn. My friend is on her back. On top of her are two large Burmese mountain dogs, you know, the ones that carry whiskey up snowy mountains. One has its jaws locked on the bottom of her jeans and is dragging her like a rag doll across the marble tiles.

Now, you know from previous dates that I have a significant flaw in my character, where I can't help but laugh at someone else's misfortune. It's not nice for the other person, but I cannot for the life of me contain the laughter, especially when it's something as shocking as this.

My laughter is mixed with my friend's screams. The wealthy old guy and my 'date' each grab the collar of one of the dogs. My friend leaps upright and as soon as her feet touch the ground, she starts to sprint, which all shoe lovers know is no easy feat in kitten heels.

At the same moment, I clock the button that leads us to freedom. I punch it with my fist and the fortress doors spring open. My friend charges past me and I follow closely behind. Thank goodness, the outside boundary doors are still open and I'm suddenly thankful there is not a moat after all. My friend flies over the square cobbled stones, like Jesus, not walking, but running on water. We reach our cars, lock the doors and speed away like robbery getaway drivers.

The one good thing that came out of the evening, was, when you are fearing for your life, you seem to get extremely focused on the present moment, which meant I didn't think of my ex, even once. I bet he never even crossed your mind during that whole date, right? See.

What I learned from this date: Firstly, concerning my ex-boyfriend. Always go for a man who is truthful, authentic and can have hard conversations. Run like the wind from someone who lives a lie and buries those lies in a box that festers in the recesses of his mind, which slowly morphs into a ticking time bomb that eventually explodes, scattering both partners' lives into a million pieces. As you can see, I'm not bitter or anything.

Secondly, Mr Hotel California taught me to always follow my gut instinct. You'll remember I didn't want to go in the first place and went against those feelings to appease my friend. When something feels off it's usually an indicator something dodgy is going on.

Thirdly, like attracts like. I went out that evening with an energy that felt out of balance, and what I experienced that night perfectly reflected my own unbalanced energy. In future, before agreeing to any dates, I will rebalance my own energy. Thank you, Abraham Hicks.

16

MR CATFISH

Age: 33
Location: Melbourne, Australia
Where we met: Online dating app
How he asked me out: Via text message

By the time this date occurred, I'd completed my master's degree in Los Angeles. This also meant I had to get the heck out of America. The US Government politely reminded me my student visa had expired and in no uncertain terms asked me to get my alien butt outta there, and pronto. Mum popped the champagne and had an all-nighter. Okay, so, I'm not sure that actually happened, but that was the visual in my head. I'd returned to Oz and within weeks had found a potential business opportunity in Melbourne. Exciting!

The epiphany to start a new venture dawned on me a few months prior during a T. Harv Eker workshop, where I'd discovered I wanted to help small business owners generate more profits. I'd also discovered a dream of wanting to build an investment property.

I already knew I was capable of starting a new business, but what about building a home? If I was to delve into my subconscious programming before I lived in LA, you'd have heard the following: 'Women aren't meant to own investment properties. You'll need a man's income to help you get a mortgage. You should be investing in a man, not a career.'

Erm. Yeah. My conscious response: 'Screw you, patriarchal programming.'

However, having lived in LA for the last three years and my two best options for a mate being between a God-fearing dwarf or a partner taking up valuable cupboard space, I had no choice but to find an alternative solution.

Cue the American dream.

There is a collective belief in the US that anything is possible. That's why people from all over the world travel to LA. Somehow, by osmosis, that belief had taken up permanent residence in my subconscious and made it to my conscious mind. Armed with this new empowering belief, I was keen to test if dreams really do come true with the right thinking.

I'd arrived in Melbourne for the business meeting, where I'd be a partner in a consultancy firm and was staying at The Crown Hotel. I'd not been on any dates for the last three months and figured, I'm here for a week, so, what the heck, let's take a dip in the Melbourne fishpond and get dirty in the trenches of online dating. Couldn't be worse than a surprise castle orgy, could it?

You know when you spot a profile and you're like, wow,

hot toddy? That was my first impression of this date. We'd exchanged numbers and after several hours of texts back and forth, I'd sent this, in response to his request for a date:

Perfect! 8 pm at The Casino Lounge Bar. See you then. ;)

I checked myself out in the floor to ceiling mirror in the hotel room, dressed to impress in my red stilettos. Only after I put them on did I realise they were of the killer heel variety, as they were new. Six pm rolled around and I figured what could be nicer than a delicious dinner beforehand?

After a final mirror check, I headed out the door.

'Thank you.' I followed as the waitress led me to my table.

Sitting at the next table were a couple of guys, professionally dressed, who were easily pushing fifty. And when I say sitting next to, anyone observing would've thought we were from the same group, that's how close the tables were. I might as well have been sat on their laps. My growing aversion to older gentlemen was thankful I was not.

I decided to have my once-a-year glass of champagne. Oh, how times have changed since my getting blottoed days in the UK. I was in high spirits because I had a meeting booked with potential business partners the following day, and maybe, just maybe, I'd move to Melbourne.

My neighbouring diners seemed surprised by the close proximity of our tables and immediately struck up a conversation, asking questions about my profession. I explained that I owned a dog walking business in Perth, but was now branching out as a business consultant, helping CEOs and business owners turn bigger profits. Fun. Turned out these two were business owners. What were the chances?

One would expect this reveal would've triggered an

extensive and lively conversation about business. Instead, I was treated to a lengthy monologue about how his wife, sorry, 'estranged wife,' or simply 'bleeping bleep,' was trying to take everything he'd got. So much for a fun and light-hearted conversation.

I did the usual nods and shakes of the head at the appropriate times. I'm well aware I have my mother's curse of being a good listener, and, as a result, I spend much of my adult life listening to other people's, let's be honest, crap. But, on a positive note, my mushroom risotto dinner was delicious so during exaggerated stories about a woman I'm sure is a lovely person, I meditated on the texture of the mushrooms. Maybe if I'm ever pre-estranged I'll make my husband mushroom risotto this good. Kudos to the chef. I made a mental note to mention that to the waitress on my way out.

I glanced at my watch, 7.45 pm. I grabbed the bill and headed down to meet that tall glass of water, my Indian head-turner from the online site. Exciting. Fingers crossed.

I wished my neighbouring diners, who were now paralytic, farewell and luck with the divorce, as one does with complete strangers, then walked to the counter and placed my bank card against the pay machine. The familiar beep of approval rang out. 'Please, thank the chef for the delicious risotto.'

'Will do, so glad you enjoyed it.' The waitress mirrored my wave.

I walked towards the steps, lit with fairy lights, carefully and one by one, given the height of my heels. I managed to reach the bottom still upright and thanked the universe for not getting me there via roly-poly—roly-polies are what little children, beginner gymnasts, and uncoordinated women do: a British term for a forward roll.

Slot machines to the left, bar to the right. The neon pink light that spelled out the name—The Lounge—caught my eye. Yep, that's the one.

I wobbled up each carpeted step towards the bar. Stilettos have that effect on me and on everyone who wears them to be honest, except for maybe drag queens who seem to have mastered the technique down to a fine art. It's not uncommon to see a woman out on the town resembling a baby giraffe trying to walk for the first time.

I reached the top. Thankfully, my date was nowhere in sight. He'd missed my less than elegant entrance. Older men lined the bar drinking whiskey on the rocks. It is a Monday night after all.

Ah-ha, two high chairs free in the far-right corner, brilliant. Perfect for stiletto wearers. After ten awkward steps to safety, I slid into one of the chairs and checked my watch—8 pm on the dot. Impressive. I'm not usually on time. I texted Mum:

Date tonight, this is his photo, and we're at The Lounge Bar at the casino. Love you mumfred. Xxx

Photo attached. Sent. Two ticks appeared next to the photo.

The Date

'Excuse me, are you...' I lift my gaze to see a medium-height chap with a bowl-style haircut staring at me. He's grasping a bottle of wine tightly with both hands. I must have had the 'do I know you' expression on my face because he follows up with, 'It's me from the dating site.' My eyes must have grown to the size of saucers because he shoves the bottle of wine he's holding into my hands and sits down opposite me.

Have you ever been in one of those moments when you're in a state of confusion? Where you're expecting one thing and you get another that's completely different? This is one of those moments. In a nutshell, this fella is not the guy from the dating site. In fact, the only thing he has in common with the photo is he's Indian and has eyes, a nose and a mouth. I've been catfished. Is my real date sick and his less attractive brother came in his place?

My thoughts are interrupted. 'So, how was your day?'

His accent is a mixture of Indian and Aussie.

How is my day? Sir, you are an entirely different person than the one in your profile and you want to open with pleasantries? That's like robbing someone's purse then asking them where they purchased it. I have to find out the truth; I have to check his profile.

'I need to grab something from my hotel room.' I fake smile and grab my handbag.

'Don't forget your wine.' He hands me the bottle.

'Oh, thanks.' I take the wine and make a mental note to leave it for the cleaners.

'Shall I come up to your room with you?'

I blink, long and hard, and widen my eyeballs fully in their sockets, so he can truly understand how absurd that request is.

I turn and giraffe walk—very slowly—back up to my hotel room and log onto the dating site. There is the face of the Adonis I was expecting, which is NOT the man sitting downstairs. I've been one hundred per cent catfished.

His profile photo was likely some Indian model the catfish thought no one would have heard of in Melbourne. But seriously, did he not think I would notice his face was a completely different face? Maybe he was hoping I suffer from face blindness.

I kick off the killer heels and fall back onto the bed; the bed bounces me a few times until it comes to stillness.

What the heck do I do now? The catfish imposter impersonating the hot guy is waiting for me downstairs. All of my instincts scream to text him and tell him what a douche bag he is for lying on his profile. How ridiculous he is to think buying me a bottle of wine would soften the blow of him being an entirely different and remarkably less attractive person, profile guy being a ten. Real person pushing a two.

This revelation alerts my brain to an article I once read on how humans select a suitable mate. Apparently, we are all seeking the most attractive match in order to create genetically blessed offspring, which was confirmed by the experiment. Every person picked a suitor who was rated within two points of their own level of attractiveness. An example would be a six could match with a four or an eight, but never a three or a nine. If I am to put my own attractiveness at an eight, the catfish is six points lower than me. What is he thinking? This goes against all of the laws of human attraction. Plus, I'll deduct another point for being a lying git. And even if I'm fair and take two points off myself for being bad at reading people and walking in heels, he's still five whole points less than me.

I take a long, deep inhale and notice another feeling kick in. Oh no! The centuries of programming of being a woman is back. Push those feelings aside, lady, and prioritise a lying stranger's feelings instead. The unconscious is a powerful weapon against change!

I shove my already aching feet back into my red heels and grab my bag. The heavy feeling of disappointment lies in the pit of my stomach, a feeling I'd gotten used to after so many disastrous dates.

Two hours later, once again, going against my intuition, I know the catfish's favourite topics: how rich he is, how much real estate he owns and the celebrities he hangs out with. Translation—he's broke, lives in a car, and is, at best, a celebrity stalker.

What I've learned from so many years in the dating game is the guy who preaches about all he has, usually has nothing, or is compensating for other lacking areas—if you catch my drift.

Based on the fact that the catfish has a different face to the man on his profile, I can confidently guess his boundaries around lying are non-existent, so, how can I believe a word that comes out of his mouth? After the second hour passes, I figure I have been polite enough to end the date.

'I have to get going. I've got a meeting in the morning.'

'What? So soon? I want to take you to this cool bar in the city. I travelled over an hour to meet you.'

Oh, here we go, the guilt trip.

'It's your first night in Melbourne. Don't you want to get a feel of whether you could live here?'

Hmmm. He makes a valid point. I would like to get to know Melbourne better. I check my watch. 'Okay, but I have to be back by midnight.' And no, I don't turn into a pumpkin.

The rest of the date isn't too bad, but not because of my date. It's because of the fabulous city that is Melbourne. We dance in cool dive bars with live bands. We walk—correction, he walks, I hobble—through Chinatown. We visit the Melbourne wheel, which has spectacular views of the metropolis, followed by a chocolate dessert at the Vegie Bar. I am in love with this city.

At midnight, we say our goodbyes. I do the hug and dash, minus the hug. He tries to maintain contact by inviting me to tennis the following day, but I don't trust him. I don't fancy him. Plus, he's not the man I agreed to have a date with. He's a stranger. So, I decline and that's the last I hear from him.

The truth is, even though I didn't fall in love with the catfish, I did fall in love with Melbourne and the city would become one of my greatest and long-lasting love affairs.

Lessons I learned from this date: Firstly, I am well aware that I still have work to do on my conditioning that prioritises a lying stranger's wants and feelings over my own. But I will add that the only reason I continued with the date was because 'I' wanted to experience Melbourne and see if it's a city 'I' wanted to live in, so I'm not going to be too hard on myself.

Secondly, and positively, this date was serendipitous because, whilst appearances may appear (literally) bad on the surface, this date brought me something much more valuable: a new place to call home—my beloved Melbourne.

17

MR BAT CAVE

Date Warning: Please dispose of all food and drink before commencing the reading of this date. This date is not for the squeamish or faint-hearted. Proceed at your own peril.

Age: 33
Location: Melbourne, Australia
Where we met: Online dating app
How he asked me out: Text message

After giving Mr Catfish the flick and vowing never to go on another online date again (again), I had the meeting with the prospective business partners in Melbourne and it went swimmingly! In my typical spontaneous style, one month later, I'd packed my belongings stored at Mum's house and driven the 3,403 kilometres across the Nullarbor Plain from Perth to Melbourne. Much to the horror of Mum.

Why was Mum horrified? Perhaps because there are hundreds of kilometres of road where there are no petrol stations, dwellings or signs of human life.

You'll be pleased to know I arrived in Melbourne safely, despite a terrifying encounter with a gigantic huntsman. Google it.

During my road trip, I stayed in what appeared to be pretty much a shack on the side of the road, surrounded by dirt and nothing else for hundreds of kilometres. There were five shacks with connecting walls and the toilet and shower was a few minutes' walk away. I'd headed to the toilet block to wash my face before bed and had arrived back at my room when the light of the moon caught a movement on the door handle. Holy crap!

It was dark, so I couldn't make out what it was, but there was no way I was touching that handle. I didn't have my phone and, therefore, no light, so I did the only thing I could do: wake up my neighbour. Lucky for me, he was a kind older gent who was not of the sleazy variety, unlike my previous encounters, and was more than willing to help a young lass in distress.

That is until he shone his torch on the handle and holy freaking moly, the huntsman was humongous. Think the size of a saucer with his legs wrapped tightly around the door handle.

From the terror on my face, my neighbour knew there were only two options. HE could relocate Mr Huntsman from his current residence to a new home, or, I'd be bunking with him and his wife for the night.

Turns out he didn't want me cosying up with him and Mrs

Neighbour, because he grabbed the longest stick he could find and with pure fear in his eyes, gently tapped Mr Huntsman off the handle, who started running for dear life across the dirt car park under the moonlight.

Every ten seconds, I'd yell, 'Further away,' as my neighbour guided the huntsman more than two hundred metres down the dirt road and into some shrubbery until I was convinced he wouldn't try and find his way back.

I kept one eye open all night anticipating an arachnid invasion.

Thousands of kilometres later, I reached Melbourne city and as soon as I drove over the Westgate Bridge, I knew I'd found home. After a few weeks of settling in and feeling like I needed to get some social interaction, I reluctantly jumped back on the dating apps and organised dates with some Melbournians. Hopefully, they were all as sweet as my spider removalist travel buddy and as willing to spend the night with me as Mr Huntsman.

After text conversations with multiple men that quickly headed south, I was desperate for a 'normal' date, as one is always hopeful. Date 17 had kind eyes: the ones that penetrate your soul. He had his own building business and seemed passionate about life, which was so attractive to me. The one thing I did find a tad odd was he wasn't smiling in any of his photos, but instead was posing with a kind of sultry look. I personally love a guy with a dazzling smile. But that aside, everything else in his profile seemed like a good match for me and after everything I'd seen, a few too many Blue Steel photos was nothing.

After texting back and forth and passing the test of not

saying anything sexual or inappropriate during the initial text messages phase, I agreed to a date—a sunset stroll along the water. Delightful.

The Date

I wander over the road onto the beachside. I see a tall, caramel-skinned man studying his watch, leaning against the railings of the pier. The sun is setting behind him, throwing off magnificent reds and oranges. It would make for a picture-perfect photo. I walk across the grass and onto the pavement in his direction. When he sees me, I pretend to take a photo with my fingers, impersonating a camera.

He responds with a tight-lipped grin and opens his arms, inviting me in for a warm bear hug. His embrace feels strong and masculine, just the way I like it, not like those weak kinds of hugs where someone stands a foot away and taps you on the back in the hope it will be over as soon as possible, although I am a fan of giving those to a special few. The hug feels wonderful, but there's a weird dog poo slash dead animal scent lingering. I initiate movement away from the area to alleviate my nose from the stench.

We commence our stroll along the waterfront, and it feels surprisingly natural when he takes my hand and interlocks our fingers. Walking side by side means we only have a side angle view of each other. At the time I didn't think anything of it—but remember this detail for later.

'Do you fancy a walk on that small pier?' He points a little way down the path and onto the beach, where a short pier darts into the water. I know his game. He's trying to get me to a spot where he can kiss me. At thirty-two years old, I'm well versed in the minds of men.

'Sure, looks pretty.'

We make our way down the path, where I see large waves breaking against the concrete pier. We step onto the beach. The sensation feels like I'm walking in quicksand. Ten strides later we reach the pier.

'Let's live a little and try and reach the end without getting wet.'

I'm loving this playful side of him. I enjoy being silly too, so, step by step we edge towards the end of the pier with the main goal of remaining dry.

'Let's go.'

My date grabs my hand and tugs me forward. We begin to run, but I hold back and point to a huge wave that's heading directly for us. We take a step back and wait again. There's another massive wave approaching in the distance, but there might be a chance to bolt to the end, touch the rail and sprint back.

'Let's go, now!'

My date pulls at my arm, and it's literally now or never. We run forward. The wave is fast approaching, and at a relentless speed. My fingertips touch the railing, and we turn. I scream, as I can literally feel the energy of the wave behind me, about to smash against the concrete.

'Run,' I yell, increasing my gait to a sprint. In the next moment, I'm in the air. My date scoops me into his arms like a princess, and bolts back along the pier, where we fall into a heap on the sand. I'm laughing so hard my cheeks are aching.

He pulls my face around to his and places his lips over

mine. A foul, metallic smell of dead animal slash dog poo is back and I pull away. We must be lying next to a rotting fish or something.

'I think we're next to something dead. Let's get out of here.'

We jump to our feet and stride off the sand until we are back on the hard concrete sidewalk. I eyeball my surroundings to check for carcasses. I don't want to step on anything.

He suggests we grab the rug from his car and lie under the stars; what a delightful proposition. I love it. Do men plan these moves beforehand? Hmm. I'd be interested to find out.

On reaching his ute, he pulls out a tartan picnic blanket, neatly folded, with a Velcro strap holding it in place.

Hand in hand we skip back to a sloped part of the park, where he arranges the blanket on the grass, takes off his jacket and rolls it into a kind of pillow for us to lay our heads. How sweet is that? He pulls me closer, and it feels natural to snuggle into him, laying my head on his bicep so I can gaze into his eyes. Ah, heaven. What more could a girl ask for than a lovely man with a backdrop of twinkling stars?

'So, are you enjoying the date so far?' He raises his hand to his mouth as he speaks. Strange. It's not the first time I've noticed him do that.

'Yeah. Love it. That was so fun at the pier, although that stench at the beach was something else. Did you notice it?'

He covers his mouth again. 'Nah, I didn't notice anything.'

Strange. It was such a potent smell, but, then again, I have a more sensitive nose than most, especially when I'm ovulating.

We continue with some idle chit-chat and for a second time, he leans forward for a kiss. I happily accept the invitation, but, once again, there's that strong metallic, dead animal, dog poo smell again. Yuck! I pull away.

'Can't you smell that?' I scan the nearby grass but can't see anything dead lying anywhere close by. Maybe it's travelling on the wind? Maybe I've stepped in dog poo? I have no idea.

'Maybe we should go. That smell is turning my stomach. On the next date, we can go somewhere there's less likely to be something dead hanging about.' I joke and sit up.

'Oh really, so you're keen for a second date, then?' He looks away, covering his mouth as he chuckles.

'Yeah, why not.'

'Okay, let's do a café next time. Somewhere inside.' He emphasises the word inside.

He refolds the blanket, interlaces our fingers, and we stroll back to the car. At the ute, I give him a strong hug goodbye.

I enjoy being around him, but crap, that grotesque stench is following me. I've got to get out of here. I walk back to my vehicle, give him a wave and close the doors. No more stench. Thank goodness.

Our second date occurs a few days later when we meet at a local café for a morning cuppa. The table is larger than a normal café table, so there's a bit of distance between us as we sit opposite each other. You'll understand why that's important shortly.

The one thing I find strange about my date is he doesn't smile or laugh, and if he dares to chuckle, he looks away with a raised hand covering his mouth.

'You don't smile much, do you?' I'm interested to know why.

'I'm smiling on the inside.' He covers his mouth.

Alright, this behaviour might be cute on a young, female, anime character, but I'm determined to get to the bottom of this. I will make him laugh.

I respond with a hilarious one-liner and this time he forgets to raise his hand to his mouth. Got him! His lips start to separate, and I lock my eyes on his opening cavity. As I observe the sight in front of me, the feeling of revulsion grips my stomach. It feels like I've left my body, and the gasp that leaves my mouth confirms my soul has, indeed, exited. The only way I can describe how I'm feeling right now, is, I'm fighting the urge to vomit. I feel it rise in my stomach, on the realisation that the metallic, dead animal slash dog poo smell was in fact . . .

HIS. MOUTH!

Okay, brace yourself. All of his teeth are either black stumps or missing. And when I say black, I don't mean a little yellow, my American friends. I mean black as the night. No wonder I couldn't see them after dark. If they were street signs, they'd need reflective tape. What the heck? His mouth resembles a cave with the stench of a cesspit. I'm expecting a whole load of bats to come flying out to complete the picture.

He sees my expression and immediately locks down the bat cave.

'I used to smoke.'

I feel my mouth hanging open—in shock. A lot of people used to smoke and I'm pretty sure I'd have noticed if any of their mouths looked like that. Why doesn't he go to the dentist? He's supposedly a successful businessman. How could he feel confident doing business with his mouth being about as clean as an overflowing porta-potty?

'Don't you brush your teeth?' I need answers. It couldn't only be from smoking.

'If you want the honest truth, I haven't taken care of my teeth.'

Oh, have you not?

He shrugs like it's no big deal. How can he not care?

'What about visiting a dentist?'

'Nah, I've got no time and I don't like dentists.'

No time? The amount of decay and toxins in his mouth would be affecting the health of his entire body. He won't have any time when he dies of sepsis. And who 'likes' going to the dentist?

'My last missus didn't have a problem with it.'

Did she wear a hazmat suit? I have no words. I think back to the kiss and the stench. The stench that was his mouth pressed against my mouth. The metallic, dead animal, slash dog poo stink was him, and I kissed him. Twice. With that mouth. Ewwwww!

I dry retch thinking about it and know I'm going to be sick. This time, I'm the one covering my mouth as I rush to the toilet and throw up—twice. Once for each kiss. I can't stop thinking about the dead animal kisses. Yuck! Stop thinking about it. Stop thinking about it. Think of roses. Roses smell wonderful. Roses. Roses. Roses.

After approximately ten minutes of forcing my mind to think of roses, I swill out my mouth with water, pat my face dry with rough, one-ply toilet paper and walk back to the table.

'I don't feel well. I'm so sorry, I need to go.'

I grab my bag, rush back to my car and drive home at the

rate of risking a speeding fine. I seriously feel like I need to disinfect my mouth and eyes. I'll never be able to remove that image from my brain. I scrub my teeth four times, have two showers and go and lie down. I mean seriously, talk about a turn-off. I can't believe his ex-partner was okay snogging that bat cave cesspit—unless she had one too.

My phone lights up, alerting me to a message. It's from him:
Are you okay? You looked like you'd seen a ghost.

I had. The ghost of all your dead teeth.

I respond back with the truth:

I'm sorry, I don't think we are compatible. Oral hygiene is extremely important to me.

He responds by saying he'll book an appointment with a dentist, a last-ditch attempt at rescuing the inevitable crash and burn, I assume. I'll be honest, I doubt that the highest qualified dentist on the planet could fix that decayed swamp of a mouth. He'd require any remaining teeth to get knocked out and replaced with dentures; that's my unprofessional opinion.

I don't hear from him again. I guess another concern is what else doesn't he keep clean? Yeah, you know what I'm talking about.

What I learned from this date: Firstly, from this day forward, first dates will be in daylight and face to face. Note to self—always check teeth prior to snogging session. How I long for the LA dates, with men with perfect white teeth with a blueish tinge. Online dating tip—anyone who has photos where they are not showing their teeth usually has a reason, and from my experience, are hiding a decaying death trap.

Secondly, I value personal hygiene and taking care of one's appearance. Toothless hillbillies, move along.

18

MR CAMEL LOVER

Age: 33
Location: Melbourne, Australia
Where we met: Online dating app
How he asked me out: Via phone call

After being traumatised by the bat cave, I took a break for several months, in the hope the nightmares would eventually fade. Unfortunately, the gym training penis strongman and the bat cave will forever be etched on my memory, for the rest of my life on this planet. Thanks a million, online dating!

So, during my breather from being mentally and emotionally scarred by men, I took some time to discover my new city —Melbourne, which is located in the southeast of Australia.

I could write a list a mile long as to why I loved Melbourne, from the snowfields in winter to the beautiful beaches along the Great Ocean Road, the cafés, the museums, the events and that vibrant and creative energy that I love in spades.

But I discovered my greatest love of Melbourne when I took a walk around Albert Park Lake. It was springtime and the weather forecast was twenty-two degrees and sunny. Perfect. I headed out in my T-shirt and trainers and five minutes later I'd arrived at the lake. I marvelled at the large family of cygnets paddling like crazy after their mum and dad, one tiny one perched amongst the feathers on its dad's back hitching a ride. How cute is that?

I greeted passers-by with warm hellos and arrived at the rowing club a few minutes later.

The wind picked up and with all the skill of an apprentice hairdresser, it styled my hair into a bird's nest. I removed several twigs and used the elastic hairband around my wrist to tie my locks into a high ponytail, or, at the very least, to keep the bird's nest out of my eyes.

One. Minute. Later.

The wind had turned into a freaking gale and in order to make any headway, I was forced to lean and walk at a forty-five-degree angle.

Dark clouds formed overhead. It was like someone had suddenly turned out the lights. What the heck? Didn't the weatherman say twenty-two degrees and sunny? What was this place? Was this the result of some twisted kind of sorcery? Had I angered a cunning witch who swore years ago to get back at me when I least expected it? Was she in cahoots with the weather channel?

No sooner had those thoughts crossed my mind than massive globules of liquid started exploding on my head. I was about halfway around the lake by this point, and within minutes I was drenched.

One. Minute. Later.

Did you guess? Yep. The globules became hale. How is this even possible? I'd have to consult with the witch's meteorologist ally.

If you'd like an immersive experience, getting pelted by hale feels like one hundred people shooting paintballs at you, nonstop, for five minutes straight, without the comradery or the promise of drinks and good times to follow. That is until it suddenly stopped, and guess what? Miss Sunshine returned with the heat of a supernova. By now my appearance resembled a drowned rat, but within minutes my arms and face looked like a lobster. I'd never experienced anything like it in my entire life.

By the time I returned to the main road I needed to cross to reach my apartment, it started thrashing down with rain again. Mother Nature was really going through something. By the time I reached the ground floor entry doors to my apartment, I could have easily passed for a rat who had drowned after being burnt to a crisp.

I know, I know. You're wondering why on earth this is my favourite thing? Because variety is the spice of life. One thing I found so monotonous about living in Perth and California was the constant sunny days. I know I'm an outlier, and most people think I'm crazy. And even though sometimes I'm dressed like an Eskimo in summer, I wouldn't change my four seasons in one day. That is my crazy, beautiful Melbourne.

So, after learning to accommodate my new love by packing four seasons of clothing each time I'd leave the house, and with a pep in my step, I swore off swearing off dating apps and decided to go on an online dating rampage with the goal of dating as many guys who fit my main criteria as possible. After all, love is a numbers game, right? The law of averages dictates that one of these guys must be perfect.

You will also be pleased to know I did learn one thing from Mr Bat Cave, and that was to only agree to dates where prospects show their teeth in photos. Date 18 had photos of himself smiling. He appeared to have a good, clean set of teeth, so in my haste to start my late in life Rumspringa dating rampage, I agreed to a date at The Winter Wonderland at Luna Park in St Kilda.

To set the scene for this date, you know I love a good adrenaline rush. Those good ol' feelings of butterflies in my tummy. Love it. FYI, I went paragliding a few weeks back and my oh my, what a wonderful experience. I reckon it's the closest feeling a human can get to flying, apart from aerial yoga, but we don't need to revisit that now, do we?

The reason I bring up my love of adrenaline is because I was excited about this date. We'd be attending the Winter Wonderland held near St Kilda beach, with ice rinks, pretend snow and a Santa's grotto. Santa's grotto was giving me some LA castle orgy flashbacks, but thankfully I wasn't overly interested in any of those things. Oh no! I was interested in one thing and one thing alone: the massive ride known as the Super Spinner.

Let me paint the picture: there are four seats, two side by side, facing in one direction and two facing in the opposite direction. After clicking in the seat belt, a heavy bar that sits over both shoulders, descends over your head and clips into your seat belt buckle. You can recall the Mr Incredible Hulk date, right? Then there's the anticipation. They are sneaky in the way they hold the ride for several minutes to increase your level of fear. We've all been there. So, I was excited to be experiencing this ride.

The Date

It's a chilly evening, so I decide to wear my long winter red riding hood coat that's pink, not red. It's so cosy and elegant. I peer in the bathroom mirror; my pink blush and lips match my coat. I look so adorable there's no way this guy isn't going to appreciate the effort I've put into my appearance. I give the reflection a wink. 'Love you, gorgeous girl,' I say out loud and blow a kiss in the mirror. I read that technique in Louise Hay's book, *Mirror Work*. Love Louise Hay. Her voice sounds like a loving grandmother and is so soothing and nurturing to my heart. The reason I started this practice was not because I'd summoned Bloody Mary in a bathroom mirror and become close friends with her, but because I noticed I'd say lots of wonderful compliments to my friends and family but was critical towards myself. I deserve those loving words too, so I decided, why not give them to myself? So, one day, I started. At first, it felt a bit strange, but now, it's like second nature.

I grab my handbag and shuffle the contents. Where are those pesky keys? I hear the jingle at the bottom, but still no dice. You know the movie *Mary Poppins*, where she keeps pulling stuff out of her bag until she pulls out a coat stand? That's like my bag, only fuller. That's why I call her my Mary

Poppins bag. Gosh, I love that movie. I should watch it again. I feel cool metal on my fingertips. My keys. Hooray. Elevator. Enter car. Off I go.

A cool whoosh of sea air fills my nose. I brush away strands of hair from my eyes and tuck them behind my ear. So much for my attempt at a professional hairdo. Having a convertible means you have to become accustomed to two styles, hat hair from wearing a baseball cap, or a bird's nest, but heck, it's so worth it feeling the wind on my face.

The flashing lights of Luna Park and the screams from the Super Spinner mean I'm close.

I glide my hands around the steering wheel and reverse park into a tight spot, next to a scratched-up silver moped. I sprinkle some abundance dust over the scooter, a technique I read in Rhonda Byrne's book, *The Greatest Secret*. I hop out and admire my gorgeous Beamer, such a lovely way to move about the city.

I begin my commute past Luna Park to the Winter Wonderland.

Dashing through the snow on a one-horse open sleigh, sings through the air. A smile creeps across my lips. This is going to be fun.

A medium height, handsome, dark-skinned guy stands at the entrance. That must be him. Yay, he's attractive. I wave. He grins and waves back. He seems happy and has all of his white teeth. But I won't get too excited in case they're dentures. I open my arms and embrace him.

'Hey, so nice to meet you. I'm excited for the Winter Wonderland.' I rub my gloved hands together with enthusiasm.

He looks pleased with my delight. 'Shall we go in?' He

holds out his arm, inviting me to link it, so I take his lead and slide my arm through.

'Two tickets, please.' He takes a fifty out of his wallet and pushes the bill through a small window and into the hands of the attendant.

She slides his change out. 'Enjoy.' She has an adorable, warm way about her.

I'm impressed. One, he was kind to the attendant. Two, he took the lead. Three, he paid for the tickets. I do love a guy to pay on the first date, as it shows me he wants to protect and provide. Not that I need someone to provide for me, I do well for myself. But I love those masculine traits in a man, as it means if we ever have a family, I know those are his values and it makes me feel safe. So, tick, tick, tick.

As we enter, we are immersed in the festivities of Christmas, even though it's only July. Christmas holds such fond childhood memories for me. A memory of making the tallest snowman on the block with my mum and sisters enters my mind. It's so interesting how those magical moments get tethered in the brain and can be brought back to the present at any moment.

'Let's go in the snow.' I feel his gait quicken and a few steps later, tiny silvery-white sparkles float past my eyes. I blink my eyelids closed, gaze up towards the sky and open my arms out wide. The cold flakes lightly touch my skin and melt into water droplets. Oh, these beautiful moments. I open my eyes and see my date observing my joy. After so many dates, I'm convinced guys love to see a woman appreciating and enjoying the moment. He grabs my hand, we skip out of the snow, and I find myself at the hot chocolate stand. Despite my traumatic experience with hot chocolate in the past, I'm seduced by the sheer spirit of Christmas that's in the air and I'm all in.

'Two mugs of hot chocolate please, with almond milk.'

Wow, this guy is really impressing me.

'I'll get these,' I chime in, touching his arm lightly.

'Your money is no good here, miss.' He takes out his card and taps the pay machine.

'Well, aren't you the gentleman? Thank you so much.'

I feel a warmth growing in my tummy, a lovely feeling I don't often get on a first date.

This date is going well. He grabs my hand and it's warm and strong. He's got those generous masculine hands, the ones that are large with meaty fingers. I once read an article about how a person's hand reflects their values. This article said a meaty palm and fingers means the man is generous and loving, whereas slight, spindly fingers means the man is a scrooge. Not sure if it's true. Spindly fingers could also mean he's built like Jack Skellington. But I'm personally a fan of the meaty variety. We sip our hot chocolate, and it tastes divine. We finish up our drinks.

'Let's go on the Super Spinner.' I point at the ride with green flashing lights at the other side of the Wonderland.

'Are you sure? It's a spinny one and we've just had a big drink.' He sounds like a concerned father as he raises the empty mug, grabs mine and places both on a side table.

'Oh, it will be fine. It'll be fun!' I laugh and take a few steps towards the ride, and then feel a strong tug, and I was back in his arms.

'Okay. You could sell ice to Eskimos with that smile.'

'I have been told that once or twice.' I give him a wink.

He hugs me in close and slides his hand down my arm and grabs my hand as we stroll round to the ride, grab our tickets and wait in line until we're motioned up by the attendant.

Click. The buckle slots in. The attendant pulls the bar over my head and pushes it in tight. I glance over at my date, feeling a whirling in my tummy. He half-smiles and then we're off, straight up at breakneck speed. Oh, the exhilaration. Heaven. My body floods with wonderful sensations as we are tossed and rolled, followed by free falls on repeat.

I'm trying to focus on the ride, but I'm distracted by the high pitch yelling of explicit swear words on a never-ending loop. Is it my date? Please, not another Mr Tunnel of Terror moment? Why do guys go on rides if they are so afraid? I peer over to see if the offending sounds are coming from my date, but his face is expressionless, and his eyes are closed. Is he trying to zone out? Is he testing his meditation skills?

The terrifying screaming jolts me out of my thoughts, and the foulest language imaginable is clearly being expelled from one of the men sitting behind me. I make a mental note to clock what he looks like, so I never agree to a date with him. I also pray that Mr Incredible Hulk didn't emigrate to Australia to convince me to have a second date and is sitting behind me on this ride.

I must admit I am laughing so hard because the guy behind is clearly fearing for his life, but I am secretly happy my date has restraint and is more refined in his expression. Three long X-rated profanity-laden minutes later, we rock to stillness, and the platform raises to meet our feet.

The attendant hurries to unbuckle us as a long line has

formed. I hop out and collect my bag from the locker and turn to find my date is still in his seat with his eyes closed and head resting to the side.

'Hey, it's over. You can open your eyes now.'

He doesn't move. It's like he's frozen to his seat. Crap! Please don't let him be dead. It's concerning how many times I've had that thought on dates.

'Mate, we need to get the next riders up.' The attendant grabs him and slings my date's arm over his shoulder and drags him down the steps like he's trying to get a wounded soldier to safety. My date is still unresponsive. Is he concussed? The attendant kicks open the gate and lays him down onto a grassy area. This is clearly not the attendant's first rodeo transporting a patron off the ride.

'Are you alive?'

His skin is translucent, and he looks ghostly. Please be alive.

My date's eyes open into slits.

Thank goodness he's not dead.

He seems to be trying to speak, 'I . . . I . . . I.'

He sounds like a person who has knocked back one too many rum and colas. All the spinning must have jumbled his brain.

'I love camels,' he blurts out, then lays his head in his hands.

'Camels? Random, but yeah, they are cool animals.' I rub his back.

'Camels at the beach.'

I shake my head, trying to figure out why he is deliriously confessing his love for camels, which are now apparently at the beach.

'Yeah, camels live in the desert.'

Camels make me think I should get him some water.

'Camels at the beach.' His tone has changed to assertive.

Am I liable if the ride scrambled his brain into early-onset dementia?

'I love seeing camels at the beach,' he's slurring.

'We should get you home.'

I pull him to his feet. Blimey, this guy is not light. I feel the weight of him hanging off my shoulders. I internally curse my attraction to heavy set men.

'Where did you park?' Fingers crossed he's in a good enough mental state to remember.

He points. The supposed direction appears to be back towards the Winter Wonderland, where there is not a single car to be found. Okay, how the heck am I going to get this guy home? If I could get him to my car, I could drive him back, but only if he can remember his address. It's the only plan I have, so we shuffle, very slowly, in the direction of my vehicle.

What feels like an eternity later, we arrive at my car and I click the unlock button on the remote, causing the lights on the door handles to light up. One step closer to getting him home.

'I love camel.' This time he yells it.

An elderly couple walking by speak in hushed tones then quicken their gait.

'Let's get you inside.'

I cannot begin to explain how difficult it is to navigate a medium-sized man's body into a convertible when they are incapacitated. He might as well be made of lead. His brain is. I have to literally pick up his leg and place it into the footwell, push his shoulders down into the seat, pick up his other foot and place it next to the other one in the well. I close the door quietly, trying not to startle him.

'Camel.' The volume is now at a scream.

What's with this guy and camels?

'What's your address?' He stares at his feet.

'Toes,' he slurs.

I sigh and pat him down to see if I can find his wallet. Aha! I retrieve a wallet out of his jacket pocket and rummage through the cards to find his driver's licence—31 Treehouse Lane. Cute. I put the transmission into drive and pull out of the parking space.

'Toes,' he shouts.

I can't wait to get this guy out of my car. That ride must have fried his brain.

Luckily, he's local and after a few roundabouts and turns we pull up to 31 Treehouse Lane. Finally. Now, somehow I'm going to have to haul him out of the car and drag him into his place.

I have no idea how I managed to get him out. Let's just say, tomorrow's bruises will explain a lot, but fifteen minutes later I've found his keys, put them in the lock and somehow got him onto his couch.

'Okay, I'm going to head off now. Hopefully, your housemate is back soon.'

I scribble a note on the back of an envelope that's sitting on the kitchen bench and leave it next to my date so that his housemate can check on him when he returns home. Here's hoping he's a doctor.

'Hey, I'm leaving now, but I hope you feel better soon.'

My date bolts upright and like he's the announcer on *The*

Price Is Right yells out, 'I love looking at camel toes at the beach,' then falls back onto his side.

I stand there for a moment, trying to process if what I'd heard was what he'd shouted. Yep, I'm pretty certain I'd heard that correctly, and I only had one response: Ewww!

Well, at least I found out sooner rather than later that he had a creepy obsession with camels, and not the ones in the desert, I might add. I'd have preferred an unnatural obsession with those desert-dwelling creatures.

We don't communicate again. I doubt he remembers we even had a date. Probably for the best.

What I learned from this date: Firstly, I am not interested in guys that have obsessions or fetishes with parts of the body. I love a healthy, balanced mind.

Secondly, more dates don't mean better dates; it simply means more disastrous dates in shorter succession. Sigh. But I will say, it took several more rampage dates before I figured this out.

19

MR SAY IT DON'T SPRAY IT

Before I get into this date, there's a warning coming. This date may make some readers feel queasy, squeamish, repulsion, horror and disgust. So please, I encourage you to finish anything you're eating or drinking before you proceed. I apologise in advance.

Age: 33
Location: Melbourne, Australia
Where we met: Online dating app
How he asked me out: Text message

Date 19 happened in short succession of the previous date after a weekend ski trip to the mountains. Did you know that Australia has snow? Be honest. You thought it was red, sandy desert with the occasional tumbleweed rolling by and drop bears falling from trees, right?

Skiing in Australia is too strong a word. The experience was more like trying not to break my neck on the sheets of ice that Australians call snow.

I'd asked friends to accompany me, but saying my friends hated the cold was an understatement, so I put on my lone ranger hat and off I went.

On the first day, there was a rare occurrence of actual snow and as I gazed into those cloud-filled skies and felt the cool snowflakes melt on my cheeks, it was pure bliss. You know those times when everything feels perfect in the world? That was one of those moments.

Unfortunately, that perfect moment was short-lived because it continued to snow overnight. The following morning the sun came out to say hello, which caused the snow to melt. The result: an icy death trap for beginner skiers.

One plus was I did manage not to fall off the ski lift on the way to the peak. But on gazing down the mountain en route to the top, the scene resembled a cut from a war movie, with the hillside littered with fallen comrades who'd failed in their attempt at conquering their niveous enemy.

With a strong desire to keep my skull intact, there was only one way out of this dilemma.

Execute mission—get down this freaking mountain in one piece.

After being thrust off the ski lift at the peak and remaining upright, all the while avoiding the pile of children who'd stacked it at the bottom of the lift, I declared it a miracle and deployed the first step of the mission: slowly manoeuvre towards the edge of the slope. Following shortly after was step two: move to bum and scoot down the mountain inch by inch.

After nearly two hours, and approximately thirty-six near-fatal collisions at the hands of five-year-old skiers, I'd completed my final bum scoot. I unlocked my skis, cursed the five-year-olds one final time and jogged back to the hire shop just in time to make it to the bus that was headed back into town.

I boarded the bus and waved goodbye to the icy death trap and all its victims as a ping sounded in my handbag.

It was a guy from an online dating site.

'Hey, are you up for a date, tomorrow?'

I clicked on his profile. This guy had a good number of physical characteristics that I appreciate. You know, the usual, tall with a strong jawline. A day prior, I was listening to a podcast that was talking about how conditioned we are to seek certain characteristics in the opposite sex. Apparently, height is important to both sexes; women subconsciously choose taller men for the protection and dominance. And men—this one feels more disturbing—men want women who are shorter than them, as apparently, a shorter person is perceived as more subservient. Seriously? I mean, I get the psychology, but wow.

Is this the reason why we see 'short man syndrome', and why taller ladies can sometimes feel less desirable and less feminine? It seems the online dating culture is perpetuating this conditioning. My opinion is we need to be evolving towards partnership and teamwork. Both men and women bring their own strengths and complement the other's weaknesses.

Hopefully, this is the way forward, however, I am also aware that past programming is harder to shake than the image of the bat cave.

Let me continue. He had a swimmer's body, and kind eyes I liked, as well as a shock of red hair, which suited him and made him stand out against the usual blondes and brunettes. I also appreciated the fact that he had a similar lifestyle to me—check! He ran his own fitness business—that explains his physique. So, we shared some common ground and similar values. Enough to agree to a first date.

We decided to meet at the local dog park to walk his bulldog—Spencer. Brilliant idea. Guaranteed a fun date for me, being outside in nature and surrounded by doggies meant no awkward moments if the conversation wasn't flowing. What could possibly go wrong?

The Date

I park the car, which by the way I'd since named Audrey, after the classy Audrey Hepburn, and take the short stroll towards the only redhead in the park. Beside him is a large English bulldog.

'Spencer.'

I see the huge, round bulldog trying to yank a large stick out of a miniature poodle's mouth. That battle was never going to be a fair one. Spencer drops the stick and turns to face me, slobber hanging from both sides of his lips, in common bulldog fashion. His owner also turns and looks in my direction. Hmm. Handsome face, kind eyes and a very cute smile.

I crouch down, 'Spencer, come.' I pat my leg to encourage him to run to me.

Spencer's stubby legs bound in my direction, the slobber bouncing in unison with each step. He reaches me and I grab him and rub my hands over his folds of fat. He parks his bum on my leg, his brown eyes staring up at me. Adorable, even as a slobber monster.

A few moments later the tall, handsome red-headed Aussie struts over. He has a strong, powerful gait, which I find appealing.

'Hello.' He opens his arms, inviting a hug.

I stand and put my hands around his middle back as his arms fall over my shoulders. This feels organic. I step out of the hug and shift my gaze onto his face.

You know how they say dog owners usually resemble their dogs? Well, as I'm standing staring at him, at this moment, all I can think is how true that saying is, whilst at the same time trying not to vomit.

I hope you heeded my food warning because large silvery strands of saliva reach from the bottom gum to the top, and from the back of the mouth to the front teeth.

I feel my lips starting to recoil, and my eyes widen with revulsion, instinctively wanting to turn and leg it the heck out of there. I avert my eyes in an attempt to disguise my feelings, but all I can think in my mind is, oh no. I cannot do this; especially given the fact I'm still scarred by the Bat Cave.

Some people have certain things that immediately turn them off, like my mum can't drink out of the same cup as someone else, not even from her children's. My sister heaves at the sight of dog urine.

I don't know, I can't imagine being okay with that amount of stringy saliva in my partner's mouth. Have a tiny, mouth-sized gang of teens attacked his gums with silly string? I'm brought back from my mental anguish by a hit of wetness on my cheek. Please, for the love of God, let that be rain.

I peek up at the sky and there's not a cloud in sight. I wipe my cheek and see small bubbles on the back of my hand. Yep. It's his saliva. Gross!

'Let's head to the coffee shop.'

Slobber drips down his chin as he clips Spencer's leash onto his collar and motions forward. A streak of panic strikes my stomach. How the heck am I going to be able to go through with this? Maybe if I sit further away, I won't notice and it'll be okay. Please be okay. I really want to escape right now. No. I need to give him at least an hour of my time since he's made the effort to meet me. Why am I so polite? Please let the time go as quickly as saliva seems to form in his mouth.

I position Spencer between us as we walk. My desire for a speedy experience is a seriously hindered because I soon discover that Spencer is literally the slowest walker ever. Finally, after what feels like an eternity, I see the tables and chairs parked outside the café with umbrellas to shield patrons from the sun. Do they have any small umbrellas to shield people from errant spit? I feel my eyes darting from table to table. Which one will allow me to sit furthest away? I feel heat flush my face as my 'croc' brain frantically tries to figure out the best option for surviving the saliva shower. Over there, a large round table on the far right. I increase my step and point towards it so my date has no choice but to follow. I see a group of five people in my peripheral vision on my left, heading for the same table. They're not getting to that table before me! No way in hell.

I increase my pace to a speed walk, and I catch the eye of an older lady who's part of a group approaching in the opposite direction. She must sense we are heading for the same table and increases her pace.

Lady, I wouldn't care if you had two fake legs and carried a giant oxygen tank. You don't know how much I need this table! I begin to run. She's almost there. I need this dang table; I hear myself say through tight lips.

I hurl my Mary Poppins bag from two metres away onto the table, which makes contact with a loud crash. Dang. I hope my phone is still intact. Other patrons go silent and turn to look. Even slobbering Spencer looks startled, and my slobbering date has a what the heck expression on his face. Oops.

A waitress hurries out of the door. 'Madam, this table is reserved for this group.' She extends her hand out to the old lady and her family who are now standing next to me.

How embarrassing.

'Sorry.'

I avoid eye contact with the older lady, and I secretly wish the earth would swallow me whole as I drag Mary Poppins off the table.

The waitress offers a hand forward, pointing to a small bar table with two stools. Great! Could that table be any freaking smaller?

I hang my bag on the fence and drape my coat next to it whilst the waitress places two menus in front of us. I stare at my date's mouth. White pockets of saliva have formed on both sides. Why can't he wipe it? Doesn't he see all these perfectly good napkins right in front of his face? I cannot eat, I feel so sick.

'I'll get a turmeric latte. No food for me. I'm not hungry.' I lie and push the menu away as a definitive sign my decision is final.

'What are the specials?' A huge spitball hits the waitress' cheek. I know one hundred per cent she knows it's there, yet in true professional form, she pretends it never happened and continues to reel off the specials.

I notice every time he says a word beginning with 'sp' it's accompanied by a spit missile, and I beg the universe he doesn't order anything beginning with 'sp'. Unfortunately, it's not my lucky day.

'I'll have the split pea soup for starter, the spaghetti, with spinach and sprouts on the side.'

I'm only just starting to recover from this onslaught of moisture when the waitress asks if he wants water.

'Yes, sparkling.'

Of course.

On every 'sp' spit flies in every direction and I see the waitress step back in an attempt to dodge them. She's unsuccessful, and several spit bombs explode on her forehead, accompanying the first spit missile on her cheek. She grabs the menus and rushes away. I notice her scrubbing her face with her apron as she re-enters the café.

'You've got a good sprinting technique.' He jokes.

I assume he's referring to my dash to the round table. As his lips purse to make the 'sp' in sprint, a huge globule of spit lands on the saltshaker. As he laughs, he throws his head back, and I have a straight-on view of the large strands of saliva encasing his entire mouth and coagulating around the rim of his lips.

I close my eyes to block out the image and bend down to pat Spencer, whose drool is hanging from both sides of his mouth and making its way towards the ground. Is their house caked in saliva? I won't be going for a visit any time in this millennium.

'So, how long have you had Spencer?' Immediately I regret asking, as of course, this gives him licence to use the 'sp' a hundred times in one sentence.

'Oh, my beloved, Spencer.' A spitball leaves his mouth and hits Spencer square on the nose. Spencer's massive tongue pops out and licks the liquid away. Can I feel any sicker, right now?

'I was going to get a springer spaniel, but when I felt Spencer's spirit, I knew he was meant for me. He's so special.'

I counted five words with 'sp' in them and, of course, he was going to get a springer spaniel and not any other breed beginning with a different letter. Spencer is licking the remaining spit off his face. Who's to say where my date's saliva ends and special Spencer's begins.

I glance at my watch, trying to catch the time discreetly, to see how much longer I am obligated to stay. A second later, a different waitress slides my turmeric latte onto the table in front of me.

'I apologise, your waitress is not feeling well, so I'll be taking care of you.' I can't say I'm surprised. The original waitress is probably traumatised by the spit shower and is likely throwing up in the back.

In all fairness, my drink looks delightful. It has a yellow sunshine glow to it, but I don't know how I'm going to consume it without hurling all over this table. Unfortunately, this image makes me recall the moment I threw up over the beautiful twenty-person banquet during the coral reef trip the first time I visited Australia. Remember that? It's interesting how these things come full circle.

Maybe I could imagine delicious things . . . like chocolate and cake. Yes. That's an awesome idea. Chocolate. Cake. Chocolate. Cake. That kind of worked at the Bat Cave date.

'What a beautiful colour, I've never tried a turmeric latte before.'

You know where this is heading.

Before I can create a barrier between him and my drink, my date swoops my cup into the air and places the rim onto his spit-infested lips. I hear a quiet 'no' leave my mouth, but it's too late. He takes a sip. I'm living in my worst nightmare.

'It has a very specific, spicy taste.'

He clinks my cup back into the centre of the saucer as I feel a globule of spit colliding with my forehead. I stare at my cup. Bubbles of spit line the rim. It becomes clear that the closest I'll come to experiencing this latte is the turmeric-infused blobs of saliva that have just landed on my face.

'You're a bit of a spunky one, aren't you?'

More spit flies through the air. This time there are four or five spit missiles, and they are heading straight for my face. I raise my arm in an attempt to block them. Four hit my sleeve, but the fifth flies straight into my eyeball. My body has a normal reaction to something flying into my eye, but my date is oblivious to the war of spit I'm battling.

I instinctively shuffle my stool further away, in an attempt to create more distance. Bad idea because he does this . . .

'You're so far away, spunky, why do you need so much space?'

I count six large spit bubbles that land on the table. He grabs my stool and drags it towards him, so I am literally within a foot of his face. This cannot be happening. I lean back as far as possible until an ache in my lower back intensifies into a deep throb. My watch shows forty-three minutes. I'm going to have to cut this short because every cell in my entire body is screaming to get the heck out of there, and pronto, as this guy seems to use every word in the dictionary that starts with 'sp'.

'I'd better head off.' I stare at my watch, trying to give him a solid hint that I need to be somewhere else.

'You haven't touched your latte.'

My face has, though. I don't respond, and feel sincere gratitude there were no 'sp' words in that sentence.

'Shall we split the bill?'

Of course, he's the only date I've ever been on who wants to split the bill. Any excuse for another word starting with 'sp'.

We pay, and I immediately feel a sense of relief as we leave the confines of the seating area.

I have an idea. I grab Spencer's leash and start to jog towards my car. 'Spencer, let's run.'

Within a few minutes, we're close to my car. Perfect strategy. I intentionally stop a good five paces from Audrey so I can deploy the hug and dash. I don't even know if I can do the hug and dash with this guy as I'm feeling so queasy. I need hypnosis to erase the last hour of my life. I feel him coming closer and the repulsion in my stomach intensifies. I realise I can't get that close to him.

'Thanks for the date.'

I take steps backwards towards my car. My date continues to move in my direction.

'Bye, Spencer.'

I scramble for my keys. Where are you? Not now keys, please, let me find you!

I locate them in the side pocket and slam the button that opens the car. I hear the sounds of the locks, jump in, and press the ignition button. Audrey purrs loudly. I'm almost free from the spit war.

'Hey, spunky.' Spitballs make contact and descend down the passenger side window. He's bending down. I see more spit bubbles ready and waiting to fire.

'Didn't you feel a spark?' More missiles hit.

My car needed a wash, anyway.

I force the transmission into drive and press my foot firmly onto the accelerator. The vehicle roars forward. I feel the tension in my lower back instantly ease, my tight shoulders relax into my seat and my body breathes a huge sigh of relief.

After a double car wash to remove the literal remnants of my date, I'm back in the safety of my spit-free home. I check my online profile and see he's back on the app. Thank goodness he got the hint.

What I learned from this date: Firstly, the reality is I'm human. I have things that turn me on and things that turn me off. Spit missiles turn me off.

Secondly, moving forward, I need to process the trauma

from previous dates, so I don't keep attracting the same crap, as I'm discovering that the law of attraction is real.

20

MR NINETY-YEAR-OLD BUM

This date has a warning on it. It may be triggering for those of you who have experienced unwanted sexual advances. Read on at your own discretion.

Age: 34
Location: Melbourne, Australia
Where we met: Online dating app
How he asked me out: Text message

First, let me tell you about a mind-blowing experience I had at the beach—no, my prince charming didn't wade out of the ocean with water dripping off chiselled abs like they do in movies. I was reading a book—no shock there—and I observed a strange sight further down the beach. There was a young guy, around twenty-years-old, moving between groups that had gathered to take in the sunset. What the heck was he up to?

As he came closer, I heard him asking to borrow their phone because he needed help. Why wasn't anybody helping him? And what did he need help for?

My nurturing instincts kicked in. I scooted on my bum down the sand dune, got to my feet and jogged in his direction.

'Hey. Are you okay?' His eyes welled up with tears.

'I need to borrow a phone to call the lifeguard. I've buried my keys and phone in a box when I went out for a swim and now I can't remember where they are. I've been out here for five hours, and no one will help me.'

What's wrong with these people? I immediately called the lifeguard, but the sun was setting, and it was after 5 pm, so I doubted anyone would be there.

The number rang out.

'They aren't answering.'

'My car keys, house keys and phone are in that box. My dog is in the house on his own.' It seemed he couldn't hold back the waterworks a moment longer. They exploded like rockets from his eyes.

'Hey. Don't worry. I'll help you.'

He gazed up at me with a glimmer of hope.

'I've spent the last five hours digging. When I was swimming, I may have drifted quite a distance, so they could literally be anywhere along the beach. But thanks for offering.'

'I WILL help you find them,' I spoke in a strong and confident tone.

I'm excellent at finding things, well, everything but a decent man.

'But I need you to do one thing: ask your gut where the keys are, and I want you to draw a circle in the sand roughly in that area.'

His expression was one of finding the only crazy woman on the beach, but he had two choices, embrace crazy or spend the night freezing, homeless and sandy.

He got to his feet, and we traipsed through the sand about five hundred metres back up the beach. He drew a circle with a circumference of about ten metres.

'Okay.' I drew a line through the circle to separate it into two halves. 'I'm going to do something a bit weird now.'

In my head I rehearsed a small prayer, asking the universe to show me exactly where the keys were located. Simultaneously to being sprayed with sand from the frantic endeavours of the young man, I closed my eyes and started to take a few steps until I felt an impulse to stop.

Stop. A voice in my head said—loud and clear.

I knelt down, pushed my hand into the sand and guess what? I hit something hard, grabbed a curved edge and pulled it out. It was his box of keys. It must have taken me all of thirty seconds.

'I found them.' I held the box above my head.

The young guy's eyes darted up and widened in shock when he saw what I was holding. He jumped to his feet, ran over and hugged the living daylights out of me whilst shouting thank you on repeat.

We walked back to the car park. 'Are you magic?' He squinted and moved closer like he was trying to see into my soul.

I laughed. 'I believe we're all magic. All I did was use a meditation technique to ask universal intelligence where the keys were and quietened my mind long enough to hear the response.'

'Meditation. I'm definitely going to try that. You've got good karma coming your way, that's for sure.' He got in his car and waved goodbye.

The question I asked myself... why must my good karma come in the form of the universe helping me find some stranger's keys and not a perfect man? Could it be so I had enough content for this book, so I could entertain you? I like that theory, and I'm sticking with it.

Speaking of book fodder, several months had passed since I'd survived the Spit Missile battle, and after a couple of lobotomies to process the two revolting previous dates, the nightmares started to decrease, and I re-entered the world of dating apps. I'd started chatting to a nice man whose profile photos showcased broad shoulders and a fantastic smile. As an added bonus, during our text chats, he'd made no obscene or sexual references. Yes, the bar was that low. Shouldn't the bar be getting higher as I get wiser? It feels like it's getting lower, as men seem to grow more and more feral. No one is getting swept off her feet any time soon. No Cinderella story here.

First impressions count, and unfortunately, the online dating world has made a whole industry out of swiping left or right based on whether the swiper likes the look of the *swipee*.

I made up swipee, so best not to use it in any important reports or papers. But appearance is all you can go off initially, especially since ninety-nine per cent of men's profiles have literally no written content of any substance and are often a collection of emojis. Am I looking for a date or chatting with a six-year-old who has discovered his mum's iPad? Step up your bio game, gentlemen.

Anyway, back to date 20. He'd checked the appearance box, or so I thought, and had not said anything obscene, plus, he'd done something else I find so attractive. He'd asked me out on a date and, wait for it, planned the date. It's so sad I am impressed by this. I don't get why Australian men: (a) take five thousand texts to ask you on a date, and (b) don't organise a date, time and location. Do you know what a massive turn-off that is? Is it too much to ask to be asked out and then taken out?

Anyway, it seems like I had matched with one of the few men who takes initiative. Woohoo! It's nothing fancy, a coffee date at a nice lake location. Delightful.

The Date

It's chilly on the water, so I put on my denim jacket over my strapless dress and lean against the wooden fence whilst I wait. My watch shows I'm a few minutes early, which is a miracle, so maybe another miracle is around the corner and this date will go well.

A text rings through on my phone: *Hey, Lady, where are you? I'm on the balcony, back right. Xxx*

I push off the fence and peer around the corner. Dark

hair slicked back, beautiful brown eyes, broad shoulders. Good start.

He gets up and greets me. His hug is long and close. I feel his muscles pressing against my body. It feels nice. Masculine.

'You're a good hugger and nice arms, too.' He flexes them, inviting a squeeze.

'I didn't used to have arms like this. I used to weigh one hundred kilos more than I am today. Lost a bunch of weight and hit the gym. I feel great now.' He pulls the chair out for me.

'Thank you, kind sir and congrats on getting healthy.' I give him the thumbs up and take my seat. I clock a steaming drink in front of me. Ah, bless him, he's already ordered me an almond chai latte and hasn't even taken a sip out of it.

'Thanks so much for ordering me a drink.' I touch him lightly on his forearm in appreciation. I'm so impressed he went above and beyond to make sure I feel cared for.

The conversation flows as we sip our drinks and watch the rowboats float by.

'Do you fancy hiring a boat?'

He points towards a small shed with red shutters and a counter off to the right of the building.

Do I, heck? I love random stuff like this. 'Sure. Sounds like fun. You know how much I love to have fun.'

I gulp the last of my latte and place the empty mug on the tabletop. He grabs my hand and pulls me up to stand. Ten steps later, we are in front of the boat hiring kiosk.

'A boat for two, please.' He hands over his credit card.

'Can I give you some money towards it?' I take out my purse.

'No, no. My treat, my lady.' His laugh is loud and hearty, which is pleasing to my ears.

The kiosk guy drags the rowboat off the grassy embankment and pushes it into the water, then holds out his hand to me. 'Ladies first.'

I take his hand and step one foot into the boat. I gain my balance with his support, bring my other foot into the boat and take a seat.

My date takes a running jump, leaps from the verge and almost misses the boat. The boat rocks violently from side to side, creating waves on the water. I let out a giggle, and he seems happy that I'm not annoyed by his boyish antics. I would have cried with laughter if he'd jumped too far and landed in the water—you know my wicked sense of humour.

The kiosk guy hands my date two paddles and waves us off. 'Have fun, you two.'

My date manoeuvres the handles of the paddles through the holes on the side of the boat and begins to glide them smoothly through the water. We drift beneath canopies of trees with delicate, white star jasmine blossoms cascading from branches. Their floral fragrance floods the air, adding to the feeling of romance that's blossoming within me. Crikey. He's so manly and cute, rowing away.

We enter what I can only describe as an enchanted lagoon, like the one in the movie *The Notebook*, where they are surrounded by white swans, but instead, we're surrounded by white flowers. The water is crystal clear, and tiny fish swim in shoals beneath us.

My date lays the oars down and the boat slows to a slight rock. He shuffles closer to me, takes a knee and curls his hand around the back of my neck and pulls me forward into a kiss. The kiss is light and gentle and then deeper and more passionate. We are unquestionably compatible in our kissing styles, and it feels so romantic in the heavenly surroundings.

As we continue to float and drift, the journey consists of a mix of taking in the beauty of nature and kisses. It's going so well; I don't want it to end.

After docking the boat back onto the grass, we head over to my car and share another long, passionate embrace.

'I booked something for us, but I didn't know if you'd feel comfortable.'

'What did you book?'

His cheeks blush slightly.

'I hope this was not presumptuous, and I don't expect anything.' He holds his hand up, I assume as a gesture of innocence. 'I booked a hotel. I thought if the date was going well, we could order dinner and that choc royale cake you said you love so much from the Vegie Bar and enjoy some cuddles in the comfort of a hotel room.'

Hmm. What to say? What to do? Is this a trap? He's been so gentlemanly all day thus far, but Mum always says watch out for the 'nice guys' as you don't see them coming. Crikey, there's no hope. The jerks and the nice guys both end up being jerks? Surely not. Can't a woman enjoy a perfectly romantic date and leave a hotel room perfectly intact? There must be some genuine guys out there. Maybe this is one of them? Please let this be one of them. Mum, if I do end up in tomorrow's news, please forgive my naivete, you can always say I got this trait from Dad.

Could cuddles really mean cuddles? If he only wants to eat

and share some cuddles that might be nice, but I don't want to get into a situation where I feel uncomfortable.

'I'll be straight up with you.' Cue serious face, accompanied by an assertive tone, 'It's so sweet of you to make that booking and dinner and cuddles sound lovely. Plus, choc royale, you're pulling out all the stops and I appreciate it, but let's be clear, if I do agree, that's all that will be happening, okay? Dinner, cake and cuddles, with our clothes ON.' I nod to emphasise my seriousness.

'Yeah, of course, I don't expect anything, honest.' His hands are back in the air, pleading his innocence.

'Let's shake on it.' I hold out my hand and he shakes it firmly.

'Okay, I'll meet you at the Vegie Bar.'

Forty-seven minutes later, after picking up dinner and dessert, I pull into a parking spot outside the hotel. Looks luxe. The rooms will probably be swanky. I see the headlights of his car pull in behind me and he gets out, the takeaway bag dangles from his fingers. I step out of Audrey, and after locking his car he grabs my hand and interlaces our fingers. His hand feels nice in mine. He gets me to hold the bag of takeaway whilst he jogs into reception to grab the room key, next we head up to the second floor to the room he's booked. On entering, I was right, the rooms are super fancy. He's got luxury tastes like me. Tick.

My date heads into the bathroom and closes the door.

I pop the bag of takeaway onto the desk, take a few steps back and mentally prepare for the elite gymnastics move I am about to perform. I run towards the bed, hurtle myself through the air and then execute the perfect army roll, landing safely on the pillows. So comfy. I trace my hands across the pillowcase enjoying the mix of softness and silkiness. Nice. Definitely a high thread count. Bad things don't happen on high thread count sheets.

The smell of food wafts into my nose, it smells delish. Can't wait to dig in.

No sooner have I had the thought then I hear the bathroom door open. I can't quite believe my eyes because he enters the room and guess what? He's nude. I mean starkers. Zero clothing. Nothing. Butt naked.

I feel my jaw drop. What the heck? Why is he naked? Surely, he'll give an explanation for this behaviour like 'I'm so sorry. My clothing caught fire while I was in the bathroom, and I had to strip naked. There were no towels, either. I'll have to give this hotel one star.'

Instead of acknowledging his nudity, he acts like everything is fine and turns towards the desk to unpack the food, and that's when I see what he means about losing weight superfast. The top half of his body is of a fit, thirty-year-old man, but from the waist down, and I feel terrible for saying this, but I'm going to describe the view:

His bum rivals one you'd find on a ninety-year-old man. It's as flat as a pancake and large amounts of skin sag from it down onto his legs. Oh. My. Goodness.

He turns around and sees my surprise. 'Are you okay?'

Where to begin? You're starkers and acting as if nothing out of the ordinary has occurred.

The feeling of alarm that he's completely naked consumes me and I feel nervousness build in my chest. 'Why are you naked? I specifically said, clothes on cuddles.'

'Relax. You look so delicious, I thought it would be fun to have cuddles without clothes.' He crawls onto the bed and tries to steal a kiss.

Inside I am freaking out. All I can think about is his nakedness.

'Please could you pass the cake? I'd like to eat some cake, please.' Focus on the cake.

He hands me a slice and when I try to take it, he pulls it away attempting to be cute. 'Kiss first, my lady.'

I Do. Not. Want to kiss him.

'No. Cake first.' I snatch the cake out of his hands and shove half of it into my mouth and swallow, which sends me into a fit of coughing. I need to get out of here.

'I need water.' I grab my bag in between coughs.

'Babe, there's water here.'

I thrust open the door and jump down two steps at a time for a speedy escape.

I never saw his naked body or his ninety-year-old bum again, but this date has been added to my growing list of nightmares.

What I learned from the date: Firstly, when a man goes back on his word, doesn't respect my boundaries and shows his true nature, that's a sure sign of a lack of respect and integrity, and, as I've mentioned previously, I love a respectful and integral man.

Secondly, I have to be attracted to my partner physically, and the ninety-year-old bum didn't do it for me.

Thirdly, I will never go back to a hotel room with any man on a first date until I know he's a man of his word.

Fourth, cake is fantastic comfort food and an excellent diversion tactic.

21

MR MILLION DOLLAR BOGAN

Date Warning: Similar to Mr Ninety-Year-Old Bum, this date heeds an equivalent warning for those who have been unfortunate enough to experience unwanted sexual advances. It is graphic at times.

Age: 34
Location: Melbourne, Victoria
Where we met: In the lift in my apartment building
How he asked me out: I can't remember as my brain went blank. All I know is by the time I'd got out of the lift; he'd got my number and had texted me.

ROADTRIP!
My girlfriends and I decided to take a drive to the

regional Victorian town of Daylesford. A quaint little spot lined with boutique stores and healing hot springs. A perfect girlie getaway.

That was until we got there, and my girlfriend announced she'd be going on a date. That night. At a stranger's house. In the middle of the woods. For a dance party. And you thought I was naïve. I didn't anticipate a girls' weekend ending in a battle with Freddy Kreuger, but life really throws you curveballs, doesn't it?

Being good friends, we agreed to accompany her on the last date of her life and our last dance party.

To stay aligned with the end of days theme, the party wouldn't commence until midnight. What that translated to was three attractive women driving along dirt roads, at midnight, with no streetlamps, on a deadly mission to find Mr Frederick Krueger's house.

My friend was not the best with directions in daylight, let alone in pitch darkness driving through woods.

It spiralled quickly as she thought she'd found the place and continued up a steep, dirt driveway. Where the heck were we? I'm certain we'd arrived at Fred's residence, and three stranded women at his front door was the perfect start for a horror movie. I was already drafting the pitch e-mail to all my acquaintances back in Los Angeles on the off chance I'd survive.

Freaked out didn't suffice as we drove past burnt-out cars and motorbikes that pretty much yelled, 'This is where I hide the dead bodies.'

'This is not right, turn back, like pronto.' I tugged at the steering wheel.

My friend put her foot on the accelerator, which started spinning the wheels in the mud. Pellets of dirt splattered the nearby trees as the car started sliding backwards down the hill we'd just made our way up.

To add more stress, Freddy K's two Dobermans heard the racket, bolted outside and began jumping and barking aggressively at the car. Our screams—perfect for the horror movie we were officially in.

Goodness knows what defensive driving course my friend had done in the past, but somehow she performed a 360-degree turn that warranted a scene in a *Fast and Furious* movie. This was turning into a genre-hopping masterpiece.

We skidded onto the dirt road, and the menacing barks from the Dobermans faded as we gained distance.

'STOP!' A shadowy figure lurked in the middle of the road. Holy crap, was that Freddy?

No. It was my friend's date, who more closely resembled a skinny Santa Claus. Now, my friend is eleven years my senior, so it would make sense that she'd date in a decade above mine, but this guy was at least two, even three, decades older.

'What's with dating the coffin dodger?'

Skinny Santa got in and directed us up another dark dirt road.

I counted my last breaths to our inevitable demise, but I needn't have worried, because on arrival, the stranger's home resembled Frodo's house from the *Lord of the Rings* and in fact, we wouldn't be dying that night at the hands of Freddy Krueger, but of boredom. The midnight dance party was more like those you'd have at an old folks' home, except the old folks were all high on weed and stared into space as we swayed on the makeshift dance floor to 'Tip Toe Through the Tulips'.

Note to self: do not make a habit of going on friends' disastrous dates in addition to my own. The goal is less disastrous dates, not more.

Feeling grateful to come away from my friend's date with my life intact, I was in good spirits, so it was no surprise that my good vibes attracted my next date a few days later. It was an old school ask out, real life, face to face in an elevator. The in-person dates are good because you can see two areas where guys lie—their actual height and their actual face.

I will note that he was not Australian, because asking women out in real life, it seems, is something Australian men don't do. I was getting my new couch moved into my apartment and humming 'Tip Toe Through the Tulips'—dang, when will that song get out of my head—when a tall, handsome guy with a killer smile held the lift open for me. You know when someone smiles and their whole face lights up, and you're so mesmerised that you go into a trancelike state? That's what happened.

When I got out of the lift on the tenth level, I realised within the thirty seconds between the ground floor and tenth floor, I'd handed over my number and agreed to a date, that night, at his apartment. He was in the penthouse, floor nineteen, and due to the lockdown restrictions because of COVID, we couldn't go anywhere else. The guy must have been loving the lockdown rules, as I wouldn't normally go to a man's apartment on a first date, let alone after a thirty-second lift ride, apart from the time I went to Mr Muscle's house . . . but let's forget that one.

The couch looked brilliant by the way—if you were wondering.

The Date

Eight pm arrives and we agree to meet downstairs in the foyer, as I can't get to his apartment without the lift fob—our building has outstanding security. Think Alcatraz.

I sit on the lounge that looks out onto the garden and water feature in the courtyard. The sounds of the lift opening and voices draw my attention behind me. An attractive man steps out of the lift and my date hugs him goodbye. The trancelike state this man's face induces in me has me thinking it's appropriate to hug this stranger too, which he seems to enjoy, as a huge grin spreads across his face as he holds me tightly.

'Steady on, bro,' my date hollers, whilst holding open the lift doors. I pull away and meet my date in the lift giving him a big hug.

'Is that your brother?' He nods.

Wow, his family has exceptional genes. Maybe if this doesn't work out, I can run down the line of brothers. Statistically speaking, it's not the worst idea.

A minute later, the lift opens onto the penthouse floor. It's grand. Floor to ceiling windows. Wood flooring, 360-degree views of the city and ocean. Impressive. My viewing is cut short by large biceps wrapping around my body, followed by being manually turned around to face him, where he goes straight in for a full-on snog. Talk about moving fast. We've literally spent a total of one and a half minutes together and I'm not even sure lift minutes count as real life.

I pull my head back. 'Crikey, give me a second, won't you?'

I wriggle out of his grip and attempt to distract him with a game of foosball, you know the game where little plastic men are in lines? You have a tiny ball, and you have to spin the handles to try and score by getting the ball in the opponent's goal. He takes the bait, but, unfortunately for me, I have exceptional hand-eye coordination skills and within minutes I've scored five goals and beat the pants off him. Dang, my natural sporting abilities. I should have played at half effort, because as soon as I win, he rushes around the table, picks me up and places me on the kitchen bar stool, drags the other stool so close our knees are touching and you guessed it, goes in for another kiss.

'Mister, please, let's get to know each other. I'm not ready to kiss you. Give me some time.'

'Okay. Okay. Let me get you a drink then.'

'Tea, please.'

He looks surprised. 'Tea?'

Two minutes later, steam rises from my mug, and I breathe in the strong scent of peppermint, but guess who's back? He puts his arms around my shoulder and leans in with gusto, this time he catches the side of my lips.

I push him away. 'Let me drink my tea.'

I feel like an animal in the wild trying to fight off a horny male. I guess the only difference is I'm in a fancy penthouse trying to drink tea. I take a sip and sigh. Is this one of those men Mum warned me about in the Mr Yogi date? The ones that want to bonk your brains out 24/7, and you spend your days trying to evade capture.

'Let's watch a movie.'

He heads into the entertainment room and starts playing around with the remote. Does he seriously think I don't know this game? This is male move 101—get her snuggled into you on the couch, then lay it on her.

I rise from my seat, watching my tea with laser focus, don't spill it. I reach the couch and place the mug onto a coaster. He's clearly house proud, as most guys wouldn't use coasters. I must admit, I find that appealing.

My date grabs me. 'Come here, you.'

The next minute I'm within an inch of his face as he tries to force my cheek, so my lips are facing in his direction. I stick my hand up between our faces as a shield. 'No.'

My date rolls his eyes. 'Do you want some nuts?'

As I start to think, *He'd better be coming back with almonds*, he gets up to go to the kitchen. Thank goodness, he means food nuts. But, as he rises, there's one large thing that catches my attention . . . the large erection poking through his pants.

Think pitching a tent. It's a substantial size, and of course my eyes go straight to it. Anyone's would. It's right in my eye line. If I were trying to watch a movie it would be blocking my view.

He comes back from the kitchen with his nuts and his pocket rocket like nothing has happened.

'Why are you staring at my erection?'

I've never been asked that question on a first date. Or a second date. Or any date. What does he want me to do, avert my gaze and ignore it like it's a child in time out?

'Erections are normal when I'm sitting next to an attractive girl.'

I guess it's a good sign his body is functioning normally? Let's put a positive spin on this.

He sits back down, adjusts his pants around the erection and presses play on the TV.

I'm trying to focus on the movie, but I can feel his erection staring at me. It isn't going away. What's this guy thinking about? Possibly old people cuddling?

Ten minutes later, yep, it's still staring at me and in the next second, he is pulling me in and trying to kiss me. I'm so exhausted.

He's on his feet again and is now staring at his erection. I guess he's allowed to stare at it. I'm still figuring out the rules.

'What are we going to do about this?' He shifts his gaze to me.

'Sir, there is no "we" in this equation. Your erection, your problem.'

'It's not going down. Can't you help me out?' He proceeds to pull down his pants and present it in full view. Turns out I had literally beat the pants off him at foosball. And let me tell you: it looks mad.

The next few seconds are a bit of a blur as I can't believe it's happening.

He steps forward with it in his right hand. 'Look, he likes you.'

Yes. He has personified his penis.

Next, he leans forward and bops me on the forehead with it.

Yes, you read that right. He bops me, a grown woman he's

known for twenty minutes at best, on the head with his erect, grown man penis and makes the 'bop' sound when he does it.

What in the world? My brain can't compute. I jump off the couch and grab my belongings.

'What's the matter? Most girls would have jumped on it by now.'

Who does he think he is? Ginuwine? And show me the women who eagerly jumped on your penis after you bounced it ON. HER. FOREHEAD.

'I don't know what kind of girls you date, but just no, in every sense of the word. I'm going home.'

I find myself back in my apartment. Dang, what am I going to do now if I see him in the lift? Note to self: do not make eye contact with any other men in the building during the time I live here.

I hear my phone buzzing in my handbag. I grab it, accidentally pressing the accept video call.

'Someone wants to say hello.'

All I can see is the angry erection staring down the phone lens.

He starts talking on behalf of his penis in a strange Kermit the Frog voice, 'Roger Ram Jet is sad that you didn't want to hang out with him tonight. He is going to be sad. All. Night. Long.'

Roger Ram Jet? He's named his penis Roger Ram Jet.

I interrupt his weird puppet commentary, 'I don't think this is going to work out.' I shake my head vigorously from side to side, every inch of my body rejecting him and Roger.

'Well, if you want hugs, give me and Roger a call.'

I press the red reject button on my phone.

I'll never be requiring hugs from you, sir, like never. Also, please revisit your definition of a hug. You and Roger both.

Ever since the date, when I needed to take the lift, I would check to see if it was on the penthouse floor. If it was, I would wait until it had moved to another level. This was the only avoidance strategy I had, other than climbing ten flights of stairs every day or moving house.

I did have to run and hide several times after the date—if you can call it a date. Lucky for me, nine months later he moved out and I can't tell you the relief I felt. Note to self: don't date where you sleep.

Lessons I learned from this date: Firstly, even during a pandemic, do not go to a man's apartment on a first date.

Secondly, bopping the penis on the head is now a deal-breaker. Maybe I should put that in my online profile.

22

MR ANCIENT BABY

Age: 35
Location: Melbourne, Australia
Where we met: Online dating app
How he asked me out: Text message

My aunty had visited Melbs for a night on a work trip, and I'd bought us tickets to go and see *The Adventures of Priscilla, Queen of the Desert* at Her Majesty's Theatre. My aunty and I have the same love of movies, theatre and doing random things like going to silent discos.

We sat in our AAA seats at the front of the theatre and settled in for a fun evening gobbling down popcorn.

'Been on any dates lately?' My aunty is single too.

'Well, I wouldn't call them dates. I had one guy who invited me for dinner, and I ended up painting his house. Another guy kept making excuses not to be alone with me.

Later, I found out he was impotent. And I had several dates with another guy who was like a dog on heat, where I'd get no sleep because all night, he'd poke me in the back with his erection. I didn't think at sixty I'd be dealing with this.'

When I told her about my recent dating escapades and this book, she loved the idea and wondered if a sequel was in order, *28 Disastrous Senior Dates*. What do you reckon?

The lights faded and the intro came over the speaker announcing the commencement of the show, and the curtains were drawn.

I had no idea what a treat we were in for. The show was spectacular with glitter, colour, vibrancy and fun. It was a feast for the eyes.

About three-quarters of the way into the show the lead made an announcement, 'We need some volunteers to attend tonight's barn dance.'

At the same time, one of the ripped, shirtless performers, who could easily have been the model for a Roman sculpture, jumped into the audience and pretty much dragged me onto the stage, much to the delight of my aunty. Yes, she has the same wicked sense of humour as the rest of the family.

Deer in headlights was an accurate description of my experience, with the stage lights literally penetrating my retinas. I didn't have time to execute an in-depth analysis on how it was possible for performers to see, as well as dance, under the burning lasers of the stage lighting because the Roman sculpture was teaching me dance steps. I was certain I was not getting paid for this, and now I was an integral part of the act. What had I gotten myself into this time?

The steps were simple. However, I was wearing the highest

heels in history. If I'd known I'd be dancing in front of hundreds of paying customers I'd have worn my special Salsa heels. Dang it.

The steps were fine when they were slow, but as we started to move and the music gained speed, the combo of mega heels and steps was an impossible feat and I could dance no more. I'd linked arms with the Roman sculpture guy on my left and another stocky framed guy linked my arm on my right. The music got faster and faster until my dance partners had no choice but to drag me around the circle, their faces getting redder and redder with each rotation, both staring at me with looks of despair that screamed, 'Woman, put your feet back on the ground.'

I stared back with a look that screamed, 'Well, give me a pair of flats and a cut of the ticket sales!'

I was getting dragged so fast now that my feet slid under the dance partner to my left. He tripped over my dragging feet and like dominos, each person in our circle crashed one by one to the ground.

When I gained my composure and took in my surroundings, the Roman sculpture glared at me like I'd destroyed his entire career. A hurried voiceover ordered all participants to exit the stage immediately.

My aunty—of course—was holding her stomach as tears rolled down her cheeks. Let's be honest. I'd be in a fit of hysterics if I were in her shoes. And if I'd worn her shoes, I wouldn't be in this mess.

After chatting to my aunty about dates and waving her off at the airport, I was inspired to give a new online dating app a go. My theory—I couldn't risk having any more exes roaming my apartment building. So, a copy and paste of a past profile later, and I was back online.

Now, we've all been caught out with online dating, where daters have put photos on their profile that are clearly fake. Remember Mr Catfish? Or the ones that have model shoots, where they are positioned at the perfect angle, with the perfect lighting, with the perfect background. Who goes around getting a professional photo shoot anyway? Everyone in LA, that's who. Ninety-nine per cent of the time, these, too, are swiped left. Then, there are those that do those weird Snapchat filters that erase any imperfection on the skin or decorate themselves with a cat nose and whiskers. Please, I'm seeking a date, not a cat who's had Botox and fillers. Cringe central. Not my cup of tea.

But, what about the ones that put photos of themselves, and you think, okay, you look alright, and you agree to a date where you're expecting one thing, but instead, you get the likes of Benjamin Button. For those who don't know who that is, Brad Pitt played the lead character in a film of the same name, and, spoiler alert, this person starts off as an ancient baby who ages backwards. Keep the ancient baby image in your mind in preparation for this dating story.

So, I'd done my usual checks, which he'd passed, and he seemed attractive enough in his photos for me to say yes to a tandem bike ride by the ocean, followed by a picnic at a waterside park. We agreed to meet at the bike shop at 10 am and I was looking forward to enjoying an active outside date, as well as basking in the sunshine. You know how much I love nature.

The Date

White sneakers on, jeans ripped at the knees and a white T-shirt styled with a French tuck. I taught my mum the French tuck after watching *Queer Eye*. Boy, she can definitely pull it off for a sixty-four-year-old. I reckon she could give Tan a run for his money. I'm anticipating a chill on the water, so I hang a light, sand-coloured cardigan around my shoulders, like men do on yachts (or so I assume—I still haven't returned to one).

I arrive at the entrance and check my watch, 10.05 am. I'm late as usual. I might text to see where he is:

Are you inside?

My phone beeps: *Yeah. Come in. I'm grabbing the tandem.*

Coolio. I type. Press send, push the door and swing it open.

I check to the left and right. Someone's fiddling with a tandem in the far-left corner. He's bent over, so I can't see him clearly. I pass bike after bike until I'm standing above him. He glances up and our eyes lock. I gasp as I take in his face.

You know I mentioned the ancient baby from *The Curious Case of Benjamin Button* movie? Imagine that face staring up at you when you were expecting a thirty-eight-year-old face. Deep furrows line his forehead and mouth. Sagging bags under his eyes seem like he hasn't slept in a decade. His skin is sallow and translucent. What's happened to this guy? Has he lied about his age? If he's lied, I'm fuming. What a waste of my time. I didn't realise there were so many subcategories to catfishing.

I feel irritation growing in my throat as I want to scream, 'Liar' for the entire bike shop to hear. I try to appear normal in my conversation and not show my intense disappointment and feelings of betrayal. How am I going to find out his age?

Lucky for me, the universe provides an instant manifestation, as the assistant behind the counter asks for his driver's licence.

He retrieves the wallet from his back pocket and rummages through the cards, eventually locating his licence. He places it on the counter, facing the assistant. I try to lean forward to check his birth date, but the assistant immediately swipes it off the counter and into the air. Dang. Opportunity lost.

The assistant enters a few digits onto the computer screen and places the licence back on top of the counter in front of A.B. (ancient baby). All I want is to know how old he really is, so, I summon all of the acting skills I absorbed via osmosis while in LA. I pretend to go for a map and 'accidentally' knock the licence to the floor. Silly me! Must pick it up for him whilst laser focusing on the birth date.

I locate the numbers. Now I've got you, you lying . . .

What the? His birth year is only three years earlier than mine. That means he is thirty-eight. How in the world is this possible? Had he angered a sorcerer who'd body swapped him with someone much older? Or, the perhaps more likely explanation of, too much sun? Even then he'd have had to bake in it every day, without sunscreen, to look twenty years older than his real age. How can a man in his late thirties look late fifties? I'm dumbfounded. This is a serious mystery. Time to channel *Nancy Drew*.

A.B. has set the bike up outside and it's ready for me to mount. 'All aboard.'

I swing my right leg over the back and park my bum on

the seat; my two legs swinging about a foot off the ground. Reminds me of my first bike when I was a kid.

The bike shop assistant positions his feet in a solid stance in front of the bike and holds the handlebars steady to keep the tandem supported. Probably because he thinks my companion is in his twilight years. A.B. jumps on like a cowboy mounting a horse, and then off we go over a small, wooden bridge that connects us to the ocean bike path. The sea air hits me, and it feels wonderful to be riding along, the wind flying through my hair, but I'm distracted by the face of the ancient baby that's imprinted on my mind. Investigation time.

'Do you work outside?' I try not to sound too conspicuous.

'No. I'm in the office all day. I should get more sun.'

Sir, I'm telling you right now, you do not need more sun. Period. Even if you have rickets.

My mind churns with the possibilities. So, if he's not melted twenty layers of skin through sun baking, how did his face transform into the Ancient Baby? What else could it be? Maybe bad genes? I'll figure this out one way or another. It's hard to hear him on the bike and it makes me uneasy when he turns back to talk to me, as the bike wobbles when he's not facing front on, so, for the next fifteen minutes I put Ancient Baby to one side and enjoy the view.

I feel the bike shift to the left. We must be nearing the picnic grounds as we take a hard turn and slow to a stop near a picnic table. He taps me on the leg, which I take to mean to dismount, which I do.

The picnic hamper is strapped on the back of the bike, so I untie and start to unload the contents, neatly positioning each one in the centre of the table.

'Are you close with your family?' My hidden agenda planted firmly front of mind.

'Yeah. Really close with my parents and siblings. I go around for lunch every Sunday.'

He pops down paper plates and cutlery, so we are sitting on the same side of the picnic table. This is good for a closer skin inspection.

'Do you have any family photos? Do you look like your parents? How old are they?'

I'm hoping he'll show me a few snaps so I can see if he's inherited bad genes.

He takes the bait, and I slide in closer to view a photo of him, his mum and his dad. I take the phone out of his hand and enlarge the shot for closer inspection of his parents' faces.

'You look more like your mum.' I attempt to distract him from the fact I've expanded it to the maximum to perform an extensive examination. Hmm. Seems the genes aren't the problem. His parents look fine. What happened to his skin to make it so ancient? Mystery unsolved.

He leans down and pulls out two wine glasses, lifting one up as an offering.

'None for me thanks, teetotaller these days.' I smile and grab the paper cup to be filled with water. He sets down the glass, picks up the bottle of water and pours it into my cup. After which he fills his glass with red wine, right to the brim.

Maybe this is the reason. Alcohol is dehydrating. He chugs it down as we make small talk about our lives, and he continues to refill his glass for a second and third time. I notice myself unconsciously pushing the bottle of water in his direction as I feel his skin screaming for hydration.

'Do you drink a lot of alcohol?' I stare at the fourth glass he's pouring. How the heck is he going to safely ride us back if he's intoxicated?

'Yeah. I love a good red. I squeeze in two bottles a night.' I feel my eyes widen.

'Two bottles a night? That seems like a lot.' Not seems like a lot, is a lot.

'I don't like any other drinks. Can't stand water. Never drink the stuff.'

Hmmm. A piece of the puzzle has emerged. Alcohol dehydrates the skin and there's no water intake to rehydrate it. No wonder his skin is screaming for H2O. I'll also bet he hasn't done a number two in twenty years.

'I could do with a ciggy. Nothing better than a ciggy with a glass of red.'

What? His profile clearly stated non-smoker; otherwise, I would never have even considered a date. Absolute deal-breaker.

'Gave up yesterday, but hanging out for one right now, used to smoke four packs a day.'

The pieces of the puzzle to the ancient baby face are becoming apparent: heavy drinker, insane smoker, zero water intake, all equal a twenty-year-jump in your biological appearance.

He starts slurring his words that sound like gibberish. He is becoming more of an ancient baby by the second. Move over Brad Pitt.

How the heck are we going to get home?

Shortly after this thought, A.B. passes out with his head resting on the picnic bench, the sun beating down on his skin. Hmmm. He may think he gets no sun exposure, but if this happens frequently, he'll be getting sunburnt every day as well.

My watch suggests we are twenty minutes away from getting fined by the bike company, so I pack up his picnic hamper and place it next to his head to try and create a bit of shade from the sun. No need to traumatise local children with his sunburnt old baby face. I grab the handlebars and swing my leg over, but dang, the seat is too high, and I can't stay upright. So, after a few minutes of trying to adjust the seat with zero luck, there's me pushing a tandem bike back to the shop, solo.

Later that afternoon, I got the following text:

I am so sorry for passing out. Forgive me?

I didn't bother replying and never saw Ancient Baby again. But I was reminded of him when I enjoyed a girl's trip to Lorne and watched the movie, *The Curious Case of Benjamin Button*.

What I learned from this date: Firstly, I seek an honest man who puts up-to-date photos of himself online, and represents himself accurately, for example, if you're thirty-eight, don't put photos of when you were eight on your profile.

Secondly, this date taught me that I'm not interested in a man who smokes, drinks heavily and doesn't like water—the elixir of life in my opinion, and the opinion of most health professionals. Wellbeing is an absolute must.

23

MR RICH GUY, POOR GUY

Age: 35
Location: Melbourne, Australia
Where we met: Online dating app
How he asked me out: Phone call

Between this date and the last, I'd been spending time with a wealthy businessman whom I'd met at the local badminton club. I think he was impressed by my overzealous technique of smashing the shuttlecock right at his forehead, which was a nice change from having any type of cock smashed against my own. Our physical chemistry was electric, but it didn't take long for me to realise our mental chemistry was zero, and I was in fact dating Mike TV.

A typical exchange looked like this:

Me. 'Let's go on a hike.'

Him. 'I'm tired, let's spend the day watching a new TV series.'

Me: *Kill me now.*

My theory—he'd achieved massive financial success, had become complacent with life and was now living through the characters on the small screen.

He had no interest in any topic other than his favourite characters from the current TV series he was watching. As a result, our conversations were as deep as a puddle. I was also concerned I'd already lost a significant number of brain cells from all the radio waves pummelling me from the idiot box. Couple that with the lacklustre conversation, and within weeks, my IQ would be lower than seventy, and that's something I wasn't willing to risk after all the lobotomies I'd had to erase the ghosts of dates past. So, after three excruciatingly boring months, I threw this dead fish back into the sea and dove back into the dating pool.

All was not lost because I could always rely on my trusted online dating pool of average to horrendous matches to fall back on.

But then there are moments like these when you read a profile, and you feel a glimmer of hope. The hope that wipes out all memory of past dates and convinces you this one will be different. He's the ultimate man online that's perfect for me. He's the outlier. I was simply wading through the dross to find this Adonis. It was all worth it.

That's what I felt when I read his profile, which came as a

welcome relief from wanting to throw myself off a tall building rather than spend another minute watching TV. This is what he wrote:

Successful business owner and real estate investor. Love adventure and new experiences. A kid at heart, and I promise to make you laugh every day. Family values. Love animals. My lady is always at the top of my priority list. Seeking a woman who is beautiful inside and out to build an extraordinary life with.

The profile photos were wonderful too. One showed him feeding a lamb, and in another, he seemed to be attending a prestigious event in a tailored suit; gotta love the James Bond look. In a third, he's completing a marathon, and the last one is a photo of the most gorgeous, emerald green Harley Davison motorbike I'd ever seen, with him standing next to it. This guy sounded like the man of my dreams.

I was so excited to meet this guy, and it seemed he was too because we organised a phone chat within a few texts and a date within a few minutes of chatting. We agreed to meet for dinner that evening at one of my favourite restaurants. Could he be the one?

In everything I do, I like to put my best foot forward, so I made a massive effort: hair straightened to perfection, bright red lips with matching shoes and bag, along with my black, fitted knit dress that created a striking contrast against the red. I was feeling smoking hot and ready to rock.

The Date

I pull Audrey into a parking space around the corner from the restaurant. Lucky for me, Audrey has a rear-view camera to make pulling into the tight spots effortless. Love how my car makes my life easier. Nope, no Beamer endorsements are coming my way. I'm simply expressing my gratitude for its features—although I won't say no if they reach out.

I step out onto the tarmac. I grab my Mary Poppins bag, hoist myself out of the driver's seat and press the lock button on the remote. I haven't taken more than a few steps before a loud honk startles me, followed by a wolf whistle. What can I say? I am looking fine tonight, but crikey, that scared the crap out of me.

I reach the entrance of the restaurant and push open the door. The waitress asks for my name.

'Follow me. Your date is already seated.'

I follow her to the back of the restaurant, where she points to a red booth, which I notice perfectly matches my shoes, and wishes me a good evening.

I peer around the corner of the booth and see my date for the first time.

Oh no, what an anti-climax. My first thought is, *Did he just get out of bed?* My second thought is, *Maybe that's where he belongs.*

My date is sporting a beige tracksuit top and matching tracksuit pants. I notice a large ketchup-looking stain on his top.

He must have noticed my disappointment because the following words tumble out of his mouth, 'Babe, you look like you're going somewhere flashy. You look stunning. I'm so sorry about my togs, I came straight from the gym as I wanted to be on time for you. Apologies. I feel so underdressed right now.'

I sit opposite him. 'Okay, no problem. It's nice to meet you anyway.'

He has a lovely face, and I can see muscles through the tight parts of his tracksuit, so at least that's attractive.

We check out the menu and place our orders. I must say, I'm excited about the food.

I'm keen to know more about his business as it's a topic I find fascinating, being an entrepreneur myself. Business and self-development books are my favourite go-tos for motivation and improving my skill set.

'So, tell me about your business. How long have you been running it?'

My sparkling passionfruit drink arrives, and I take a sip. Yum. Fruity and fresh.

My date appears a little uncomfortable. 'Well, I haven't started it yet.' Then he's silent.

Okay. Maybe he's had other businesses in the past and this is a new one.

'What industry is it in? What are the other businesses you've had in the past?'

My date shifts in his seat. 'No, this is my first one. It's a business where I get people to sign up for charities in shopping centres.'

Are you kidding me? He's one of those charity canvassers you see in the shopping centres, where customers do everything in their power to try and avoid catching their eye? No wonder he's had to use dating apps. Everyone avoids him like the plague in the real world. Seems we have yet another case of misrepresentation on a dating profile.

'Oh, right.' I try my best to stay positive, but I feel annoyed that I've been misled yet again. Let's see if he also lied about investing. 'So, what do you invest in? Real estate, stocks?'

Oh crikey, there's the seat shift. What is he about to say? He doesn't invest in stocks because he thinks they are wooden frames used to punish the British locals for swearing and drunkenness? He shifts again in his seat before answering.

'Well, my plan is to invest in real estate.'

What that means is he doesn't invest in anything. I'm pretty certain I'm on a date with a wannabe.

Our meals arrive and it's the one thing on this date I'm excited about, so I dig in and enjoy.

'What would you say are the three top things you would recommend to make a business successful?' My date questions, staring at my red lips.

I feel like if he had a pen and paper handy, he'd be frantically writing down every word. Unfortunately for him, I responded with this:

'Well, I usually charge a lot for client consultations, so if you want to book in I'll give you my business card.' I joke, but I'm dead serious. I can't tell you how many dates have wanted free business advice when they hear that I'm a partner in a business consultancy company. Cringe.

An awkward silence follows. I try and eat faster than I normally would, as I'm already done with him. I scoff down the last of my food in record time and I'm usually a slow eater.

'Shall we go?'

'Really?' Disappointment is written all over his face.

Welcome to my world, matey.

We walk to the counter, and he stands there. He doesn't reach for his wallet. I glance over. He gazes. Straight ahead.

The waitress prints out the bill and places it in front of us on the benchtop. I hand over my card. 'Can you put half on my card, please?'

'Sorry, we don't split the bill,' she apologises. Of course, you don't. My date still hasn't moved an inch.

'So, how are we going to do this?' I turn and direct my words to his face.

He pats the pockets of his beige jogging pants and does a fake surprised look. 'Oh no, I've forgotten my wallet, I'm so sorry. Can you pay, and I'll send you a bank transfer?' He takes a few steps away from the counter.

Clearly, he was expecting me to pay, for us both, from the start. Free business advice and a free dinner. A productive date for him.

I tap the screen and pay the full amount. I can't believe his cheek. Even though it's nice when a man pays, I never expect them to and always offer my share.

I thank the waitress, and we walk outside. I sincerely hope to see the incredible motorbike from his profile photo, but I'm not holding my breath.

You will not believe what is sitting there instead; remember the clapped-out moped from the Mr Camel Lover date? That's his ride. What are the odds? It's so old it's probably a prototype from forty years ago. Scratches cover the paintwork; foam is splaying out of a rip in the seat. It's filthy dirty. I can't hold my words in any longer.

'Why did you blatantly lie in your profile? Where's the motorbike from your photos? I don't understand why you'd lie and deceive someone like that.' I cross my arms feeling extremely annoyed.

'I didn't lie. I created a profile of my future self, and one day I will become that man.'

I've heard of faking it until you make it, but this is another level.

'Sorry, but that's not how it works in dating. You should be presenting the man you are right now, so you aren't wasting people's time.' I shake my head. 'If you don't change your profile to make it accurate, I will report you.'

'I'm so sorry. If you give me a chance, you'll see I'm a great guy,' he begs.

'Sorry, but I don't date liars. All the best.'

My date's face drops, and I turn and begin the commute back to Audrey. I glance back and see him swing his leg over the back of the moped and attempt to turn on the ignition. Nothing happens, a few clunky sounds emerge from the engine. After three more failed attempts, my date pushes the bomb along the street. I feel sorry for the guy. But I can't tolerate liars.

I know this is a bit naughty, but I'm intrigued to see where he lives, so I hurry back to Audrey, turn the headlights on low and in stealth mode follow him. After a few lefts and rights, he pushes the kickstand and parks the moped outside a small, dated flat. I can hear a screaming match coming from the neighbours. I pull in behind a car a few doors down so I can watch where he goes.

Weirdly, he knocks on the door. Where's his key? The door swings open and a lady who looks like she's in her sixties stands at the entrance. My date hangs his head and moves into her arms, where she cuddles him and strokes his hair. That must be his mum. He lives with his mum? And clearly, he hasn't got the memo to get his own place by the fact she hasn't even given him a set of keys. Wow. His actual life could not have gotten any further from his aspirational profile. What a joke.

My phone pings, and I see there's a text in my inbox from my date. *I'm sorry for lying, if you give me another chance, I promise I'll make it up to you.*

My response: *How about transferring the money you owe me first.*

I never got a response and never got my money. I did, however, see him the following week walking along the beach, hand in hand with a woman, pushing a stroller. What the heck? He wasn't even single. And he had a child, to boot! This guy was clearly lying to everyone. Luckily, I saw him before he saw me, so I cartwheeled into the nearest bush to avoid him. It seems I need to increase the radius of the men I date as they are getting too close to home, although maybe I should trash dating apps altogether, as I read a stat that claimed forty-two per cent of people on dating apps aren't even single. What an absolute joke!

Lessons I learned from this date: Firstly, Mike TV affirmed I need a good conversationalist and an avid reader who's into self-growth and expansion. I'm not into a man who's happy to be found dead on the couch, holding a bag of Cheetos watching Seinfeld reruns.

Secondly, actions speak louder than words, and I admire a man whose actions back up his words. I also want a man who has his life together, like I do and can at least pay for his own dang meal.

Thirdly, never wear a ketchup-stained tracksuit to a date.

24

MR THIRD WHEEL

Age: 36
Location: Melbourne, Australia
Where we met: Online dating app
How he asked me out: Text message

I'd spent the day enjoying a round of golf with a girlfriend. Golf skills—highly questionable. All was not lost because my abs were well on the way to a solid six-pack after laughing so hard at our poor hitting technique. Let's just say the ball became good friends with the grass since they never left each other's side.

It didn't help that we'd arrived late, and it was already dusk. Because our hitting skills were so dismal, it meant if the par for the hole was three, we'd get there in three plus a zero on the end. After the second hole, the golf attendant did the rounds of closing up shop and removed all the flags. So, in a nutshell, we were playing golf in the pitch darkness and had no idea where the hole was. I'm certain that thought has crossed many a man's mind.

Having such a good time gave me a cracking idea regarding future dates: only agree to dates where I was guaranteed fun, irrespective of the man who showed up. After all, I'd been the best part of every one of my dates so far, so I figured I would lean into that, date myself and let a man tag along. If he ends up being the one, that's a lovely bonus.

I deployed this new plan and agreed to one of my favourite kinds of dates—one that involves the furry kind. No, not that kind. Dirty mind!

By now, you know I'm a passionate and devoted animal lover. That's the reason I don't eat them. Makes sense, right? And that's the reason I started a dog walking business, because I had so much fun being around those furry little munchkins. So, I was excited to meet date number twenty-four because the handsome date had a handsome standard poodle called Gerald.

This date checked my superficial boxes, and I liked that his online profile featured his dog, who was in every photo. The only thing I thought was a tad strange was several of the pictures showed Gerald draped around his neck, like a scarf. Not sure what that's all about, but it wasn't enough for me to discard a date.

The Date

We arrange to meet at Brighton dog beach. The sun is shining, and it feels wonderful with the warm rays caressing my cheeks, especially after several days of rain. There are lots of dogs romping around, playing, swimming and generally living life to the fullest. It's a wonderful sight.

I keep checking the entrance for any newcomers and to see if my date is arriving. A large, white standard poodle claws at the gate. He pushes his nose at the handle, and, as the owner undoes the latch, the poodle gallops straight over the sand dunes and dives headfirst into the water. That must be handsome Gerald.

My date shuts the gate behind him and yanks on it twice; I assume to make sure it's securely locked. Security conscious. Nice. I know that feeling of triple checking everything from days working in my dog walking business. I smile and wave him over.

He puts his hand up in acknowledgement, but instead of coming over to greet me, he walks over to the section of the beach where Gerald is demonstrating the perfect doggie paddle, splashing like crazy, swimming after another dog's ball. Okay, is my date expecting me to go over to him? I take steps in his direction. How awkward. Why wouldn't he come and greet me first?

I'm about ten strides behind him when he shouts, 'Look at Gerald.'

I hurry until I'm beside him. Gerald is still frantically splashing around like he has been for the last ten minutes.

'He's such a magnificent swimmer.' He gazes out lovingly at Gerald.

'So, how has your day been?' I am aware I am risking interrupting Gerald's recital in an attempt to strike up a conversation.

He keeps his eyes firmly on Gerald. 'Well, Gerald woke me up early this morning, at 3 am. I spent the morning making him his favourite breakfast, then I massaged and brushed him for two hours.'

'Crikey, must be a special day for Gerald!'

'Oh no, this is part of our daily routine. Though every day with Gerald is special.' He pauses to gaze at Gerald before continuing on. 'We then went clothes shopping, for Gerald, and we bought the cutest outfit. I'll pop it on him after his walk so you can see.' His eyes remain fixed on Gerald. Does he even know what I look like? I could have black teeth and lip spittle for all he knows. Rookie mistake.

'Impressive, you've got a lot done given the fact it's only 9 am.' I do my best laser eye focus on the back of his head to try and will him to even glance in my direction. It doesn't work. Note to self: must practice mind control later.

'He's so graceful when he swims.' He claps his hands together in delight.

I wouldn't personally attribute the word graceful to describe Gerald's swimming technique as it has all the grace of a large, grown man learning to doggie paddle for the first time, but as the saying goes, love is blind.

I'm about to ask another question when he pipes up, 'Gerald, Gerald, come to Daddy.' He waves his hands around his head, wildly. Gerald eyeballs his owner, makes a U-turn and starts doggy paddling towards the beach. He reaches the shore and removes the excess water with a long shake, all over my pretty dress. Lucky for my date, I'm not too phased as it wouldn't be the first time or the last time it happens, that's for sure.

'My little Gerald, you are such a good boy. Who's the best boy in the entire world?'

By any chance could it be Gerald? Eye roll.

Gerald jumps up with his paws on my date's chest. This catches him off balance and he stacks it backwards, onto the sand.

'Gerald. You little terror.' My date's expression of joy embodies a man who's just realised he's been accepted into heaven, as Gerald pounces on him and licks his face.

Is it possible to be the third wheel with a man and his dog?

Five or so minutes later, my date crawls onto his knees and then to a stand. 'Let's go to the café, I already took Gerald for a two-hour walk this morning, but I know how much he loves the water, so I had to bring him to the beach.'

So, what you're saying is, you're here because Gerald wants to swim and not because you wanted to have a date with me? I feel about as special as a dying houseplant.

He pats Gerald on the head, honks him on the nose and kisses him as we head to the outdoor shower outside the gate, where he clips Gerald's leash to the post and turns on the water. He checks the temperature several times, I assume to make sure it is just right for Gerald. Gerald apparently likes his water at thirty degrees Celsius—no more, no less.

I thought he was only hosing him down, but instead, my date reaches into his bag and pulls out organic shampoo and conditioner.

'I don't use any old crap on Gerald.' He squirts the creamy liquid into his hands and rubs them together. 'Only the best for my champion.'

The one positive thing I can say about my date so far

is he'd clearly be a doting father. There's a silver lining in every storm.

I'm wearing a cute, floor-length floral maxi dress, so I don't help him with the lathering but instead perch myself against the fence that creates a boundary between the dog park and the rest of the beach. I study my watch. I feel like I'm back at work for my dog walking business, not on a date. How did my plan to go on an enjoyable date fail so quickly? Fifteen minutes have gone by, and I'm now best friends with the owners of a cocker spaniel named Tango and Doug the golden retriever who have been waiting patiently in line for the shower. My date seems oblivious to the holdup. They've got places to be, mate. This is the dog equivalent of the shower at the gym. Not a full-service spa. Get a wriggle on!

Gerald has enjoyed his third and final rinse and is untied and moved to the side, where I'm asked to hold the leash, which means he remembers I'm here after all. My date retrieves a towel from his bag and hand dries Gerald, whose tail is whizzing in a circular motion at approximately fifty kilometres an hour. At least someone is enjoying this date.

He packs the towel away and pulls out Gerald's brand-new outfit—a blue doggie onesie with—can you guess what is on it? Yep, tiny poodles, all over it. Righto.

After Gerald is adorned in his fresh new outfit, and Tango and Doug have finally gotten to take their showers, Gerald and my date take off at a good pace, which means I'm walking several paces behind them because apparently Gerald enjoys walking fast. Where was Gerald on my Say It, Don't Spray It date?

On route to the café, I feel like I'm a servant walking

behind a king, or more accurately, behind the king and his dog. My date doesn't look back during the entire walk, and all I hear the whole way is, 'Oh, don't you look magnificent, Gerald, in your new outfit.'

Never mind my cute outfit. I could have clad myself in a bin liner. Would have had the same effect on my date. I spend the walk rolling my eyes behind him.

I once had a client with two miniature poodles and whenever I'd rock up to take them for a walk, she'd have them dressed in the most ridiculous outfits. One day the male dog was dressed in a jester costume, complete with a tiny jester hat with bells hanging from it. The dog seemed to have had enough because he stood facing the wall and refused to move. I removed the offending costume, and oh, the joy of that little dog. He performed about ten figure-eight zoomies around the living room in celebration. Gerald and this dog would not have gotten along.

We reach the café and the waitress gushes over Gerald's new onesie, and I'm offended that she's not on my side, which she should have known telepathically. She sits us next to a sleeping Pomeranian. Gerald, I assume, will lie down and have a snooze.

Nope. That's not what happens.

My date pulls out a deluxe blanket and places it on the chair next to him.

'Up Gerald.' He pats the seat. I notice Gerald's bum fills the entire seat as my date pushes the chair closer to the table edge.

The waitress returns with a notepad, holding her stare on Gerald in what seems to be amusement. That makes two of us.

'I'll take the avocado on toast, please.' I point to the dish on the menu.

'I will have the scramble on toast, with the bacon on the side.' He hands the menu back to the waitress and pats Gerald on the head.

I begin to speak, but I'm interrupted.

'Gerald has food allergies, you know, so I need to be careful with what I feed him. I don't want him getting sick, now, do I?'

Of course not. However, would you get him to the most exclusive dog hospital in all the world in time?

He shakes his head and lowers his gaze as he plants a kiss on Gerald's nose. 'He loves fresh avocados . . .'

I quickly interrupt in my attempt to get any amount of airtime on this adventure.

'I had a client that has this wonderful avocado tree in the garden, and whenever I turned up to walk the dog, there were loads of avocado seeds lying on the ground. One day I turned up and Larry—the Great Dane—was launching himself in the air, trying to reach the fruits. He succeeded, put it between his paws, carefully tore off the skin and consumed the fruit and spat out the seed. He had the shiniest coat I had ever seen on a dog.' I chuckle as I recall the scene in my mind.

'Gerald adores avocados, don't you Gerald? I make him guacamole at least once a week.'

I stick my tongue out at my date to see if he'd notice. Nope. He's still one hundred per cent focused on Gerald and probably mentally preparing his next batch of dog guac.

The food arrives. Hopefully, we can get to know each other over some civilised conversation. The waitress slides plates in front of us. Yum. But my date pushes the plate away from him and slides it in front of Gerald's nose.

'Wait, Gerald.' He holds his hand up, displaying the universal stop sign and proceeds to retrieve what appears to be a baby's bib that he ties around Gerald's neck. 'We don't want to get any food on your new outfit now, do we?' He bops Gerald on the nose. Gerald licks his lips, his eyes transfixed on the steaming scramble and bacon.

My date picks up his fork, slides on some scramble and nods. Gerald opens wide, like a baby, as my date places the fork into Gerald's mouth. 'Good boy, Gerald.'

I realise that there will be no riveting conversations happening on this date, and, in fact, I can confirm I am the third wheel.

My date seems perfectly content talking to and feeding Gerald, which I am convinced will be his fate for the rest of his life. I may as well not have gotten out of bed this morning. He and Gerald would have still had the same magnificent time. But the most ironic thing happened after the date when I received this text:

Hey, Gerald and I loved meeting you. We had the best date. We'd love to do it again sometime.

My response, *Thanks for the offer, but I'd always come second to Gerald. It seems you've already found the love of your life. All the best.*

I never heard back. He probably read my text and figured I was right.

Lessons I learned from this date: I'll never settle for second best. I've had men who put me second to friends, their work, the gym, but this only leads to resentment. I once watched a documentary about Mt Everest, and the lead woman interviewed believed her husband loved the mountain more than her and their children. That's another level of coming second. Just, wow! Sure, there are times when other things take priority; however, I am seeking a man who is at a stage in his life where he prioritises and wants to invest in our relationship.

25

MR HYDE

This date has a warning on it. This date includes criticism and verbal abuse and may trigger some readers. Read on with caution.

Age: 36
Location: Upper Swan, Victoria
Where we met: At a golfing clinic
How he asked me out: Face to face, after one of our golf classes had finished.

After being blindsided by so many heinous online dates I was grateful to have met date 25 in person. This date began at a golf clinic—yes, I started taking lessons. With a handicap of over one hundred, the insurmountable evidence suggested I needed them.

The date ended at a rescue horse riding stable.

I'd ridden horses from a young age, back in the UK. Thanks, Mum. Not a cheap activity, Mum will tell you so. As a child, my sis and I spent our weekends mucking out stables and getting free rides for labour. There was nothing more joyful than being on the back of a beautiful horse, cantering through the woodlands. That's when I started loving that feeling of freedom one experiences when going fast, out in nature, with an element of danger involved. I'm certain that's why I love motorbikes now as an adult, as it's a similar physical sensation. With a horse, you have the extra danger of the animal having a mind of their own, which, at any time, could turn in an opposing direction than one is intending. Over the course of my lifetime, I've been thrown under gates, over jumps and through fences, but hey, that's the risk you take when riding a live animal and is still more enjoyable than some of the dates I've been on. So, this date occurred on horseback, out in the wild countryside of regional Victoria.

My golf date was attractive—physically. He was my ideal type in appearance: half-Mauritian, half-Irish. Gorgeous combo. Flawless caramel skin, curly, dark hair, and the sound of his voice could make me weak at the knees.

I watched a doco once that said when a woman is ovulating, she is more attracted to men with a lower tone, as it implies there's more testosterone in his body and more likely to produce healthy offspring, but me, I love that tone All. Month. Long. I could listen to his voice for days.

We'd met through our mutual love of golf. We clapped eyes on each other during a golf clinic, and let me tell you, sparks flew. Instant chemical reaction. Don't you just love it when that happens? Because for me, it happens so rarely.

During the golf sessions, we realised we shared a love of horses and, of course, he leapt on the opportunity to ask if I'd like to go on a hack in the Victorian bushland. YES. Zero hesitation. It was his birthday on the day we would be attending the hack and he asked if I minded driving so he could have a beer afterwards. Being the sweet person I am, I had no problem with that arrangement.

The Date

On the morning of the date, I send this text:

Happy birthday, Mister. 39 years young. You don't look a day over 25. Let this be the most wonderful year of your life, filled with love and joy. Excited for today. See you at 9 am.

Pretty cute, right? I'd date me.

I jump in and out of the shower as I'm already running late. No surprise there. Light makeup applied. Hair in a loose braid to fit under helmet. Jodhpurs on and riding helmet and boots in bag. Ready to go.

Before heading out, I grab the rainbow cake from the fridge I've bought for his birthday—he did mention it's his favourite. I purposefully found out this information because I like this guy and I want him to feel special on his birthday.

I boil the kettle and make two flasks of tea and pop everything into a picnic hamper and head out the door.

I'm outside. I press send on my phone.

The text isn't required as he's already walking towards me. I wave and he's beaming. Oh, those beautiful brown eyes. Pools of heaven.

He opens the door, gets into the passenger side and leans

in for a hug. He smells divine. I'd noticed his pheromones at golf, and I'm sure you would agree there's nothing more intoxicating than a scent that drives you absolutely bonkers. I'm not certain he hasn't already impregnated me with his smell alone.

'Happy birthday!' I kiss him on both cheeks.

'Thanks, sweetheart.'

He's already calling me sweetheart. There's nothing more magical than beautiful words leaving the mouth of a man you admire.

'How was your morning?'

The question was simple enough, but with his tone and cadence, I wonder how I'm going to drive for two and a half hours with that velvety Barry White-sounding voice in my ear. This might be a more harrowing journey than that fateful ride with Janet. I'm pretty certain he could make a living as a hypnotist or radio announcer. If I could marry a voice, it would be his. Do they make tuxedos for voices? Will be googling this later.

'Anybody home?' He waves his hands in front of my face, which startles me out of my thoughts.

'Oh, sorry. Yeah. It's been brilliant. Even better now.' I give him a cheeky wink, which he seems to appreciate and returns the favour.

I push the ignition button, and the engine kicks in with a low purr. I plug the location into the GPS on my phone, pop it into its carrier next to the hand brake, and we're off. So excited!

'I brought you some tea.' I hand him one of the flasks, and he takes a sip.

You know the story of Dr Jekyll and Mr Hyde? What happened next mirrors that exact story.

'Yuck! Tastes like dirty dishwater.' He winds down the window and chucks the entire contents out, spraying the tea all over Audrey and the car behind us.

I'm currently stunned in shock. Who does that? How freaking rude. All these years I've been politely sipping grotesque concoctions so as not to offend waiters I don't even know and apparently, you can just pour a date's kind gesture all over their car.

He takes some water out of his satchel and takes a long sip.

A feeling of embarrassment envelopes my stomach. Was my tea that bad? I feel so rattled by his sudden and mean behaviour I'm stunned silent for the next thirty minutes while he, I assume, is recovering from the apparent assault on his delicate taste buds.

For the next half hour, I intermittently check the GPS who I've affectionately named Susan.

'Why do you keep looking at your phone when the GPS is telling you where to go?' His words are sharp, and his tone has shifted from smooth and velvety to rough and irritated.

'Habit, I guess.' I smile outwardly but feel churning in my stomach. Not a good sign.

We approach the lookout point where I want to stop so I can surprise him with the cake. Fingers crossed; this will lighten the mood.

'I've got a surprise for you.' I manoeuvre Audrey off to the left and the beauty of the rolling hills comes fully into view. What a glorious sight. I love nature's greenery. Apparently, when humans view the colour green in nature, it releases chemicals in the brain that give us an instant sense of well-being. I love how the planet and humans are so inextricably connected.

My date gets out of the car to check out the scenery. He's unimpressed. Apparently, the inexplicable divine connection between Earth and humankind doesn't float his boat.

'Close your eyes, Mister.' My date follows my request, albeit reluctantly.

I open the boot and grab the rainbow cake out of the cooler bag and light the candle in the centre.

'Happy birthday to you. Happy birthday to you,' I sing, as I make my way to where he's standing.

My date opens his eyes. At last, he expresses some degree of happiness, and makes a silent wish while blowing out the candle. I assume it's the same wish as the Tin Man from *The Wizard of Oz*, based on his recent behaviour.

I set the cake down onto the picnic table that's close by and cut a large piece, put it on a plate and hand it to him. He takes a sizeable bite and then a weird expression creeps across his face. Oh no, it was resembling the one I'd seen when he took a sip of my tea. He grabs the plate with the remaining cake off the table, walks over to the bin and throws both his piece and the rest of the cake into the rubbish can.

'It's dry. I can't eat that.' He shakes his head with an expression of disgust.

You couldn't have spit out the bite you'd taken and leave the rest? The mere existence of a cake that's not up to your moisture standards is so offensive to you, you needed it destroyed right away? I hadn't even tried it. I hadn't even smelled it. Maybe if I inhale deeply, I'll get a slight whiff of it and use my imagination. As I ponder this, I have no words. My brain is still trying to compute whether my eyes had deceived me.

'Let's go.' He gets back into the passenger side, slamming the door.

I'm stunned by his behaviour and quietly make my way back into the driver's seat, start the engine and remain silent. Not surprising, but clearly his wish had not worked.

The silence doesn't last long because, for the rest of the journey, he proceeds to tell me about all of these beautiful and mesmerising women he has met over his lifetime, including the most stunning of all, his best friend's wife. His favourite word to use is, 'stunning'. She's absolutely stunning. Have I told you she's stunning?

Clearly, he needs to add the Scarecrow's wish to his list, as evidently, he has no brains to draw on in order to select appropriate topics of conversation to use around a woman.

I feel the energy drain out of my body and feel sadness form in the pit of my stomach. What about the woman who is stunning—right in front of you? Who brought you a freaking cake on your birthday?

At that moment, he points to my feet. 'Oh my God, you have the hairiest toes I've ever seen. Oh my God, they are disgusting. You should get your toes waxed.'

I glance down at my delicate feet. I've never noticed the hair on my toes because they are light blonde. I take a peek at his trotters and who the heck is he to talk? His gnarly hooves resemble those found on the likes of trolls. Talk about projection!

When we arrive at the stables, I feel defeated, a mixture

of sadness that morphs into anger and then back to sadness. I push the helmet firmly down onto my head, change into my riding boots, register, then pay at the counter.

My horse is one of the first, my usual, Lightning is her name, and she's a rescued racehorse. We had an instant connection the moment we met. Kindred spirits, plus, we both love going fast, and she doesn't insult my toes.

This particular horse sanctuary rescues all of its horses, and they seem to love being outside in the native bushland. I give my beautiful Lightning a cuddle and stroke her neck. Her nose immediately goes to my pocket. Dang, she knows me well. I retrieve the carrot, and a second later, it's in her mouth, and she's crunching away in delight. She hasn't rushed to the bin to spit it out, so I'm feeling optimistic about our reunion.

'How are you today, my angel?' Her ears flick from side to side as I put a foot in the stirrup and hoist myself into the saddle.

'Love your boots.' I hear a male voice coming from behind.

I turn around to see my very own Arabian Knight straddling a magnificent black stallion. Okay, he wasn't wearing armour, but he felt like a knight because he'd said something complimentary and had rescued me from the thoughts of my critical date.

'Oh, thanks.' I smile. 'They're cute, aren't they?'

I glance back to see my date is still unmounted and is staring at me and the knight with a glare on his face, but you know what, he's been an absolute jerk this whole morning, and I don't like him, so I'm already done.

The Arabian Knight continues to compliment, which is

a welcome change given the criticism I'd received on my journey here.

My date is called forward and mounts a dark horse named Fred. Fred appears to have a bee in his bonnet—just like my date. Like attracts like as the saying goes.

The horses start to form a line behind the guide and off we trek into the bushland. Lucky for me, it's single file and the sweet Arabian Knight chit-chats away to me along the route.

As I bob along to the rhythm of Lightning's gait, all I can think about is the extensive criticism I've experienced throughout my life and conclude that critical people usually feel inferior or threatened in some way. I've noticed men who've criticised me in the past favour subtle digs and put-downs or intentionally build up other women in an attempt to steal my energy, because THEY don't feel good enough. It's so insidious. I've had enough criticism in my life, and I don't want a partner who so freely dishes it out—and on a first date, which means the worst is yet to come. No thanks.

After several canters through the wooded areas, we come to the most exhilarating part of the hack, where all of the horses stand in a line at the bottom of the hill and on the guide's command, they gallop to the top. I see my date far over on the right. He still has that glare on his face. *Get over yourself. And while you're at it, gallop away and get some cake with perfect moisture levels and leave us all in peace.*

Three. Two. One. Go. Lightning knows those words well, and all I do is lift my bum out of the saddle, loosen the reigns and let my girl fly.

The Arabian Knight on the black stallion is on our tail and Lightning senses them and I feel her kick up a gear. You know when you move a stick shift car through the gears? That's how it feels when Lightning is galloping. It must be the programming from her race days.

'You're wonderful, Lightning.' I place my hand on her neck lovingly. Her mane flies wildly in the wind.

We are almost at the top and the Arabian Knight falls back into second place as we reach the peak.

Winner, winner, chicken-free dinner. I glance back and give the Arabian Knight a winning smile. I squeeze my hands gently on the reigns. My girl is sensitive to touch, so I apply only a slight pressure in my hands, and she feels it and immediately slows to a trot.

'You were fast.' The Arabian Knight pulls up alongside me.

'Team effort.' I lean forward and stroke Lightning's neck.

I hear a commotion and see one of the instructors galloping back down the hill. What's going on there? In the far distance, I see a horse cantering in the opposite direction of the group. The rider's foot seems to be stuck in the stirrup as they're getting dragged along the grass, yelling their head off until they hit a bend and the rider gets flung into a hedge; then there's silence. Crikey! I hope they're okay. That would be hilarious if it was my date. I feel naughty for having the thought, but karma is real.

'The horses always run back to the stables, it's under control.' The leading guide shouts to the group, 'Let's keep going.'

I see the other two guides who were positioned at the back of the group galloping after the runaway horse. One guide stops next to the fallen rider. I see the hands of the person who's stacked it waving them frantically around their head, accompanied by a barrage of curse words. Yikes! He reminds me of my date. Where do folks get off thinking it's okay to abuse other people like that?

The remaining riders transition into a trot and enjoy the rest of the ride back to the stables.

Thoughts of my critical date fade until we walk back into the yard, and I remember I've got to suffer his company for the two and a half-hour drive back. Fun times ahead. Why did I agree to drive? Where is he anyway? I turn around to see the final horses appear around the corner. He's not on any of them. I dismount and place a second carrot that had been zipped in my pocket into Lightning's mouth. She chomps away joyfully.

'Goodbye, my sweet girl. Thank you for an amazing ride.'

I kiss her on her nose, and she breathes hot air into my face. I walk back to the office where we paid. On entering, I see someone bent over and covered from head to toe in mud with an ice pack on his hand.

He looks up and, oh crap, it's my date. Was he participating in one of those marathon mud runs while I was riding Lightning? I successfully hold in my laughter.

Our eyes meet and he glares, then, in a loud, brash tone he starts shouting, 'I can't believe you didn't come to see if I was okay. You were too busy flirting with that idiot to even notice I was being dragged for miles by that bleeping horse, and you carry on as if nothing has happened. You are the worst date I've ever had.'

There was more to that rant. A lot more. But his abuse doesn't deserve any more space on this page.

Out of the corner of my eye, I see someone entering the

office. It's the Arabian Knight. He calmly walks over to my date. He must have heard what was being said from outside, which I'm not surprised about, as my date's enraged voice projects more loudly than a seasoned Broadway performer aiming for the back row. He stands squarely in front of my date, asserting a strong, power pose. I'd seen it before in one of those body language books. He interrupts him, 'Mate, what are you doing? You don't speak to people like that. She had no idea what had happened to you. Have some respect and stop being such an abusive d*ck.'

My date immediately goes silent. He clearly isn't used to feeling vulnerable and having someone call him out on his behaviour. Plus, the Arabian Knight is like two feet taller, and his biceps suggest he goes to the gym a lot more frequently than that puny excuse of a man.

My date stands, barges past the Arabian Knight, and stomps out of the office. I watch him as he kicks pebbles on the way to Audrey. His behaviour mimics a small, sulking child. Poor thing needs a juice box and a nap with his *favouwite bwanky*.

I automatically hug the Arabian Knight and then step back and grin. 'Thanks for sticking up for me. No one has ever done that for me before.'

He puts his hand on my shoulder like a supportive father. 'Please, don't let anyone speak to you like that.'

He's right. I vow to never tolerate abuse ever again, from anyone! But especially not from grumpy troll hooved men who hate birthday cakes and can't ride horses.

I walk past the lady behind the counter who is nodding in agreement, I'm assuming at the scene she'd witnessed. I wave goodbye and step out of the office and head towards my car. My date is leaning against Audrey with his arms crossed. His face is flushed and there's that scowl again. I press the button to open the door and he climbs in, getting mud all over the interior. I guess this is payback for the Alfie date.

He chirps up as soon as we start to drive. 'I can't believe that idiot said that to me. What an absolute . . .'

I slam my foot on the brake so hard that Audrey screeches to an emergency stop and pebbles fly off the wheels.

In an assertive voice, I cut him off and feel the power of a thousand women surging through my stomach as intense heat, and I say this, 'Stop, will you. He had every right to say something to a man who was being verbally abusive. You have criticised me from the moment you got into my car this morning. I won't tolerate this for one second more, so if you want to continue, you can get out of my car right now and find your own way home.'

His expression is wide-eyed. He doesn't apologise, instead, he shakes his head and stares out of the window. I keep my eyes on him a few seconds longer, so he knows I mean business.

I press the accelerator and the car speeds to 60 kph in a few seconds.

I feel powerful. I feel so proud for standing up for myself.

As you might have guessed, we don't speak for the two-and-a-half-hour journey home and, frankly, it's bliss. I drop him home and he doesn't return to the golf clinic. Hallelujah!

I am eternally grateful for the Arabian Knight showing up for me, and you'll be pleased to know, I've not attracted another critical man since. Hmmm. Is it because I'd stood in my power and made the decision to never tolerate that kind of behaviour again? Did the universe know I meant business and as a result, I was free of it, and so I wasn't compatible with mean guys anymore? It feels good, so I'm going to stick with that theory.

Lessons I learned from this date: Firstly, verbal abuse is not natural, it's not healthy and it's not okay. I will not tolerate this or any kind of abuse. I deserve a man who is kind and considerate, who will treat me equally and with respect.

The other interesting thing I discovered from this date is that because I'd experienced a lot of criticism and abusive behaviour from people since childhood, I'd normalised those abusive kinds of behaviours. After the Arabian Knight had called out the abuse, I'd realised, at that moment, that verbally accosting another person is not a normal or healthy way to communicate, and from this date forward, I will not allow another person to speak or treat me in that manner.

26

MR TIKKA MASALA

Age: 38
Location: Melbourne, Australia
Where we met: He was jogging by whilst I was reading a book in Audrey.
How he asked me out: Face to face, through the car window.

I was smiling from ear to ear when I said these words on the phone, 'Mum, guess what?'

'You got the land!' Mum never fails to showcase her psychic abilities.

'YES!' At this point, I was jumping around and screaming 'yay' in Mum's ear.

'Congrats, my lovely daughter. I'm so proud of you.'

I felt so happy because never in a million years did I think this was something I could accomplish without a man by my side. Thanks, the American dream. Yes. My very own slice of land in Australia.

My intention was to build the most beautiful house imaginable to provide community housing for ladies over fifty-five who may be struggling financially or are single and want the companionship of other ladies around their age. Australia had a high rate of senior females who were homeless, so I wanted to use my home to help some of those ladies in my community.

According to my building contract, the house would be built in approximately twelve months. How exciting!

After finishing up with Mum on the phone, I jumped into Audrey and headed to the bay. It was a beautiful day at St Kilda beach, where I was reading Celestial 911 with the windows down. You are well aware that I love to read, and you'll be pleased to know I'd achieved another goal. If you came around for a cuppa, you'd think you'd stepped into a public library. Home library accomplished.

I'd read all of Robert Stone's books, but I'd clearly left the best 'til last. It was about visualisation, and I was loving it.

This particular place was my daily relaxation spot that I would visit after I'd finished work for the day, a special place to unwind and enjoy the view. Picture 180-degree views across the water. It felt so relaxing watching the boats bob up and down on the waves.

There was a paved walking track that lay in front of the beach, where the locals strolled with their dog or jogged along the waterfront. I was observing a stand-up paddleboarder floating past, thinking that would be a fun activity to pick up during the summer, although you know by now that a summer day in Melbourne can be a sunny forty degrees with a high chance of hale.

FOCUS woman! A handsome guy jogged by and moved into my eye line. Flirty eyes. Engaged!

A few minutes later, he reappeared at my car window. Flirty eyes. Success!

'Miss me already?' I joked.

He laughed, which gave me the opportunity to inspect for a bat cave, excessive saliva production or a wedding ring from a dog marriage. All clear. Nice, white and no teeth missing.

'I saw that pretty smile and had to come back and see if you were single.'

He spoke in a strong northern English accent and had the same pasty white skin like me. If we ended up together we could invest in a sunscreen company since our purchases would keep them in business, along with every other English person living in Australia.

'Well, you're in luck, I am single. Are you asking me on a date?'

'That would be a yes.'

'Let me give you my contact info.'

'Wow. That was easier than I thought it would be.' He laughed.

As he leaned into the car to plug my number into his phone, a poignant aroma of curry filled my car. He must have had curry for lunch. Wow! Potent stuff.

We exchanged numbers, and since we lived pretty close to each other, he thought it would be fun to go visit the fairy penguin colony at St Kilda pier. It was a fantastic idea since

I hadn't seen fairy penguins before. We met after dinner at around 8 pm.

The Date

It's 8 pm, I see him and hold my arms out for a hug. 'It's a tad chilly, isn't it?' I rub my shoulders with my hands to generate some heat.

Like a true gentleman, he immediately takes off his jacket and places it around my shoulders. The smell of curry wafts into my nose. Maybe he'd been wearing his jacket over his jumper when he ate curry earlier? I let the thought pass through my mind, and we meander onto the pier. The sounds of water lapping against the wooden frame of the pier is soothing to the soul, but the salty ocean air mixed with the potent odour of his curried jacket is less so. They don't make 'Sea Breeze and Curry' scented candles for a reason. At least it's not dead animal slash dog poo. Just saying.

The fairy penguins' squawks alert us to the fact we are close to the colony. They sound like wives scolding their husbands for being late for dinner. Adorably cute doesn't suffice, and my date glows at my delight in watching them waddling around and telling each other off.

He puts his arms around my shoulders and before I can appreciate the embrace, back into my nose goes the curry scent. He must have worked up a sweat from the walk and the curry smell is steaming out of his pores. Either that or he's hidden bits of curried potato into his pockets like a hamster.

I discreetly plug my nose with my fingers as I embrace

his hug. I've got to give it to him, he's an excellent hugger and his heat provides welcome relief from the cool autumn temperature. I only wish he didn't smell like an Indian spice market on restock day.

He guides me backwards until I feel my back against the rails, and he leans in for a kiss. All I can smell is curry. Curry. Curry. Curry. He tastes like curry. He smells like curry. He sweats curry. All I can think about is curry. Could he be a fan of curry?

We head back to our respective cars, arrange to meet the following evening at my place to play board games and eat non-spiced snacks, and I wave goodbye as I speed away in Audrey. Maybe he'll eat something different tomorrow.

The following evening rolls around and the buzz of the intercom sounds.

'Press level ten in the lift.'

Three loud knocks reverberate through the apartment. I swing open the door and twirl, showcasing my lovely flowery maxi dress that is consistently a hit with the men.

'Wow!' His eyes take in my outfit. 'That dress is gorgeous.'

Told you.

I immediately notice he's wearing the same jumper he wore on his jog the previous afternoon as well as on our evening date. Maybe he's washed it since yesterday? Maybe he has two?

I lean in to give him a welcome hug.

Well, if it's been washed his detergent is made with two parts soap and ten parts curry. I swear this guy must eat curry for breakfast, lunch and dinner.

'What did you have for dinner?' I need to know if my assumptions are correct.

'Tikka Masala. Curry's my fav.'

You're not kidding.

I put the thoughts of curry to one side and avert my attention to setting up the Monopoly board on the carpet. A night of competitive purchasing of prime real estate and whipping my date's butt! What could be more fun? I will add, I'm not the type to let a man win so as not to bruise his ego. It's actually a great way to establish compatibility. No wimpy egomaniacs for me.

No sooner has he sat down he grabs his stomach. 'Where's the bathroom?'

I point down the corridor. 'First door on your right.'

Emergency bathroom visit already? I thought I was through with dating children posing as grown men.

He gets up to check out the bathroom then pokes his head out. 'Could you put the TV on . . . loudly?'

Why does he want me to put the TV on loudly? He'd better be planning on practising a private opera in there and not what I think.

I scoot along the carpet to grab the remote and turn on the song *Follow You* by Imagine Dragons.

'Louder,' he hollers from the bathroom.

I turn the volume up and sit staring at the Monopoly board for the next ten minutes. My living room is already starting to smell of curry. I hear the toilet flush and the tap running. At least he is—hopefully—washing his hands. And fingers crossed this isn't Mr Yogi, *numéro deux*.

I hold my breath as he re-enters the living room.

'Did you hear anything?'

'Nope.' I lie. 'Let's play Monopoly.

He crouches down to make his way into a seat and stops halfway. 'I'm so sorry, can you give me another minute, and could you put the sound on louder this time and plug your ears with your fingers.'

He scurries back into the bathroom for another fifteen minutes and pokes his head around the corner with the toilet flushing in the background. 'So sorry, it's the curry.'

My immediate thought: stop eating curry for breakfast, lunch and dinner then. It clearly doesn't agree with you.

Fast forward six hours, I am currently standing outside, shivering my butt off on my own balcony with my fingers in my ears. The music is at the highest volume blaring out *Follow You* for the thousandth time. My neighbours probably think I'm drunk, cooking curry and listening to *Follow You* on a never-ending loop. My whole apartment stinks of curry. I have no toilet paper left and neither of us had even gotten around the Monopoly board once. This is not the game night I had envisioned. Why doesn't he go home and use his own toilet? Or dig a hole in the ground outside for all I care?

He emerges from the bathroom, and I charge towards him, holding my breath as I hand him his belongings. 'You should go home, you're clearly not well.'

I manoeuvre him to the door. 'You're right. I think it's the curry.'

Astute.

I push him out of the door, then race like a lunatic around my house opening all the windows and doors, lighting incense, turning on air diffusers, spraying sage and lighting as many candles as possible. My neighbours know I have now reached the witching hour of my strange evening ritual.

The smell of curry doesn't leave my apartment for several —what seemed like—months and understandably, I haven't eaten a curry since. I'm not sure if I can stomach a curry ever again after this date.

What I learned from this date: Experiencing the same behaviour across multiple days usually indicates a pattern. This guy didn't have a problem wearing the same smelly clothes on each of our dates. Uncleanliness is a habit I cannot live with. I love a man who takes pride in his appearance and the way he smells. My friend insists that the first few dates are when a man is presenting his best self and it only goes downhill from there. So, if this is true, goodness knows what he'd smell like after ten dates. Thankfully, I'll never find out. You'll also be pleased to know I was able to eat my favourite curry about six months after this date. There is justice in the world!

27

MR WORK DATE

Age: 39
Location: Melbourne, Australia
Where we met: At the office where we were both working
How he asked me out: He didn't technically ask me out.

Oh, my goodness, I'm so happy! My house is complete. I'd spent the last three weeks over in Perth furnishing the internals and landscaping the gardens with the family. I must say, it's affirmed that I am definitely not cut out for manual labour. Mum on the other hand, at sixty-nine years old, was digging and carrying massive boulders of limestone out of the earth in forty-five degree temperatures (Celsius), whilst the twenty-year-old male labourers and I were trying not to pass out from sunstroke. Even my four-year-old nephew helped by throwing bricks down my new drains. Love that little terror. Thanks, family!

One week later, my first investment property was rented. Patriarchy, go take a running jump.

In other good news, remember the business venture that I came to Melbourne for? Well, it went so well, I decided to set up shop and start my own consulting firm. I'd acquired ten clients on my highest monthly package and with my help, their results were skyrocketing. I found nothing more satisfying than helping others and seeing them thrive.

I truly believe finding my passion for business at ten years old was the greatest gift I've received—remember my first venture, Skimmers? It's meant my life has been filled with joy, and nothing ever feels like work. I wonder what would happen if the school system spent more time helping students find their passion instead of training them to enter the rat-race and being okay with making other people rich. How wonderful if everyone was waking up in the morning excited to do what they love.

Speaking of passion, date 27 occurred in my interactions with a colleague of a new client I was consulting for. Drum roll. Let the games begin.

This wasn't exactly a romantic date. It all began at a work lunch with a colleague at my new contracted position. He was a similar age to me, smart and had a charm about him that was magnetising. There was instant chemistry when we first met. He was passionate and loved business, two things we had in common, but there was a catch. He was married, and he was the man I reported to during my contract.

My morals and values meant there was zero chance of me going there, and even though there was an obvious attraction, there was no way I would ever act on it.

The guy, on the other hand, had questionable morals and was one of those fellas that used his smarts to his advantage. Unlucky for him, I was smarter.

When you began reading *28 Disastrous Dates*, you may recall the following text message that I received, which prompted this whole voyage of journalling dates:

Let's skip dinner and go back to yours and play Postman, and I'll put my big package in your tiny slot.

Just a quick note on the text. As we've discovered in previous dates, a man's idea of big is subjective, and secondly, how does he know my slot is tiny? Very presumptuous, don't you think?

Some guys are blatant and crude in their intentions, and to be honest, to me it reads like an unrefined bogan. Instant turn-off.

But this guy. This guy was much subtler in his manipulations, so subtle, in fact, you could blink and miss it.

The Date

It all begins on my first day. He stands beside me, and I can feel his energy charging out towards me. You know that feeling, right?

He's pointing at the computer screen. 'Can you go down on,' he pauses, 'me, for example, I would say.' Then he continues with some sales blurb.

You know when you hear something that sounds out of place, but it's masked in the context of a normal sentence? Well, if you reread what he said without the pause and stop after the word 'me,' you'll see what I'm talking about.

I take a moment to process. Did he just ask me to perform fellatio on him in the middle of an office building? Surely this is not an approved Safe Work Australia training practice.

I barely know the guy, so I give him the benefit of the doubt and figure it's just a coincidence, even though I don't believe in coincidences.

The second three occurrences happen in short succession, only a couple of weeks after the first. He calls me into his office looking pleased with himself.

'I'm so excited to show you my big package.'

Again, my brain takes a pause. His big package? What the heck? This is not appropriate work talk.

He pulls out a large cardboard box, opens the lid and pulls out an advertising flyer.

'I would appreciate it if you could give the flyer a once-over and provide feedback. Once I get it back from you, I'll make the adjustments and slip it into your box for a final once-over.'

Am I hearing things or what? Yes, each person in the office has a box, where paperwork gets placed for their attention, but if I were bringing someone a sandwich I wouldn't say, 'here's something for your hole.'

I shake the sentence out of my head and turn to leave.

'Let's do lunch today. It's raining, so bring your umbrella, we don't want you getting too wet now, do we?'

This CAN NOT be a coincidence. No freaking way.

It's 12.30 pm and the alarm on my phone starts to sound, indicating it's time to get a move on. It's a five-minute walk, so all good. I grab one of the large umbrellas from the stand by the door as I leave, the company name embossed in golden letters on the black fabric. I don't want to get too wet now, do I?

I enter the café and see a hand waving at a table on the far back left. He's dressed especially dapper today in a sharp tailored suit. He knows how to dress to leave a lasting impression.

'I hope you didn't get too wet.'

'I'm one hundred per cent bone dry,' I respond with a smirk.

'Sit. Let's get some lunch. I'm going to get a muffin. I love to munch down on delicious muffins.' He chuckles with no sign that what he's saying is in any way sexual.

Maybe it's me. Maybe I have a dirty mind? Have I been single too long?

The waitress takes our order, and he chats away about the current sales.

'It's important that we go deep today, and understand how to penetrate the market. It's important to get in and out, you know, as fast as possible. Do you know what I am saying?'

All I hear is him describing one thing:

S.E.X.

And what's worse, he's describing the worst variety—humping like a jackhammer. What's wrong with me? Should I make an appointment with a psychologist? I discard the thoughts in order to communicate a coherent response.

'I don't agree on getting in and out as fast as possible. The market has changed. We need to be focusing on building long-term relationships. People require more touchpoints before buying nowadays because they have so many more options available to them.'

A smile emerges across his face. 'Steady on, you're riding me hard and it's only your third week.'

I feel like I'm in some sort of sexual nightmare. If he jumps up and rips off his shirt, I'm definitely dreaming.

I wait.

He remains seated. Shirt remains intact.

Our food arrives and I watch him devour the pistachio muffin; he clearly does love munching down on them. The meeting ends, and we head back to the office and for the rest of the day, I can't help but go over his words in my mind. It can't be in my head, can it? I'm starting to doubt myself.

I walk back to Audrey, click the remote, slide into the driver's seat and press the Audible app on my phone that gives me access to his library.

I notice a book with an intriguing title, *Seduce Anyone*. Interesting. What's this? I click on it and the audiobook begins. It's not a business book at all, but more about how you can use NLP (Neuro-Linguistic Programming) to manipulate and seduce people. What the heck? Why is this in here?

The book talks about Cleopatra and Mark Anthony, and how Cleopatra used the techniques taught in the book to get Mark Anthony to ask for her hand in marriage. Firstly, did Cleopatra have Audible? Secondly, what the heck? Is this what he's doing to me? Is he trying to manipulate me through the careful placement of sexual words into normal-sounding sentences, so my subconscious accepts them and associates sex with him?

This is exactly what he's doing. What an absolute jerk. How manipulative. He's clearly been doing it from the get-go and what's worse is I'd started believing I was the issue. That's crazy. I do feel a sense of relief that I'm not going insane, although my feelings about muffins have suddenly changed drastically.

Armed with this new information, this guy was going to have a real problem on his hands. We were both now equipped with the same knowledge. He clearly wasn't that smart because he didn't think about the fact that I had access to his reading material. Fool.

I completed the audiobook that night and it sparked a memory from my past—about my creepy English teacher at the private girl's school I'd attended back in the UK.

The English teacher was talking about a piece of literature. I recall him saying, 'He slipped his finger into the edge of her silk glove.' He accompanied these words with hand gestures, moving his middle finger up and down the centre of his palm. Yuck! He then locked eyes with me. 'He then took a sip from her cup.' Gross! I guess this wasn't my first time experiencing this manipulation technique at the hands of men in authority.

The next day, armed with my new knowledge, I count how many times he attempts to infiltrate my mind, and over the following weeks I recall these statements.

When I told him about the astronomical sales results: 'Blow me down. That can't be true.'

At lunch: 'Can I try your sauce?'

After tasting it: 'Yum, your sauce tastes delicious.'

When we are taking a tram to see a potential client and miss the tram stop: 'We need to get off, right now.'

After I tell him that his biggest client called and cancelled his services: 'It's so hard, right now.'

Every Wednesday: 'Happy Hump Day!'

When the team doesn't hit the sales quota: 'We need to go faster and harder.'

During the sales meeting: 'I am erecting a sales strategy that is going to arouse and delight.'

Needless to say, none of these got past me, and I realised the reason he was trying to manipulate me was that not only did he find me attractive, but he was intimidated by me. Also, he apparently had a lot of free time on his hands to be coming up with these half-baked innuendos.

One late night at the office, he confessed if he was single, I'd have him wrapped around my little finger, which created an even weirder dynamic, but seems I am equally as skilled as him in manipulation techniques.

Another time he gloated that he could easily mess with his wife's emotions and could get her to do anything he desired. This affirmed he was intentional with his manipulation, and he was also using them on his poor wife. How messed up is that?

After enduring him and his behaviour for twelve months, the contract ended, and I didn't have to see him again. The last time I heard, the company was being sued by five employees on sexual harassment charges. I figure those smart ladies had clocked onto him and had done something about his manipulative ways. Good on them!

Lessons I learned from this date: Firstly, this date awakened me to the fact that some men can be cunning and devious, as can some women. I knew both men and women could be manipulative, but never dreamt it could be done in such a bizarre manner, using a technique that is meant to be used for good.

Secondly, never again will I question my sanity if my female intuition is giving me a strong indicator that someone or something is off. Note to self: always listen to and follow intuition over logic.

28

MR SPEED DATE(S)

Age: 40
Location: Melbourne, Australia
Where we met: Speed dating event
How he asked me out: There were multiple men fighting over me.

I'd bought Mum a flight over from Perth to celebrate her birthday. We'd driven up to the Dandenong Ranges for a hike.

Mum might be seventy in chronological years, but let me tell you, she has the body and mind of a thirty-year-old. Anything I can do physically, Mum can do better. She is an absolute powerhouse of a woman and an inspiration to the world that biological age should have no bearing on health, strength and wellbeing.

The reason for her surprising feats of strength is not

pumping iron in a gym seven days a week, it's in the way she thinks. She thinks she can do anything physically, so her body complies. Remember the landscaping?

Mum and I were chatting about my dating life as we were hiking up a two-kilometre, forty-five-degree hill. Mum leading the way, of course.

'You've heard the quote by Albert Einstein, haven't you?' Mum turned to face me.

'He's said loads of impressive things, which one?' I take in a big gasp of air.

Mum's about to inform me of this poignant quote when a lyrebird casually walks across our trail and lets out an almighty sound.

Of. A. Chainsaw.

Holy heck.

Don't worry—there wasn't a terrifying, murderous man wielding a chainsaw behind the lyrebird. Here's a fun little aviary nugget for you: lyrebirds mimic sounds they hear. David Attenborough is calling your name. But on a serious note, Earth is in big trouble when the wildlife is mimicking chainsaws.

As the lyrebird disappeared into the bushland making the sound of a pneumatic drill, Mum continued, 'Insanity is doing the same thing over and over and expecting a different result.'

I'm pretty certain I'm not diagnosed as insane; however, according to Einstein, my dating behaviour is. So, at that moment, I decided to change up my dating regime, axe online dating and delve into something radically different.

Speed dating.

Insanity averted. Phew!

Mum had a fantastic time by the way before she headed back to Perth. I'm visiting for Christmas so it will be wonderful to see her and my family again soon.

So, here we are at the final date, or should I say date(s), given there were copious disastrous dates all occurring over the course of one unforgettable evening. Picture this, not one, not two, but twenty dates—all in the same room. Yep, that's right, welcome to the 'alternative' speed dating event and my personal hell. We may as well end on multiple disastrous dates and go out with a bang, right?

Thanks for the suggestion, Mum. Just kidding. I'm a grown woman and I take full responsibility for my actions! There will be no blame cast here.

Most people would have experienced, or at least seen on TV, the 'normal' version of speed dating. You know the drill, the women sit at the table, the fellas move from one lady to the next and spend a few minutes chatting to each person. Sounds simple, right? Well, the speed dating event I attended was, how do I put it, it was out of the box—no, not my box. We're still recovering from Mr Work Date's innuendos together.

The Date(s)

I decided to wear my long, red maxi number. It doesn't show a lot of cleavage or legs, but it's form-fitting and screams the girl next door.

I'm running late (no shock there), and as I enter the building, I'm met with about forty pairs of eyes; twenty male and twenty female—well nineteen female, I was the twentieth. I make my entrance confidently. I showcase my brightest smile and check the room for the host.

'Please write your name on the form provided and take a seat on the floor.'

As I fill out the form, the host stands so close anyone would think we were lifelong friends. Personal space would be scarcer than hope, this evening.

I avoid eye contact and make my way towards a friendly-looking Indian chap, sit and cover my legs with my dress, taking care not to flash him.

'So, today's speed dating experience won't be your typical speed dating experience,' the host announces.

Little did I know how true that statement would be.

'I invite you all to stay open to everything I suggest and to give everything a go. Please partner up and sit cross-legged in front of one another. Ladies, sit with your back against the wall, and men, face the ladies.'

Sounds of shuffling follow as people scoot into position.

'Your first date will be to stare into your partner's eyes for ten minutes.'

I'm familiar with this technique. It's a tantric technique to create connection through the eyes. That's okay, I'm happy to do it, but ten minutes is a bit rich for first-timers. Yikes! I haven't even stared into my own eyes for ten minutes straight.

My first date has a kind face, and I can already tell he fancies me. A girl just knows these things.

'Your ten minutes starts now.'

I gaze into my date's eyes, feeling wholly present. A few

seconds into it, my date's face starts to redden until tears stream down his cheeks.

I grab his hand to comfort him. 'Are you okay?'

'I think you're my soulmate,' he stutters quietly under his breath.

'No talking during this exercise.' The host glares at my date.

Do you know how awkward it feels to continue staring into the eyes of a crying man you've only known for five seconds, and who has professed his love for you? I didn't either until I was experiencing it. I remove my hand from his and pray for time to get sucked into a black hole.

For the remaining nine minutes and fifty-three seconds, I watch the tears fall down my date's cheeks, that drip and form a puddle on his polished dress shoe.

Ten minutes feels like ten hours, and when the host rings the brass bell that signals time is up, I'm ready to collect my belongings and bolt for the door, but, unfortunately, another lady beats me to it. Great. Now it'll be awkward if I leave. I remain put, both seething and respecting the heck out of her.

'Men, in silence, please stand, move clockwise and sit in front of your next lady.'

My date keeps his gaze on me with a sad, longing expression. His eyes remind me of Bambi.

I do my most convincing friend wave—the fast one that I nicked from Mr Oh My God—and avert my eyes to the floor.

My date sits down in front of the next lady, but his stare is still on me. Oh, please fall in love with her now. She's got perfectly lovely eyes to project an entire made-up life onto.

I keep my eyes focused on the carpet until a bald-headed

man takes a seat in front of me. I smile. He has no expression. Okey dokey! Date number two and the awkwardness continues.

'For your next date, please confess the hardest experience you've ever faced. You have ten minutes. Off you go.'

Gees, Louise. This is full-on. Crikey! What to confess? What to confess? My thoughts are interrupted by my date's voice.

'I haven't told anyone this before,' he starts. 'I feel like I was born on the wrong planet. I don't feel like I belong here, and this is not my real home. I know I'm an alien, and I hate humans and I hate this planet and . . .'

Maybe he should go to LA as all the foreigners are classed as aliens there.

As my date continues to rattle off everything he hates about the planet and the human species, I observe each participant in the room and wonder if any will result in a second meeting. I catch eyes with the host, who is staring directly at me. I get the ick immediately and so turn my attention back to my date, who is now crying about being destined to be a lonely alien forever. Maybe I should tell him about LA?

Have I come to the right place? Have I accidentally wandered into the social hour for a group of test subjects of a highly experimental psychoactive drug?

'Time.' The host jingles the bell.

I never got the chance to tell my date about my hardest life experience, which is for the best as I might have said, 'Listening to you.'

My date rises to his feet, wiping away tears as he escapes

to the bathroom. Both of my dates have cried and it's of no credit to me.

'Okay, for your third date, everyone please stand up. This date is about trust.'

The only thing I can trust is it'll be as horrid as the last two.

My next date stands in front of me. He's staring at his feet, which are shuffling from side to side nervously. His forehead is sweaty. Third time's a charm is not looking good.

'Okay. Ladies, please collect a blindfold from me and place it over your date's eyes.'

What are we doing now? Please don't let it be anything S&M. I'm still recovering from the cupboard date.

I walk over to the host who stares deeply into my eyes, lingering his hand on mine as he hands me a red blindfold. Can this night get any weirder? You'll be delighted to know, it can.

I take the red blindfold and quasi smile at the host out of politeness and head back to my date whose forehead is sopping wet with sweat. Where are the Australian Open ball kids when you need a towel?

'Are you okay?'

'Not really, I'm freaking out. This is not the kind of speed dating I was expecting. This is really out of my comfort zone. Put the blindfold on and let's get it over with.'

Righto, sir. I hear you. At least we're both singing from the same hymn sheet. I place the blindfold over his eyes and tie it into a bow at the back.

'Okay, everyone, please grab your date's hand. You will now manoeuvre your date around the room as fast as you can, avoiding bumping your date into obstacles or other people.' And aliens, I add mentally.

Wowsers! Well, okay, if you say so. I grab my date's hand, which feels like grabbing a wet fish, and start to run around the hall.

Soon after we begin, my date starts to scream as we run. Is he enjoying it or is he afraid? He doesn't stop running, but his hands are thrashing around like a mad man, so, I up my speed to a sprint, dodging a pole here, a person there. Everyone else in the room is either laughing, crying or moving in silence. My date and I are the fastest, and his screams echo loudly off the walls.

'STOP!' the host shouts loudly to be heard over my date's screams.

My date tears off his blindfold that is now a dark maroon colour from absorbing all of the sweat.

'I. Am. Done!' my date yells at the top of his lungs and storms out of the hall.

Another one bites the dust. I guess a second date is out of the question.

The host shakes his head with a look of disgust on his face.

'If anyone else wants to go, get out now.' His tone is stern, and he points with a straight arm towards the exit.

Everyone is silent. Is this a cult? How did I end up here? Are there at least snacks?

'Right. Move to your next partner. Role play is next.'

I once again pray it's not anything related to S&M. It seems I'm still scarred.

'Men, you will now take the role of a dog. Get on all fours. Ladies, you are the dog's master. Your ten minutes start now.'

This is just plain weird. It feels like I'm playing out some sordid fantasy. Maybe I should pass on the details to the cupboard date.

My date doesn't seem phased at all and is already in character, panting and barking. Next, he simulates humping my leg. Holy heck, what has this got to do with dating?

I grab my pretend leash and start to walk my dog date around the hall. I feel like an absolute twit. My canine date is disobedient and jumps on top of my previous 'alien' date and starts barking and wrestling. To be fair, the alien guy is giving as good as he is getting. Maybe he feels more at home being a dog!

The other female partner and I share a moment, telepathically exchanging the following information . . . What the actual heck are we doing here?

I yank my date off the alien guy, and in retaliation my dog date decides to simulate peeing on my leg, which makes the host release a bellowing laugh from the front of the hall.

After the ten minutes is called, it's break time, and as soon as I take a step towards the kitchen to make myself a camomile tea, to calm my brain, my first crying date is back by my side asking if he can make me a cuppa.

I'm going to sleep well tonight, that's for sure.

He continues to tell me how he knows, without a shadow of a doubt, that we're soul mates, how he knew instantly to the core of his being, and there's no one else here he likes. Dang it! I guess the second woman's eyes didn't measure up. I gulp down my tea and seriously consider hurling myself out of the kitchen window for a speedy escape. Goodness knows what the host is going to get us to do next.

I try and slink away by excusing myself to use the bathroom. I grab my bag and tell the host I've got to go.

'I'll walk you out.' He follows me through the corridor and onto the porch.

'Why are you leaving?' He crosses his arms with one eyebrow raised.

'It's not for me. I don't see any potential husbands in there.' I chuckle in an attempt to make it light-hearted.

'What about me?' He points at his own chest.

'You?'

'Yes. I saw you when you entered and you have this tantalising, regal energy about you, like a real lady, you know. It's so attractive. I've been watching you all night and I think we'd be a good match.'

How left field is this?

He continues, 'I've been with my wife for five years, but after meeting you, I believe you might be the one for me.'

Is this a joke?

'I'm sorry, did you say you're in a five-year marriage, but you are going to give that up for me?' I had to double-check I wasn't hearing things.

'Spot on. You're a goddess in my eyes.'

Just wow. I thought this night couldn't get any stranger but it just did. This night is a record for weirdness.

'I'm sorry, I have to go home. It's been an odd night.' I start to walk back to my car.

Instead of humbly accepting my rejection and leaving me to it, the host follows. I continue walking the fifteen minutes back to Audrey with him trying to convince me to give him a chance. Goodness knows what the remaining participants are thinking now he's MIA. Maybe they're trying their hand as cats now.

For the next half hour whilst I'm trying to escape, he continues to tell me how special I am, how it's destiny, and how his wife will understand.

Sir, I'm pretty certain your wife will NOT understand.

'I'm sorry, I have to go.' I click the button on the car remote, get in and drive off. I glance in the rear-view mirror and see him standing in the middle of the road watching me speed away, like breakups that happen in movies.

This evening can be described as weird if weird were a concoction of steroids, cocaine and whatever experimental drug they were all taking. That was the last alternative speeding date I will ever attend. Like ever!

Lessons I learned from this date: This dating experience made me realise I am not a fan of the extreme. I like balance. Having my partner behave like a dog is not something I take any joy in or having someone disclose their most traumatic life event to me inside of one second of meeting is not conducive to creating attraction—it actually creates repulsion.

FINAL THOUGHTS

So, there you have it, 28 disastrous dates, spanning over twenty years. I'll be frank, I never thought I'd still be single at forty, but here I am, and the reality is, I couldn't be happier. My life is brilliant! I've created a wonderful life, filled with fabulous friends, a loving Mum and family, businesses I'm passionate about, and I'm living life based on my values, and on my own terms. I fulfilled a personal goal of building my own investment property and you'll be pleased to know, I'm on to the second.

Yes, it would be wonderful to meet a great guy and share our lives together, but if it doesn't happen, my life will still be filled with all the wonderful things I put in it.

So, whilst I hope my disastrous dating escapades have entertained, but more likely disgusted you, I hope during your own disastrous dating experiences you realise the intentions written at the beginning of this book:

You are not alone.

Every bad date will lead you to know what you don't want, which in turn leads you to know what you do want.

Each date has the potential to reflect your conditioning and that understanding can lead you closer to finding your true self and your life partner—if you want one. You can still lead a happy, fulfilled life as an amazing single person, or even as an ordinary one.

I wish you bon voyage on your own dating journey, filled with colour and flavour. After all, having weird and wonderful experiences is what life's all about, right?

A big thanks to my lovely Mum, family and girlfriends who listened to each of these disastrous dates in explicit detail and offered encouragement and loving support along this journey. What would I do without you?

And finally, thank you to all the men out there who are consciously moving beyond the old paradigms of the outdated patriarchal system and treating women like the beautiful and deserving human beings we are. You guys rock!

On the other hand, if you're a man who has done anything that even remotely resembles anything in this book, I once again ask you to immediately cease what you're doing and pick up that phone. A psychologist, doctor or dentist in your local area is waiting for your call.

SUMMARY OF LESSONS

Size does matter but not in the traditional sense. I believe there is a perfect size for every person, think of Cinderella and the slipper.

We are all human, just because a man is afraid, doesn't make him less of a man. A man has all the same emotions as a woman and should be allowed to freely express himself in a healthy and respectful manner.

No men who are emotionally dead inside.

The experts were right. Experiencing something terrifying with a date, definitely creates a bond and an attraction right off the bat.

If a man doesn't have a natural protective instinct, it usually means I have to take the masculine role and then sexual desire goes out the window, followed by the relationship.

First dates should only be for an hour in a public place, although, I don't think I'll ever follow my own advice on this one as coffee dates are so dang boring.

Stress shows the true nature of a person.

No druggies.

If someone displays bad behaviour towards someone else, one day it'll be directed at me. Steer clear.

Deceit is sometimes packaged in kindness. Be aware. Very aware.

Only date confident men.

Skip men who only want maids and surrogates.

Pick a man who can keep his ego in check.

No controlling men.

Pick a man who is considerate to my needs as well as his own.

Stand in my power, and use my voice to communicate if something doesn't feel right.

Never sacrifice my own feelings in order to protect someone else's.

Never agree to an activity where I can't easily escape.

Never tolerate liars.

If a guy shirks his fatherly responsibilities, he's not a decent person. Run!

No two hundred per day farting machines.

Pick a man who responds, instead of reacts.

Pick an emotionally intelligent man.

Pick a man who's happy to take the lead.

Date locally.

Have compatible sex drives and similar sexual tastes.

Pick a man who is honest and isn't afraid of having hard conversations.

Follow my gut.

Before going on any dates, rebalance my own energy.

First dates need to be in daylight and face to face.

Check teeth prior to snogging session.

Be cautious of men who don't show their teeth in online profile photos.

Become conscious of where I am conditioned by society, and make new choices from a place of authenticity and personal power.

Immediately axe anyone who participates in anything that reduces a woman's body to a sexual object.

More dates don't mean better dates.

NO SPIT MISSILES!

If there's no physical attraction, don't waste time with further dates.

Axe any man who doesn't keep his word and lacks integrity.

Never have a first date in a man's apartment.

Axe any man who doesn't respect my boundaries.

Axe any man who uses his penis as a weapon, figuratively and literally.

Only date men who have healthy habits—no heavy drinkers or smokers.

Must be capable of intellectual and thought-provoking conversation.

Pay attention to a man's actions over his words.

Never settle for second best.

Zero tolerance of verbal abuse and critical men.

Pick men who take pride in their appearance and have good standards for themselves.

No stink bombs.

Intuition over logic.

ABOUT THE AUTHOR

Poppy Mortimer is a self-proclaimed humour addict who often finds herself startled awake in the middle of the night from the sound of her own laughter. She earned an MFA in creative writing during a three-year stint in Los Angeles and finds joy in making people laugh by sharing stories about her bad dates. She inherited her entrepreneurial spirit from her dad, has multiple businesses and dabbles in real estate. She's an avid reader and is passionate about acquiring knowledge and wisdom. She is still dating and remains hopeful that the next man will be the right man.

To connect, please visit our Facebook page: facebook.com/28DisastrousDates.

A NOTE FROM THE AUTHOR

Thank you so much for reading 28 Disastrous Dates. If it made you laugh or you could relate to any of the dates or lessons, I'd love to read your review. If you have any friends who want to feel better about their own dating life or need a jolly good laugh, please refer them to buy this book.

If you would like to connect with other singletons around the globe, you can find us at facebook.com/28DisastrousDates.

I'm excited to connect with you to continue the conversation, and I can't wait to hear about your own disastrous dates.

Lightning Source UK Ltd.
Milton Keynes UK
UKHW020628110722
405680UK00009B/857